K

A Researcher's Guide to the National Statistics Socio-economic Classification

A Researcher's Guide to the National Statistics Socio-economic Classification

Edited by
David Rose and David J. Pevalin

⑤SAGE Publications
London • Thousand Oaks • New Delhi

For David Lockwood and John Goldthorpe

Selection, editorial material and Chapters 1, 2, 12 and 13
© David Rose and David J. Pevalin 2003
Chapter 3 © 2003 Abigail McKnight and Peter Elias
Chapter 4 © 2003 Colin Mills and Geoffrey Evans
Chapter 5 © 2003 Anthony P.M. Coxon and Kimberly Fisher
Chapter 6 © 2003 Kimberly Fisher
Chapter 7 © 2003 Peter Elias and Abigail McKnight
Chapter 8 © 2003 Justine Fitzpatrick
Chapter 9 © 2003 David J. Pevalin
Chapter 10 © 2003 Helen Cooper and Sara Arber
Chapter 11 © 2003 Anthony Heath, Jean Martin and
Roeland Beerten

First published 2003

SAGE Publications Ltd
6 Bonhill Street
London EC2A 4PU

SAGE Publications Inc
2455 Teller Road
Thousand Oaks, California 91320

SAGE Publications India Pvt Ltd
32, M-Block Market
Greater Kailash - I
New Delhi 110 048

British Library Cataloguing in Publication data

A catalogue record for this book is
available from the British Library

ISBN 0 7619 7322 2

Library of Congress Control Number: 2002102788

Typeset by Photoprint, Torquay, Devon
Printed in India at Gopsons Papers Ltd, Noida

Contents

Foreword

This volume forms part of the story of a remarkable social science collaboration.

In 1994 the Economic and Social Research Council was commissioned by the (then) Office for Population Censuses and Surveys to undertake a review of government social classifications. The widely used and long established 'Registrar General's Social Class' categories were a prominent focus of the review.

An extensive programme of rigorous investigations established that there was a strong case for replacing the existing class categories, and indeed the associated 'Socio-economic Groups', with a more reliable, valid and useful schema. The new National Statistics Socio-economic Classification (NS-SEC) duly came into official being in 2001 – in time to inform the design and analysis of the decennial National Census.

The decision to replace fundamental components of the UK's official socio-economic classifications was of course not taken lightly. It could be justified, but only after detailed and systematic inquiry into the logic of the theoretical bases of the different classifications, the availability of sound indicators for the key concepts, and the utility of the descriptions and explanations that could be derived from applying the classifications in empirical analyses.

Supported by joint funding from the office for National Statistics and the ESRC, a broadly based team of some two dozen or so social scientists and survey research specialists set about the challenge posed by this exciting agenda, under the guidance of University of Essex sociologists David Lockwood and David Rose. Validation of the proposed new schema – in other words, establishing that the new class categories measured what they claimed to measure, and therefore that they could yield useful empirical findings – formed a central plank of the case for its adoption. The UK now boasts probably the most exhaustively validated socio-economic categories in the world. The reasons why will be evident from the chapters collected together here.

The venture has also provided striking proof of the importance of high quality basic social science research. Having systematically explored the alternatives, the researchers involved in this project concluded that the new NS-SEC categories should be derived from an existing social class schema, devised by John Goldthorpe and his collaborators in the early 1970s as part of an ESRC-funded study of social mobility in England and Wales. Some thirty years later, the new official socio-economic categories for the UK are supported by the same theoretical framework but offer updated and better-validated measures of employment relations and conditions, yielding new insight into a wide range of health and other social outcomes. In social science, no less than the life or physical sciences, basic research often generates applications that were wholly unenvisaged at the outset. It is for this reason that the ESRC reserves fully one-third of its research budget for these 'curiosity-driven' or 'blue skies' projects. The story of the new socio-economic classification for the UK confirms the wisdom of this funding policy.

I therefore welcome this publication warmly, as a testimony to the virtues of a fruitful collaboration between funding agencies and researchers, and of the scientific and civic value of basic research.

Dr Gordon Marshall
Chief Executive
ESRC

Preface

This volume is designed as an introduction to the National Statistics Socio-economic Classification (NS-SEC), its validity as a measure of socio-economic positions and its usefulness as a research tool. It is therefore a primer for future users of the NS-SEC. A companion volume, discussing the history of the ESRC Review of Government Social Classifications that led to the development of the NS-SEC as the new official socio-economic classification for the UK, has also been produced, as discussed in Chapter 1.

The book is divided into four parts. The two chapters in Part I offer a description and explanation of the NS-SEC. The four chapters in Part II examine the adequacy of the NS-SEC as a measure of its underlying concept of employment relations. The five chapters in Part III are concerned with the NS-SEC's construct validity and thus with its usefulness as an aid to the investigation of various types of social inequality. In addition, the chapters in Part III offer a guide, both explicitly and implicitly, to the use of the NS-SEC, as well as providing an indication of its flexibility. Finally, the two chapters in Part IV offer some further reflections on and conclusions about the NS-SEC. Each part of the book has its own introduction, setting out the general issues relevant to the subsequent chapters.

We are pleased to acknowledge the help and support we have received from the following individuals in the course of both the Review and the production of this volume. Jean Martin and Tessa Staples (ONS) each played a vital role in the Review team's work, the former as both an active participant in the Review and as the liaison person between ESRC and ONS and the latter through her encyclopaedic knowledge of occupational information and its processing by ONS. In the latter stages of the Review, Roeland Beerten (ONS) assisted us with analyses of LFS data. Catrin Roberts (formerly at ESRC) helped to establish the Review and subsequently gave us unfailing support. David Lockwood (University of Essex) was the Review team's Chairperson and offered wise counsel at all times. John Goldthorpe (Nuffield College, Oxford) gave generously of his time and expertise. As the Foreword indicates, the NS-SEC is based on his pioneering basic research into the class structure of the UK. Equally, Gordon Marshall, while still at Nuffield College, and Sara Arber (University of Surrey) acted as consultants to the Review and played a crucial role in the clarification of many vital issues.

The chapters in this book were first prepared for a workshop on the interim version of the NS-SEC held at the University of Essex in December 1998. We are grateful to all the participants in that meeting for their comments and contributions.

We are also grateful to our colleagues in the Institute for Social and Economic Research, University of Essex. In particular we record our thanks to Jonathan Gershuny, Judi Egerton, Terry Tostevin, Mary Gentile, Jane Rooney, Jenifer Tucker, Eileen Clucas, Helen FitzGerald and Lindsay Moses. Most especially, we are indebted to Janice Webb, who undertook all the secretarial and administrative tasks in relation to both the Review and this book, and to our former colleague, Karen O'Reilly (University of Aberdeen), who made so many important contributions as Assistant Convenor of the Review.

We also thank the Review Committee for their contributions. If we single out Peter Elias (University of Warwick), Abigail McKnight (LSE) and Peter Goldblatt (ONS) for especial thanks, our colleagues in the team will understand why.

The support of the Economic and Social Research Council, the Office for National Statistics and the University of Essex is gratefully acknowledged. The work reported here was made possible by ESRC Grant H501 26 5031 and is part of the scientific programme of the Institute for Social and Economic Research, University of Essex.

Finally, we thank the contributors to this volume for their indispensable role in the work of the Review, as demonstrated by the chapters that follow.

David Rose
David J. Pevalin

Figures

Tables

Abbreviations

BHPS	British Household Panel Survey
CS	Cambridge Scale
ESRC	Economic and Social Research Council
GHS	General Household Survey
LBW	Low birthweight
LFS	Labour Force Survey
LLI	Limiting longstanding illness
n.e.c.	not elsewhere classified
NS-SEC	National Statistics Socio-economic Classification
ONS	Office for National Statistics
OPCS	Office for Population Censuses and Surveys
OUG	Occupational Unit Group
RGSC	Registrar General's Social Class
SC	Social Class based on Occupation
SEC	Socio-economic Classification
SEC90	NS-SEC based on SOC90
SEG	Socio-economic Groups
SMR	Standardised mortality ratio
SOC	Standard Occupational Classification
SOC90	Standard Occupational Classification 1990
SOC2000	Standard Occupational Classification 2000
SRS	Service relationship score
VLBW	Very low birthweight

Contributors

Sara Arber is Professor of Sociology and Head of the School of Human Sciences at the University of Surrey. Publications include *Connecting Gender and Ageing* (with Jay Ginn, Open University Press, 1995), *The Myth of Generational Conflict: Family and State in Ageing Societies* (with Claudine Attias-Donfut, Routledge, 2000) and Editor of a Special Issue of *Social Science and Medicine* on 'Social and economic patterning of women's health in a changing world' (2002, vol. 54, no. 5).

Roeland Beerten is a Principle Methodologist at the Office for National Statistics. He is responsible for consultancy and advice on data collection methodology for social surveys. His research interests include social classifications and survey non-response. He previously worked as a researcher on the Belgian National Election Study at the University of Leuven, Belgium.

Helen Cooper is a Senior Researcher and is currently working on a cross-cutting inequalities project at the Office for National Statistics. Prior to this, she was a Research Fellow at the University of Surrey where her research interests were inequalities in health associated with age, gender and ethnicity. She is author (with Sarah Arber and Jay Ginn) of Health Development Agency publications on social capital.

Tony Coxon is Research Professor in the Department of Sociology and Health and Human Sciences at the University of Essex. He has researched for many years on the margins of social stratification – Clergy as an occupation and the Project on Occupational Cognition (Edinburgh, with Charles Jones), which questioned the cognitive assumptions of grading and stratification scales. Recent work includes multidimensional scaling and classification and sexual behaviour and gay men.

Peter Elias is a Professor at the University of Warwick's Institute for Employment Research (IER). His research interests include employment event history modelling and the analysis of transitions between education, training and employment. Together with others at the IER and the Office for National Statistics he undertook the Revision of the Standard Occupational Classification. He is currently working with David Rose, Jean Martin and David Pevalin on plans for the introduction of a harmonised social classification for the European Union.

Geoffrey Evans is an Official Fellow of Nuffield College, Oxford. His research interests include social stratification, voting behaviour, ethnic conflict, comparative political sociology, democratisation and survey methodology. A long-time member of the team undertaking the British Election Studies, in recent years he has also conducted research into social and political divisions in Northern Ireland and many post-communist societies.

Kimberly Fisher is a Chief Research Officer at the Institute for Social and Economic Research, working in the fields of employment, living conditions of people with disabilities, and time use. Dr Fisher is also a DIW Research Affiliate.

Justine Fitzpatrick is a Health Analyst for the Health of Londoners Programme and the London Health Observatory. She previously worked as a Senior Research Officer in the Health Variations Team at the Office for National Statistics where she was co-editor of *Geographic Variations in Health*. Current work includes local mapping of the health inequalities targets across London.

Anthony Heath is Professor and Head of the Department of Sociology at the University of Oxford, a Professorial Fellow of Nuffield College and a Co-Director of the Centre for Research into Elections and Social Trends (CREST). His current research includes ethnic disadvantage, ethnic and national identity, contextual effects of ethnicity and social class, and the social bases of electoral behaviour.

Jean Martin is Director of the Data Methodology and Evaluation Division, Office for National Statistics, which includes responsibility for the official classifications of occupation and industry and for the NS-SEC. On behalf of ONS, she managed the ESRC Review of Government Social Classifications that led to the development of NS-SEC.

Abigail McKnight is a Research Fellow at the Centre for Analysis of Social Exclusion (CASE) at the London School of Economics and Political Science. Her research has focused on labour market disadvantage, inequality, child poverty, and the evaluation of welfare to work programmes. She contributed to the revision of the Standard Occupational Classification (SOC2000) and the development of the new socio-economic classification (NS-SEC).

Colin Mills holds a joint appointment in the Methodology Institute and the Interdisciplinary Institute of Management at the London School of Economics and Political Science. He has written a number of articles on social stratification and is currently carrying out research on changes in the terms of the employment relationship in the UK.

David J. Pevalin is a Senior Research Officer at the Institute for Social and Economic Research at the University of Essex. He was involved in Phase Four of the ESRC Review of Government Social Classifications and the construction of the final version of the NS-SEC using SOC2000.

David Rose is Research Professor of Sociology in the Institute for Social and Economic Research at the University of Essex. He was the Academic Convenor of the ESRC Review of Government Social Classifications. He is joint author of several books including *Social Class in Modern Britain* (Hutchinson, 1988) and *The ESRC Review of Government Social Classifications* (ESRC/ONS, 1998) and joint editor of *Constructing Classes* (ESRC/ONS, 1997).

Part I
Introduction to the National Statistics Socio-economic Classification

In the UK two socio-economic classifications (SECs) have been widely used in both official statistics and academic research, *Social Class based on Occupation* (SC, formerly *Registrar General's Social Class*) and *Socio-economic Groups* (SEG). In 1994 the Office for Population Censuses and Surveys (now part of the Office for National Statistics, ONS) commissioned the Economic and Social Research Council (ESRC) to undertake a Review of Government Social Classifications. As a result of this Review, ESRC recommended a new SEC – subsequently named by ONS as the *National Statistics Socio-economic Classification* (NS-SEC) – to replace both SC and SEG. The NS-SEC came into official use in April 2001.

This introduction to Part I provides basic information on the ESRC Review and its principal conclusions and recommendations. Rose and O'Reilly (1998) have provided a detailed account of the Review team's work leading to an interim version of the NS-SEC. Rose and Pevalin with O'Reilly (2003) have updated this volume to include the work undertaken to produce the final version of the NS-SEC as discussed and used in this volume. Together, these two volumes thus offer a more comprehensive account of the Review than we offer here.

However, before we consider the ESRC Review, first we should look at its background in terms of the previous official classifications. Here we shall provide only a summary relating to the perceived problems of both SC and SEG that led to a recommendation for a new SEC before we proceed to a discussion of the NS-SEC.

SOCIAL CLASS BASED ON OCCUPATION

The final version of Social Class based on Occupation is given in Figure I.1. The limitations of SC, which remained almost unchanged from 1921 until its demise, are legion. It has correctly been described as an intuitive or a priori scale. A plethora of articles and book chapters have appeared in the last twenty years calling attention to its problems (see Rose, 1994; 1995). Many writers criticised it because they claimed that it had no coherent conceptual or theoretical basis, a point that particularly concerned the ESRC Review team. Even the champions of its empirical usefulness agreed on this. Others have argued that the shifting conceptual basis offered for it over the years – a hierarchy in relation to social standing or occupational skill – in fact reflected

I	Professional etc occupations
II	Managerial and technical occupations
III	Skilled occupations
(nm)	Non-manual
(m)	Manual
IV	Partly skilled occupations
V	Unskilled occupations

The occupation groups included in each of these categories were selected in such a way as to bring together, as far as possible, people with similar levels of occupational skill. In general, each occupation group was assigned as a whole to one or other social class and no account was taken of differences between individuals in the same occupation group, for example differences in education. However, for persons having the employment status of foreman or manager the following additional rules applied:

(a) each occupation was given a basic social class;
(b) persons of foreman status whose basic social class was IV or V were allocated to Social Class III;
(c) persons of manager status were allocated to Social Class II with certain exceptions.

Figure I.1   *Social Class based on Occupation*

an outmoded nineteenth-century view of social structure which can be traced directly to eugenicist ideas.

Even when judged in its own terms, questions were raised regarding the validity and reliability of SC. For example, there was cogent evidence that any claim that the SC related to social standing was unjustified. This judgement was also shown to apply to the post-1980 claims that the SC related to a hierarchy of occupational skill. Consequently, those responsible in ONS for the periodic revision of SC had to make explicit or implicit ad hoc judgements about the relative position of occupations on the underlying continuum – whatever that was considered to be.

SOCIO-ECONOMIC GROUPS

Socio-economic Groups have been much less discussed in the literature than SC, yet SEG was a more social scientific measure, one that spoke theory without knowing it. As can be seen from Figure I.2, SEG had an operational requirement to take account of employment status and size of employing organisation as well as occupation. In that sense, as we shall see in Chapter 2, SEG came closer than SC to sociological measures of social class. When we note that SEGs were devised in 1950 by a social scientist, David Glass, we can see why this might be the case.

The problems that arose with SEG were somewhat different from those of SC. To begin with, there was no explanation available at all concerning the conceptual basis of SEG. References to SEG being a measure of 'social and economic status' were hardly illuminating. In fact, the seventeen groups could be collapsed to produce something like the Goldthorpe class schema on which we have based the NS-SEC. However, the lack of a conceptual rationale

Classification by Socio-economic Groups was introduced in 1951 and extensively amended in 1961. The classification aimed to bring together people with jobs of similar social and economic status. The allocation of occupied persons to Socio-economic Groups was determined by considering their employment status and occupation (and industry, though for practical purposes no direct reference was made since it was possible in Great Britain to use classification by occupation as a means of distinguishing effectively those engaged in agriculture).

The Socio-economic Groups are:

(1.1)   Employers in industry, commerce, etc (large establishments)
(1.2)   Managers in central and local government, industry, commerce, etc (large establishments)
(2.1)   Employers in industry, commerce, etc (small establishments)
(2.2)   Managers in industry, commerce, etc (small establishments)
(3)   Professional workers – self-employed
(4)   Professional workers – employees
(5.1)   Intermediate non-manual workers – ancillary workers and artists
(5.2)   Intermediate non-manual workers – foremen and supervisors non-manual
(6)   Junior non-manual workers
(7)   Personal service workers
(8)   Foremen and supervisors – manual
(9)   Skilled manual workers
(10)   Semi-skilled manual workers
(11)   Unskilled manual workers
(12)   Own account workers (other than professional)
(13)   Farmers – employers and managers
(14)   Farmers – own account
(15)   Agricultural workers
(16)   Members of armed forces
(17)   Inadequately described and not stated occupations

Figure I.2   *Socio-economic Groups*

necessarily meant that there were no clear rules to guide researchers on how SEGs might best be collapsed for analysis – hence the many, varied and often incoherent ways in which this was achieved. As with SC, SEG also relied on outmoded distinctions – those of skill and the manual/non-manual divide. Partly as a consequence of this, SEG reflected women's positions in the social structure very inadequately, with the heterogeneous SEGs 6 and 7 being particularly responsible for this. Finally, the logic of the allocation of occupation and employment status combinations to SEG seemed especially complex and opaque, with SEG 5 being particularly egregious in this respect. To all this we can add one further observation: SEG and SC did not interrelate, in the sense that SEG did not collapse into the categories of SC. They were two different classifications and thus probably one more than was necessary.

THE ESRC REVIEW

It is against this background that the ESRC Review of Government Social Classifications was conceived. The Review had the following terms of reference:

1   To review the characteristics, use and perceptions of Social Class based on Occupation and Socio-economic Groups.
2   To review existing alternative social classifications.
3   To propose recommendations for the revision of government social classifications.
4   To assess the effectiveness of recommended revisions.

The Review was conducted in four phases. In Phase 1 both the continuing need for government SECs and the weaknesses of the current ones as discussed previously were demonstrated. It was recommended that a single, new, occupationally based SEC should be devised. This new SEC should unite the most important features and advantages of both SEG and SC (see Rose, 1995). For example, in terms of SC, there should ultimately be a small number of categories; in terms of SEG, the underlying implicit rationale relating to employment relations should be retained. The new measure needed to be reasonably continuous with (i.e. bridgeable to) the existing SECs, and, although occupationally based, it should be comprehensive in relation to the adult population, with rules for allocating the unemployed and the economically inactive. The new SEC also had to be applicable to a range of different types of official data – registration data, Census data and survey data. It thus seemed sensible to develop a flexible, and therefore nested, SEC with a large number of categories, similar to SEG, which could be collapsed according to rules to a number of different SC-type analytic variables.

Phases 2 and 3 of the Review were therefore concerned with designating a new SEC and then operationalising, validating and testing it. Initially this involved specifying a classification with an explicit conceptual rationale that would render it both more useful as a social scientific and policy tool and clearer in terms of operational and maintenance rules.

In order to achieve these objectives, Phases 2 and 3 were designed in the form of six interrelated and largely sequential projects: (1) advice to ONS on the Census design requirements of the SEC; (2) the establishment of a conceptual basis, operational rules and other required properties for a new SEC; (3) as a research resource to the Review, the creation of a database on the 371 Occupational Unit Groups (OUGs) of the 1990 Standard Occupational Classification (SOC), one of the principal building blocks for the new SEC (see McKnight and Elias, 1997); (4) the creation of a new matrix relating the OUGs of the Standard Occupational Classification and employment statuses to the categories of the new SEC; (5) validation of the new SEC; and (6) bridging between current and new SECs.

Finally, Phase 4 had the task of rebasing the NS-SEC on the new Standard Occupational Classification that came into effect in 2000, *SOC2000* (see Elias et al., 2001; ONS, 2000a; 2000b).[1] At the same time, various adjustments were made to the interim version produced at Phase 3 (see Rose and O'Reilly, 1998) in the light of new evidence and some rethinking.

The two chapters in the first part of this book provide an introduction to the NS-SEC. In Chapter 1 we offer a description of the new classification in all its forms. We also discuss associated measurement issues and operational rules.

This description provides a foundation for Chapter 2 in which we explain the conceptual basis of the NS-SEC and what flows from this in terms of analytic issues.

NOTES

1 See also the NS-SEC User Manual at:
http://www.statistics.gov.uk/nsbase/methods_quality/ns_sec/soc2000.asp

REFERENCES

Elias, P., McKnight, A., Davies, R. and Kinshott, G. (2001) 'Occupational change: revision of the Standard Occupational Classification', *Labour Market Trends*, January. Coventry: Institute of Employment Research, University of Warwick.

McKnight, A. and Elias, P. (1997) 'A database of information on unit groups of the SOC', in D. Rose and K. O'Reilly (eds) *Constructing Classes: Towards a New Social Classification for the UK*. Swindon/London: ESRC/ONS. pp. 116–45.

ONS (2000a) *Standard Occupational Classification 2000: Volume 1. Structure and descriptions of unit groups*. London: The Stationery Office.

ONS (2000b) *Standard Occupational Classification 2000: Volume 2. The coding index*. London: The Stationery Office.

Rose, D. (1994) *The Registrar General's Class Schema: Characteristics and Criticisms. A Report to ESRC*. Colchester: ESRC Research Centre on Micro-social Change, University of Essex.

Rose, D. (1995) *A Report on Phase 1 of the ESRC Review of OPCS Social Classifications*. Swindon: ESRC; reproduced in Appendix 1 of D. Rose and K. O'Reilly (eds) *Constructing Classes: Towards a New Social Classification for the UK*. Swindon/London: ESRC/ONS. pp. 151–67.

Rose, D. and O'Reilly, K. (1998) *The ESRC Review of Government Social Classifications*. London/Swindon: ONS/ESRC.

Rose, D. and Pevalin, D.J. (with O'Reilly, K.) (2003) *The National Statistics Socio-economic Classification: Origins, Development and Use*. London: ONS.

1
The NS-SEC Described

David Rose and David J. Pevalin

INTRODUCTION

This chapter offers a basic introductory description of the NS-SEC. We shall outline the NS-SEC in terms of its different versions and their categories, thus demonstrating the nested structure of the classification. We also discuss various issues relating to how this nested structure operates, including those aspects that relate to continuity between the new and old government classifications. A number of important measurement issues are also addressed. These include methods for deriving the NS-SEC in the absence of some elements of its operational algorithm, as well as a discussion of the means by which the NS-SEC may be measured at the household level. Finally, we shall present some basic frequency data for the NS-SEC as revealed by the 1996/97 Winter Quarter of the Labour Force Survey (LFS). We begin with the 'operational' version of the new classification.

THE OPERATIONAL VERSION

The operational version of the NS-SEC has two purposes. First, it is the principal means by which we translate between both SC and SEG and the new classification. Second, in its basic categories, it is a classification designed to offer researchers maximum flexibility in terms of different possible and allowable collapses (within the underlying conceptual model of employment relations discussed in Chapter 2) to nine, eight, seven, six, five and three class analytic variables.

Figure 1.1 indicates the fourteen functional and three residual categories as well as the sub-categories of the operational version. The functional categories (L1–L14) represent a variety of labour market positions and employment statuses that can be collapsed into classes as defined by the employment relations approach discussed in Chapter 2 (see Figure 1.3 below; see also Goldthorpe, 1997). The 'L' prefix for each category is short for 'long' version, our initial name for what is now called the operational version. As we shall explain, L14 is an optional category and L15, L16 and L17 are the residual categories that are excluded when the classification is collapsed into classes. All the sub-divisions of categories are component codes required for bridging

L1 Employers in large establishments

L2 Higher managerial occupations

L3 Higher professional occupations
L3.1 'Traditional' employees
L3.2 'New' employees
L3.3 'Traditional' self-employed
L3.4 'New' self-employed

L4 Lower professional and higher technical occupations
L4.1 'Traditional' employees
L4.2 'New' employees
L4.3 'Traditional' self-employed
L4.4 'New' self-employed

L5 Lower managerial occupations

L6 Higher supervisory occupations

L7 Intermediate occupations
L7.1 Intermediate clerical and administrative occupations
L7.2 Intermediate service occupations
L7.3 Intermediate technical and auxiliary occupations
L7.4 Intermediate engineering occupations

L8 Employers in small establishments
L8.1 Employers in small establishments in industry, commerce, services, etc.
L8.2 Employers in small establishments in agriculture

L9 Own account workers
L9.1 Own account workers (non-professional)
L9.2 Own account workers in agriculture

L10 Lower supervisory occupations

L11 Lower technical occupations
L11.1 Lower technical craft occupations
L11.2 Lower technical process operative occupations

L12 Semi-routine occupations
L12.1 Semi-routine sales occupations
L12.2 Semi-routine service occupations
L12.3 Semi-routine technical occupations
L12.4 Semi-routine operative occupations
L12.5 Semi-routine agricultural occupations
L12.6 Semi-routine clerical occupations
L12.7 Semi-routine childcare occupations

L13 Routine occupations
L13.1 Routine sales and service occupations
L13.2 Routine production occupations
L13.3 Routine technical occupations
L13.4 Routine operative occupations
L13.5 Routine agricultural occupations

L14 Never worked and long-term unemployed
L14.1 Never worked
L14.2 Long-term umemployed

L15 Full-time students

L16 Occupations not stated or inadequately described

L17 Not classifiable for other reasons

Figure 1.1 *Operational categories and sub-categories of the National Statistics Socio-economic Classification*

and continuity to SC and SEG rather than necessary sub-categories in terms of the conceptual base of the NS-SEC.

A fuller discussion of each category of the NS-SEC in terms of (1) category descriptions, and thus face validity issues (the degree to which categories make intuitive sense), (2) conceptual and operational issues, and (3) continuity issues in relation to SC and SEG can be found elsewhere (see Rose and Pevalin with O'Reilly, 2003). Here we only present the descriptive definitions of the NS-SEC operational categories.

The NS-SEC operational categories

The following category descriptions define labour market positions (*not* classes) as determined by an employment relations approach to social classification. Necessarily, therefore, the descriptions contain references to employment relations concepts, especially those of the *service relationship* and the *labour contract*. These concepts are fully explained in Chapter 2.

L1   Employers in large establishments
Employer positions occupied by persons other than professionals where the incumbents employ others (and thus assume some degree of control over them), and delegate some part of their managerial and entrepreneurial functions onto salaried staff, in enterprises employing twenty-five or more persons.

L2   Higher managerial occupations
Positions in which there is a 'service relationship' with the employer, and which involve general, higher level or executive planning and supervision of operations on behalf of the employer.

L3   Higher professional occupations
L3.1   'Traditional' professional employees – that is, previously defined as professionals by SC and SEG
L3.2   'New' professional employees – that is, not previously defined as professionals by SC and SEG
L3.3   'Traditional' self-employed professionals – that is, previously defined as professionals by SC and SEG
L3.4   'New' self-employed professionals – that is, not previously defined as professionals by SC and SEG
Positions, whether occupied by employers, the self-employed, managers or employees, covering all types of higher professional work. Employees in this category have a 'service relationship' with their employer.

L4   Lower professional and higher technical occupations
L4.1   'Traditional' lower professionals – that is, previously defined as technical occupations and ancillary workers professionals by SC and SEG
L4.2   'New' lower professionals – that is, not previously defined as technical occupations and ancillary workers by SC and SEG
L4.3   'Traditional' self-employed lower professionals – that is, previously defined as technical occupations and ancillary workers by SC and SEG
L4.4   'New' self-employed lower professionals – that is, not previously defined as technical occupations and ancillary workers
Positions, whether occupied by small employers, the self-employed, managers in small establishments or employees, and covering lower professional occupations. Employees in this category have an attenuated form of the 'service relationship'.

L5   Lower managerial occupations
Positions in which there is an attenuated 'service relationship', and where those employed in these positions generally plan and supervise operations on behalf of the employer under the direction of senior managers.

L6   Higher supervisory occupations
Supervisory positions (other than managerial or lower professional) having an attenuated form of 'service relationship' and which cover intermediate occupations included in L7 and involve as their main task the formal and immediate supervision of others engaged in such occupations.

L7   Intermediate occupations
L7.1   Intermediate (clerical and administrative) occupations
L7.2   Intermediate (service) occupations
L7.3   Intermediate (technical and auxiliary) occupations
L7.4   Intermediate (engineering) occupations
Positions not involving general planning or supervisory powers, in certain clerical, administrative, services, technical and engineering occupations. Positions in this category are 'mixed' in terms of employment regulation; that is, are intermediate with respect to the service relationship and the labour contract.

L8   Employers in small establishments
L8.1   Employers in small establishments (less than twenty-five employees) in industry, commerce, services, etc.
L8.2   Employers in small establishments (less than twenty-five employees) in agriculture.
Employer positions (other than in higher and lower professional occupations) in which the incumbents employ others (and thus assume some degree of control over them) and carry out all or most of the entrepreneurial and managerial functions of the enterprise but employ less than twenty-five employees.

L9   Own account workers
L9.1   Own account workers (non-professional)
L9.2   Own account workers in agriculture
Self-employed positions in which the incumbents are engaged in agriculture or in any non-professional trade, personal service, semi-routine, routine or other occupation but have no employees other than family workers.

L10   Lower supervisory occupations
Supervisory positions having a modified form of 'labour contract', which cover occupations included in categories L11-L13, and involve as their main task the formal and immediate supervision of others engaged in such occupations and thus the use of minor delegated authority.

L11   Lower technical occupations
L11.1   Lower technical (craft) occupations

L11.2   Lower technical (process operative) occupations
Positions in which employees are engaged in lower technical and related occupations and thereby have a modified form of the 'labour contract'.

L12   Semi-routine occupations

L12.1   Semi-routine (sales) occupations
L12.2   Semi-routine (service) occupations
L12.3   Semi-routine (technical) occupations
L12.4   Semi-routine (operative) occupations
L12.5   Semi-routine (agricultural) occupations
L12.6   Semi-routine (clerical) occupations
L12.7   Semi-routine (childcare) occupations
Positions in which employees are engaged in semi-routine occupations that have only a slightly modified labour contract.

L13   Routine occupations

L13.1   Routine (sales and service) occupations
L13.2   Routine (production) occupations
L13.3   Routine (technical) occupations
L13.4   Routine (operative) occupations
L13.5   Routine (agricultural) occupations
Positions where employees are engaged in routine occupations which have a basic labour contract.

L14   Never worked and long-term unemployed

L14.1   Never worked
L14.2   Long-term unemployed
Positions which entail exclusion from the labour market involving (a) those who have never been in paid employment but would wish to be; and (b) those who have been unemployed for an extended period while still seeking or wanting work.

L15   Full-time students

Persons over 16 years of age who are pursuing full-time courses of study in secondary, tertiary or higher education institutions.

L16   Occupations not stated or inadequately described

There are always some cases where the occupational data requested in response to surveys and censuses are not given or are inadequate for classificatory purposes. This category exists for such situations.

L17   Not classifiable for other reasons

Whatever rules are devised, some adults cannot always be allocated to a class position within our schema. For example, if the design of a particular survey excluded (say) the elderly from being asked questions about past employment, then for completeness' sake, such cases should be allocated to this category.

Before we turn to how this operational version may be collapsed into analytic variables, we should first note how the classification deals with (1) the non-employed and (2) full-time students.

The NS-SEC and the non-employed

In order to increase population coverage, the NS-SEC treats those who are not currently in paid employment by allocating them to the class of their last *main* paid job. Thus, for most non-employed persons (the unemployed, the retired, those looking after a home, those on government employment or training schemes, the sick and disabled, etc.), the normal procedure is to classify them in this manner. The main exception to this rule is for full-time students (see below). Those who have *never worked* but are seeking, or would like, paid work should be allocated to L14.1. In the case of the 'long-term unemployed', there is an argument that they should not be classified according to their last job, but should be assigned to category L14.2 of the classification (on the grounds that they are excluded from employment relations). They are then included with the never worked when the NS-SEC is collapsed to its official eight-category version. However, it is not possible to define the long-term unemployed in any hard and fast way. Essentially, analysts must make their own decisions here, according to their research purposes. Some might not want to implement L14 at all and thus will exclude the never worked from the classification and classify all unemployed persons in respect of their last main job. Others might want to implement the class and use a six-month unemploy-ment rule related to the maximum length of time for which Jobseekers' Allowance is paid, but others might prefer a one- or even two-year unemploy-ment rule. Our recommendation, in the absence of any strong analytic or theoretical preference, would be to employ a one-year rule. The use of such a rule in health research is further pursued in Chapter 10. Of course, since we cannot prescribe on this matter, *information on last main job should be collected for all unemployed persons*. We are aware that it may not be possible to implement these rules for the allocation of the non-employed on all data sets. However, we recommend that, other things being equal, data be collected in a manner that would allow these rules to be implemented.

The NS-SEC and full-time students

Full-time students would not normally be allocated a class position, although they are recognised as a category in the full classification for reasons of completeness. Nevertheless, since many students will have or have had paid occupations, they could be classified by current or last main job if the analyst wished to do so. Normally, however, we would not expect students to be classified in this way. Conventionally, where full-time students are included in class analyses (e.g. in research on education), they are normally given their class of origin or family class position. Regardless of this, data should be collected on the current or last main jobs of full-time students. In Chapter 12 we shall indicate some of the problems associated with allocating students to a class position on the basis of their part-time occupations.

COLLAPSED VERSIONS OF THE NS-SEC

The operational version of the classification discussed in the preceding para-
graphs may be collapsed into a number of different analytic variables. Although
it has no official warrant as a descriptive name, for convenience we have
termed these *socio-economic classes*. The principal one of these 'class'
variables – the official NS-SEC as adopted by ONS – is depicted in Figure 1.2.
It contains eight basic categories, although Class 1 may be sub-divided if
analysts so choose. However, Class 8 is not easily operationalised in all
government data sets and so is not a required element of the official classification. The first two columns of Figure 1.3 show the relationship between the
operational version of the classification and the official NS-SEC.

NS-SEC category names

It will be noted that, with the exception of the three-class version, none of the
category names of any of the versions of the NS-SEC makes reference to either
'skill' or the 'manual/non-manual divide'.[1] This is quite deliberate, of course.
The notion of skill has no part in the conception of the NS-SEC; to use
category names that refer to skill would therefore be inconsistent with the
employment relations approach discussed in the next chapter. As for the
manual/non-manual divide, changes in the nature and structure of both industry
and occupations have rendered this distinction both outmoded and misleading.
As Goldthorpe (1997) has noted, although it might be argued that no great
importance needs to be attached to category names or class labels, nevertheless
conceptually neither the degree of 'manuality' of the work involved nor its skill
level are considerations that should determine the allocation of occupation-by-
employment status units to classes. And empirically the relationship between
the manual/non-manual divide and the basic positions distinguished by an
employment relations approach is less than is generally perceived. Consequently what were previously referred to in the old SECs as 'intermediate',
'junior' or 'skilled' non-manual occupations now become, respectively, 'lower
professional', 'higher supervisory' or 'intermediate' occupations. 'Skilled',

---

1   Higher managerial and professional occupations
    1.1   Large employers and higher managerial occupations
    1.2   Higher professional occupations
2   Lower managerial and professional occupations
3   Intermediate occupations
4   Small employers and own account workers
5   Lower supervisory and technical occupations
6   Semi-routine occupations
7   Routine occupations
8   Never worked and long-term unemployed

Figure 1.2 *The National Statistics Socio-economic
Classification*

Operational categories	Analytic variables			
	Nine classes	Eight classes	Five classes	Three classes
L1 Employers in large establishments	1.1 Large employers and higher managerial occupations	1 Higher managerial and professional occupations	1 Managerial and professional occupations	1 Managerial and professional occupations
L2 Higher managerial occupations				
L3 Higher professional occupations	1.2 Higher professional occupations			
L4 Lower professional and higher technical occupations	2 Lower managerial and professional occupations	2 Lower managerial and professional occupations		
L5 Lower managerial occupations				
L6 Higher supervisory occupations				
L7 Intermediate occupations	3 Intermediate occupations	3 Intermediate occupations	2 Intermediate occupations	2 Intermediate occupations
L8 Employers in small establishments	4 Small employers and own account workers	4 Small employers and own account workers	3 Small employers and own account workers	
L9 Own account workers				
L10 Lower supervisory occupations	5 Lower supervisory and technical occupations	5 Lower supervisory and technical occupations	4 Lower supervisory and technical occupations	
L11 Lower technical occupations				
L12 Semi-routine occupations	6 Semi-routine occupations	6 Semi-routine occupations	5 Semi-routine and routine occupations	3 Routine and manual occupations
L13 Routine occupations	7 Routine occupations	7 Routine occupations		
L14 Never worked and long-term unemployed	8 Never worked and long-term unemployed	8 Never worked and long-term unemployed	Never worked and long-term unemployed	Never worked and long-term unemployed

Figure 1.3 NS-SEC operational categories and their relation to the analytic class variables

'semi-skilled', 'partly skilled' and 'unskilled' manual occupations become, respectively, 'lower technical', 'semi-routine' and 'routine' occupations.

Issues in collapsing the operational version to the official NS-SEC

1 *Employers in large establishments*. These (L1) are combined with higher managerial occupations (L2) in Class 1.1. If it were possible to overcome the difficulties of operationalising the distinction between legal forms of incorporation, partnership, etc., in a meaningful way, there would be no obstacle in principle to elaborating the classification so as to remove the anomalies caused by including employers in a class that is largely composed of employees. Even so, the small numbers in L1 make it unlikely that it could ever be separately analysed as a class in survey research. Nevertheless we could have divided Class 1 into three components by giving large employers a sub-class of their own. Indeed we might have regarded large employers as being the whole of an elite Class 1, with higher managers and professionals in Class 2. This might have satisfied purists (see for example Scott, 1996: 212 and *passim*) but it would yield little in the way of analytic benefit and might even be misleading. Most of those in L1 could not be described as heroic capitalists, as we shall see later.

2 *Small employers*. Other than in the case of professionals in L3.3, L3.4, L4.3 and L4.4, employers in small establishments (L8), because they generally have only one or two employees, are combined with own account workers (L9) into a single self-employed class.

3 *Higher managerial and professional occupations*. While it would be normal within an employment relations perspective to regard Class 1 as a single class for analytic purposes, we have preserved a distinction made by SEG between senior managerial positions (1.1) and higher professional positions (1.2) so that those who wish to analyse these two elements of Class 1 separately may do so. SC also had a separate class (Class I) for higher professionals that we have isolated in L3.1 and L3.3 of the operational version. Since debate continues as to whether higher managers and professionals are merely *situs*es within one class or two different classes (see Mills and Evans in Chapter 4 and Butler and Savage, 1995; Evans and Mills, 2000; Savage et al., 1992), this distinction is further justified. A further change from the interim version of the NS-SEC affects higher and lower professionals. The final operational version follows SEG in making a distinction between self-employed and employee professionals. This is largely for continuity's sake and not because we think it brings any analytic benefit. In the real world, especially for 'traditional' higher professionals, independent practice and salaried employment are often indistinguishable so that true self-employment is difficult to identify. Finally, it should be noted that, as was the case for SC, any OUG designated as professional in the NS-SEC is professional regardless of employment status. Therefore,

self-employed higher and lower professionals are allocated to L3.3, L3.4, L4.3 or L4.4 and not to L8 or L9.

4   *Semi-routine and routine occupations.* To date, employment relations approaches have made no distinction between what we have called semi-routine and routine occupational positions (or what have been convention-ally known as 'semi-skilled' and 'unskilled' occupations) because a basic labour contract is assumed to exist for both positions. Hence, it would be normal to regard these positions as forming a unified class. The evidence that is provided by Mills and Evans in Chapter 4 appears to confirm this. Indeed, we originally proposed a Class 6 divided between semi-routine (6.1) and routine (6.2) occupations. However, SC does distinguish 'semi-skilled' occupations (Class IV) from 'unskilled' occupations (Class V). SEG makes a similar distinction. Hence, for continuity's sake, we have created L12, Class 6 and L13, Class 7 as separate classes (although those who wish to ignore this distinction will no doubt treat Classes 6 and 7 together for analytic purposes).

So how many 'classes' are there?

All the above comments beg the question, 'So how many classes are there?' Some believe a definitive answer may be given to this question (see for example Runciman, 1990). However, an employment relations approach does not assume that there are x and only x number of classes. Rather it argues that the number of classes to be recognised empirically depends upon the analytic purposes at hand. The NS-SEC is thus to be regarded as an *instrument du travail.*

As an explicit demonstration of the flexibility of the NS-SEC, the relations between the operational classification and the various analytic class variables that may be derived from it are given in Figure 1.3. We would expect that most current academic users of SC would use the seven- or eight-class versions of NS-SEC. They may want to treat 1.1 and 1.2 as separate classes, class 'fractions' or *situs*es (depending on their predilections), especially when comparing current research using NS-SEC with past research using SC. Within the conceptual model, it is also possible to have a five-class version and if analysts wish to keep professionals and managers separate, a six-class version could be implemented.

The 'manual/non-manual divide'

In the past, analysts have sometimes divided SC into two basic classes, non-manual and manual. We have already seen that the manual/non-manual distinction no longer holds in any meaningful way. For example, 'white-collar' positions are found in both L12 and L13 and some 'blue-collar' positions in L7. However, the new classification does allow for a basic three-class version, as in the last column of Figure 1.3.

We should enter a caveat here, however, concerning the three- and five-class versions. Each of these allocates the never worked and 'long-term unemployed' to the working class. Thus, if performing health analyses, users would need to be very careful about how the 'long-term unemployed' and the never worked were defined and treated. Including the permanently sick would clearly not be sensible. They should be classified to last main job. Of course, this may still leave some people who are permanently sick or disabled in the never worked category, hence this warning. The long-term unemployed should include only those who are seeking or are available for work. Analysts may, in any case, prefer to allocate these to the class of last main job for the three- and five-class versions. We would again stress the point made earlier about the need to collect data on last main job for *all* the non-employed, thus giving analysts maximum flexibility. Even more importantly, how analysts deal with problems like these must depend upon their theoretical and analytic purposes. We shall return to this point in Chapter 2 when we discuss conceptual issues and their implications for analysis. Chapter 10 also pursues the problems arising in health inequality research discussed here.

Continuity between NS-SEC, SC and SEG

At the beginning of the chapter, we noted that the operational version of NS-SEC is the principal means for relating the new classification to the previous ones. In particular the sub-categories of the operational version were created with continuity in mind. As indications of how the sub-categories relate to SC and SEG, we offer the following examples. L3 is sub-divided between positions which were recognised by both SEG and SC as higher professional – 'traditional professionals' – and those (e.g. computer analysts) which now appear to be higher professional positions on the basis of research conducted to produce the NS-SEC – 'new professionals'. L4 is equivalently treated in terms of lower professional positions (or what SC termed 'technical occupations' in Class II and SEG 5.1 referred to as 'ancillary workers'). Similarly, L7, L8, L9, L12 and L13 are also sub-divided to aid continuity with SC and SEG. This structure has an additional advantage. It permits us to look 'inside' the NS-SEC classes in our analyses, and thus at internal class variations, as we shall explain later.

In order to examine the relationships between the NS-SEC, SC and SEG, it was first necessary for us to create SOC2000 versions of both SC and SEG.[2] We did not make any other changes to SC and SEG allocations that we believe would have necessarily been undertaken by ONS simply in order to 'catch up' with SOC2000 and other secular changes. Following the creation of a few new sub-categories in the operational version in order to improve bridging between the NS-SEC, SC and SEG, continuity was assessed at 87 per cent with both SC and SEG. The levels of continuity here compare with 91 per cent for SC and 88 per cent for SEG with the interim NS-SEC.

Chapter 11 further explores continuity between SC and NS-SEC and the implications for analysts.

MEASUREMENT ISSUES

We now turn to some of the measurement issues associated with the NS-SEC.

Creating the NS-SEC

Although we have specified a new SEC, its operational requirements are basically unchanged from those used with the old classifications. With the exception of specifying the never worked and the long-term unemployed, the data required and the method used for creating the NS-SEC from the Census and from social surveys are the same as were required for SC and/or SEG; that is, data on occupation, establishment size and employment status.

Level of measurement

In measurement terms, the NS-SEC is nominal. Some analysts might see this as a disadvantage, preferring continuous or ordered scales. SC is, of course, ordinal and many researchers find this property useful. In particular, they like the health gradients SC conveniently produced. However, a price was paid for this. For example, SC never separately identified the self-employed, yet their life chances are distinctive from those of employees in the same occupations, a point to which we shall return presently. In any event, an employment relations approach necessarily involves nominal measurement and the use of appropriate analytic techniques. Why is this?

As we shall discuss in more detail in Chapter 2, we take the view that occupation (usually combined with employment status) is a reasonable indicator of overall social position. This is so because the life chances of individuals and families depend mainly on their position in the social division of labour and on the material and symbolic advantages that derive from it. The Phase 1 Report of the Review noted that there are broadly two different ways of creating occupationally based social classifications – *occupational scales* and *class schemata* (Rose, 1995: 9–10 and 38–9; and see also Rose, 1994). Occupational scales are hierarchically ordered *strata*, each of which comprises sets of occupations which are regarded as equivalent in terms of whatever the scale is measuring. Thus SC is an ordered scale in respect of (supposedly) skill or social standing. The Cambridge Scale (Prandy, 1990) is continuous, and is designed to measure generalised social advantage. Classifications such as NS-SEC, however, are designed to measure the *relational* as well as the distributive aspects of social inequality. Hence the NS-SEC relies on employment *relations* as its basis. As has been shown elsewhere (see Rose and O'Reilly, 1998: Section 5), this classification minimises (so far as is possible within the limitations of the LFS data used for this purpose) within-class and maximises between-class variation in terms of (a selected range of) employment relations measures. That is, we have determined the work and market relations typical of each NS-SEC class or category.

However, because the NS-SEC is based on social relations, its classes are not *strictu sensu* hierarchically ordered in a unilinear way. This is why we must collapse the operational version (see Figure 1.1) in the manner indicated in Figure 1.3 (see also Figure 2.2). For example, higher managerial and professional occupations (Classes 1.1 and 1.2) are broadly equal, as is non-professional self-employment (whether small employers or own account workers) in Class 4. Of course, some class categories *are* superordinate with respect to others, for example higher managerial positions (Class 1.1) vis-à-vis intermediate and working class (Classes 5, 6 and 7) positions. However, we cannot wholly order a schema such as NS-SEC. We do not attempt to describe society as a layered model in the manner of SC, but via more subtle, relational concepts similar to those that were implicit in SEG.

A 'health' warning on measurement issues

For all these reasons, we have previously offered a 'health warning' on measurement issues which we repeat here. Except in its basic three-class version, the NS-SEC should not be regarded or interpreted as an ordinal scale, not least (but not only) because of its recognition of self-employment as a separate class position. However, we recognise that some researchers might prefer to have an ordinal scale similar to SC with six classes. This could *ostensibly* be achieved, for example, by combining the self-employed in NS-SEC Class 4 with the intermediate Class 3. *We do not advocate this*, however, not least because the self-employed are distinctive in their life chances and behaviour, as Fitzpatrick in Chapter 8 and Sacker et al. (2000) have demonstrated in relation to mortality. On the contrary, we recommend strongly that analysts (1) accept the theoretical, and thus the measurement, principles of the new classification; (2) only collapse the NS-SEC in the recommended ways; (3) take advantage of the conceptual base of the model for developing hypotheses linking class to outcomes of interest; and (4) use analytic techniques as appropriate. We shall have more to say on the third of these points in Chapter 2.

Other measurement issues

There are a number of other measurement issues of which users should be aware. These concern (1) deriving NS-SEC where elements of the operational algorithm are missing; (2) the use and meaning of establishment size for generating certain NS-SEC categories; and (3) methods for producing a household or family class version of NS-SEC. We deal with each in turn.

Deriving 'reduced' and 'simplified' NS-SEC

The NS-SEC User Manual provides users with the derivation matrix needed to create the operational version of the classification.[3] However, the User Manual also provides matrices for two other methods of derivation: (1) *Reduced NS-*

SEC, similar to the former *SEGLOW* where data on establishment size are not available; and (2) *Simplified NS-SEC* (SSEC), equivalent to the old *Simplified Social Class*, for use with data sets where only occupation is recorded.

1   *Reduced NS-SEC*. Some data sets do not have all the operational elements required for the full implementation of the NS-SEC, for example birth and death registration data. Formerly, ONS used a version of SEG (SEGLOW) that could be implemented without information on establishment size. As a further demonstration of the flexibility of the NS-SEC, we have produced an equivalent of SEGLOW for the new classification based on the probabilities of managers or employers being 'large' or 'small' within each relevant SOC OUG (see ONS, 2000). When operationalised it accurately allocates 98 per cent of LFS cases in the seven-class version for those currently in paid employment (also see Chapter 8). The following are the rules for allocating managers and employers to Reduced NS-SEC:

(a)   In the case of managers, those in L3 are, of course, treated as professionals. For the remainder OUGs 1111–13, 1121, 1123–37, 1171–3, 1181, 1184, 1212, 1231 are allocated to L2. OUGs 1114, 1122, 1141–63, 1174, 1182–3, 1185–1211, 1219–26, 1232–9 are allocated to L5.

(b)   In the case of employers, the probability for every OUG is that they are small employers and should thus be assigned to L8.1 or L8.2 (L3 or L4 if higher or lower professional occupations).

2   *Simplified NS-SEC*. The counterpart to SEGLOW for SC was known as Simplified Social Class and again we have produced an NS-SEC equivalent. This is used when only information on OUG is available. In such cases, we have decided to classify OUGs to the class that is allocated for the employment status of employees, except where employees are in a minority within an OUG or an OUG has no employee status. In these cases we take the class of the most frequently occurring OUG/employment status combination. Simplified NS-SEC (SSEC) correctly allocates 84 per cent of LFS cases in the seven-class version for those currently in paid employment.

Establishment size

Employers   Like SEG, NS-SEC uses information on number of employees in the 'workplace' in order to distinguish between employers in large and small establishments. Operationalising the distinction between large and small employers has consisted, to date, of applying a size rule cut-off of twenty-five employees. Individual employers in organisations with twenty-five or more employees are deemed to own 'large' establishments; those owning enterprises below this threshold are classified as 'small' employers. While this pragmatic rule is not entirely satisfactory, there are good reasons for retaining it: analyses of LFS data suggest that it is a sensible cut-off for managers, and using the twenty-five-employee rule retains continuity with SEG.

How is the employing organisation defined? In government social surveys and in the Census organisational or establishment size is related to the workplace, that is the local unit of the establishment at which the respondent works (see GSS, 1996: 45). However, we would prefer that organisation or establishment should refer to an 'enterprise' as defined in the *Inter-Departmental Business Register* and not to a local unit (IDBR – see ONS, 1998: 3). Thus, in our view, local unit or workplace should only be used *faute de mieux*: that is, if it is impossible or impractical to obtain information at the level of the enterprise.

Large employers   It should be noted that, for the most part, the category of large employers in the NS-SEC is not dealing with the leaders of industry or the *Sunday Times*' 'Rich List'. In fact, according to our LFS data, at least 62 per cent of respondents in this category own enterprises with less than 50 employees. The most common occupations, accounting for almost 50 per cent of category L1, are restaurant owners and other service industry proprietors. Once a business becomes incorporated it is often difficult to disentangle ownership and control. Directors of large public companies usually have shareholdings, and thus are part owners, but they may well describe themselves as employees working in senior management or administrative positions and thus will be classified to L2. This is one reason why the inclusion of large employers and senior managers in the same basic class of collapsed versions of the classification (see above) makes some social scientific as well as pragmatic sense.

Managers   The interim version of the NS-SEC retained the distinction between managers in large and small establishments which SEG applied but which SC did not recognise. In terms of an employment relations approach, initially in the interim NS-SEC we followed Goldthorpe in deeming all managers in large establishments to be equivalent to senior managers and administrators in Class 1. In fact what employment relations approaches (and we assume SEG) really wish to distinguish is higher from lower level managerial positions, not whether a manager is in a large or small organisation. This conceptual distinction between higher and lower level managers is operationalised more satisfactorily in the final version of NS-SEC. This is because SOC2000 has a more refined and restricted definition of managerial occupations and we were able to identify some managerial OUGs that are in effect wholly or mainly occupied by junior or middle managers. Hence, these OUGs are now allocated to L5 (lower managerial) regardless of establishment size. This is more in keeping with the underlying concept. While small enterprises may not have many higher level managers, large enterprises are of course likely to have many lower level managers. The NS-SEC is thus rather better operationalised for managers using the new method.

The unit of class composition

Many analysts only perceive SECs as individual measures of labour market position. Consequently they only use them as such. In fact, however, many analyses would be improved if, when appropriate, researchers employed the household rather than the individual as the unit of class composition. It may be asked, however, how a measure such as the NS SEC, based as it is on employment contracts, can be anything other than an individual measure. We shall try and explain.

Traditionally the unit of class composition or unit of analysis has not been the individual but the conjugal family/household. That is, the (nuclear) family is given priority over the individual as the unit of class composition so that those living together in a family household are regarded as having the same class position. In other words, the family is the basic class structure element because of the interdependence and shared conditions of family members (see for example Goldthorpe, 1983). After all, a family member's own class position may have less relevance to his/her life chances than the position of another family member (see for example Vågerö, 2000). It is the family that is the unit of class 'fate' and the basic decision-making unit in terms of both consumption and labour market participation (see for example Erikson and Goldthorpe, 1992: 232–9). Hence, lines of division run between, but not through, families. This does not assume or imply that the family is egalitarian, but only that family members living in the same household share the same class fate. Therefore, we need to be able to assign a household NS-SEC value to all household members.

The simple practical solution to this problem has been to select one family or household member (usually the 'male breadwinner') and take that person's class to stand for the whole household. Recently, however, especially because of the increased participation of married women in the labour market, there has been much discussion about whether this continues to be an appropriate strategy. Some have advocated that the individual should now be the unit of class composition. Without entering into the details of this controversy (see Erikson and Goldthorpe, 1992; Sørensen, 1994), here we discuss different ways in which the NS-SEC can be applied to households and families. We shall amplify some of these issues in Chapter 12.

Assigning household class: 'highest income householder'

Because of the overt sexism involved in the male breadwinner approach to the definition of the household reference person (HRP), a new method has been developed by official statisticians (Martin, 1995; 1998; Martin and Barton, 1996). ONS has decided that, in the final instance, the HRP should be the 'Highest Income Householder' (HIH), thus removing sex as a criterion for determining head of household. Here the householder is regarded as the person responsible for owning or renting or who is otherwise responsible for the accommodation. Where this definition yields joint householders, the person with the highest income takes precedence and becomes the HRP. Where incomes are equal, the older is taken as the HRP. This procedure increases the likelihood both that a female will be the HRP and that the HRP better characterises the household's social position. Analysts will generally use this procedure for determining household class. When using most government data sets they will have no choice but to do this. However, it should be noted that *any* definition based on income is likely to reduce the number of HRPs classified as self-employed, since they tend to have (or to declare) low incomes.

Assigning household class: the 'dominance' approach

There is an alternative approach that regards the HRP as the one who is dominant in the labour market, the so-called 'dominance' approach (see Erikson, 1984). From a social scientific perspective, this procedure is preferable to one that relies on income in the determination of household class, but it does require that NS-SEC values must first be established for all household members.

The dominance approach advocates two class concepts. In the first, work-related concept, individuals are the unit of classification because work is uniquely related to individuals. Hence it does not matter whether the individuals are male or female; each can be assigned a *work position*. In the second, market-related concept, families are seen as the classification unit. This is called the *class position*. Everyone has a class position, whether or not they are in the labour market. The problem is thus how to determine a class position for the family and then assign it to men and women alike. Erikson argues that class position may be derived as a function of individual family members' work positions based on an order of dominance. At first sight, this may appear to contradict our earlier statement that the NS-SEC classes cannot be ordered. However, it should be recalled that the employment relation or contract only applies to individuals, that is to the work position. Employment relations do not exist within families and so do not play a part in determining which family member's work position best represents the family's class position.

So how may we determine family class position? If only one household member is in paid employment, that person's work position becomes the family's (household's) class position. Similarly, if two generations are present in the household and each has a representative in employment, the person of the senior or *primary* generation takes precedence. However, where each of two or more members of this primary generation has work positions and these positions are different (i.e. place them in different individual-level class categories), we need another dominance rule to determine (household or family) class position. As with any other method for determining the HRP, ultimately we need an ordinal variable to make the final selection. If the work positions are the same (as they often will be) then this becomes the family class position. Otherwise, we need to decide for each possible pairing of different work positions, which is likely to have the 'the greatest impact upon ideology, attitudes, behaviour and consumption patterns of the family members' (Erikson, 1984: 504). *Note that this ordering is not based on work position as determined by employment relations but on the basis of the life chances known to be associated with work positions.* It is in this sense that Erikson assumes there are dominance relations on various dimensions in which work positions may differ. Thus, higher qualifications dominate lower ones; non-manual work dominates manual work; self-employment dominates being employed; employers dominate own account workers; and professional work dominates all other forms of work. Finally, the active dominate the inactive. All these assumptions flow from long-established results of research on the relationships between class position and life chances. Erikson then tested these assumptions using data from the Swedish Level of Living Survey (ibid.: 507–11).

On the basis of Erikson's research, where the NS-SEC work positions (i.e. the individual class assignments) differ, the rules of precedence we suggest are as follows. First, individual work positions derived from full-time work are dominant over those from part-time work. Second, if each is in full-time work, or each is in part-time work, something like the order of precedence in Figure 1.4 should prevail from highest to lowest. Note, however, that this order has not yet been validated, but could be by following similar procedures to Erikson's.

Joint classification   It will be noted that all three procedures we have discussed ultimately involve the assignment of a household or family class position in terms of the characteristics of one member of the household. Where more than one person has a work position, and especially where cohabiting partners each have a work position, why do we not advocate some kind of joint classification? As Erikson (1984) has observed, it is doubtful whether an average code of the individual class position of two or more members of a household is meaningful. Are a husband in NS-SEC Class 2 and a wife in Class 6 ('average' = 4) in the same household class as, say, a husband and wife who

L3	Higher professional occupations
L2	Higher managerial occupations
L1	Employers in large establishments
L8	Employers in small establishments
L9	Own account workers
L4	Lower professional occupations
L5	Lower managerial occupations
L6	Higher supervisory occupations
L7	Intermediate occupations
L10	Lower supervisory occupations
L11	Lower technical occupations
L12	Semi-routine occupations
L13	Routine occupations
L14	Never worked and long-term unemployed
L15	Students

Figure 1.4 *Projected dominance rules for assigning household NS-SEC*

are each in Class 4? Joint approaches to classification such as this, as well as more complicated alternatives, have been suggested. However, it is hard to see how these approaches could ever square with the sort of concept that underpins the NS-SEC (see Erikson, 1984; Erikson and Goldthorpe, 1992: 238; Marshall et al., 1995).

DATA RELATING TO THE NS-SEC

In this final section of our introduction to the NS-SEC, we present some basic data on class distributions. Our data come from the 1996/97 LFS.

Table 1.1 shows the frequency distributions in total and for men and women for the seven-class version of the NS-SEC. Table 1.2 shows results for the

Table 1.1   *Distributions of the NS-SEC classes (column per cent)* *

NS-SEC classes	All	Men	Women
1 Higher managerial and professional occupations	11.1	16.0	5.5
1.1 Large employers and higher managerial occupations	(4.3)	(6.4)	(1.9)
1.2 Higher professional occupations	(6.8)	(9.6)	(3.6)
2 Lower managerial and professional occupations	23.5	21.8	25.4
3 Intermediate occupations	14.0	7.3	21.9
4 Small employers and own account workers	9.9	13.7	5.8
5 Lower supervisory and technical occupations	9.8	13.9	5.3
6 Semi-routine occupations	18.6	13.9	23.9
7 Routine occupations	12.7	13.2	12.2

* Data: Those currently employed, Labour Force Survey Winter Quarter 1996/97 (excluding Northern Ireland), n = 63,233 (may not add to 100% owing to rounding).

Table 1.2   *Distributions of the NS-SEC operational categories (column per cent)* *

NS-SEC operational categories	All	Men	Women
L1 Employers in large establishments	0.1	0.1	0.1
L2 Higher managerial occupations	4.2	6.2	1.8
L3 Higher professional occupations	6.8	9.6	3.6
L4 Lower professional and higher technical occupations	14.2	11.7	17.1
L5 Lower managerial occupations	6.7	8.3	4.8
L6 Higher supervisory occupations	2.7	1.9	3.6
L7 Intermediate occupations	14.1	7.3	21.9
L8 Employers in small establishments	2.3	3.1	1.4
L9 Own account workers	7.7	10.6	4.3
L10 Lower supervisory occupations	6.1	7.5	4.5
L11 Lower technical occupations	3.8	6.4	0.8
L12 Semi-routine occupations	18.6	13.9	23.9
L13 Routine occupations	12.7	13.2	12.2

* Data: Those currently employed, Labour Force Survey Winter Quarter 1996/97 (excluding Northern Ireland), n = 63,233 (may not add to 100% owing to rounding).

operational version. We can see from Table 1.1 that overall Classes 1 and 7 are similar in size at 11 and 13 per cent respectively. The two largest classes are 2 and 6 at 24 per cent and 19 per cent. Classes 4 and 5 are almost identical in size at just under 10 per cent. Finally, Class 3 constitutes 14 per cent of the LFS sample. Thus the overall distribution of the sample is reasonably even across the classes.

However, and unsurprisingly, the picture is rather different when we examine men and women separately. For men, Classes 4 to 7 are of very similar size at 13–14 per cent. Class 1, at 16 per cent, is only slightly larger. Class 2 is by some margin the largest at 22 per cent and Class 3 by far the smallest at 7 per cent.

For women there is a less even distribution. Here we have a tri-modal pattern with Classes 2, 3 and 6 ranging from 22 to 25 per cent. Classes 1, 4 and 5 are also similar at 5 to 6 per cent. Class 7 lies in between at 12 per cent.

We can learn more about the differential distributions of men and women by looking inside the classes, using the data for the operational version in Table 1.2. For example, we see that there is a higher proportion of women than of men in the lower professional category (L4, 17 per cent and 12 per cent). However, this position is more than reversed among both higher professional in L3 (4 per cent and 10 per cent) and higher managerial occupations in L2 (2 per cent and 6 per cent). Even among lower managerial occupations, there is almost twice as high a proportion of men than of women. We could perform more detailed inspections using the sub-categories of the operational version of course.

CONCLUDING COMMENTS

We have now explained the basics of the NS-SEC. We have shown that it is a nested classification that offers analysts flexibility in both its operationalisation and use. It also has a very high degree of continuity with both SC and SEG, thus assisting with time series analyses. However, a full appreciation of the NS-SEC requires that users understand its conceptual base and various related issues. This is the concern of the next chapter.

NOTES

1 Originally, we designated the third category of the three-class version of NS-SEC 'lower occupations'. Subsequently, ONS decided to rename this class as 'routine and manual occupations'. Nevertheless, this class includes many 'non-manual' occupations, too. Analysts should thus not be misled by its name. Needless to say, we would still prefer our original name for this class.

2 These unofficial, LFS-based SOC2000 versions of SC and SEG are available through the University of Essex Institute for Social and Economic Research web site at:
http://www.iser.essex.ac.uk/ons/ns-sec/index.php

3 Available at:
http://www.statistics.gov.uk/ns-sec/derivation-tables.asp

REFERENCES

Butler, T. and Savage, M. (eds) (1995) *Social Change and the Middle Classes*. London: UCL Press.

Erikson, R. (1984) 'Social class of men, women and families', *Sociology*, 18: 500–14.

Erikson, R. and Goldthorpe, J.H. (1992) *The Constant Flux*. Oxford: Clarendon Press.

Evans, G. and Mills, C. (2000) 'In search of the wage-labour/service contract: new evidence on the validity of the Goldthorpe class schema', *British Journal of Sociology*, 51: 641–61.

Goldthorpe, J.H. (1983) 'Women and class analysis: in defence of the conventional view', *Sociology*, 17: 465–88.

Goldthorpe, J.H. (1997) 'The "Goldthorpe" class schema: some observations on conceptual and operational issues in relation to the ESRC Review of Government Social Classifications', in D. Rose and K. O'Reilly (eds) *Constructing Classes: Towards a New Social Classification for the UK*. Swindon/London: ESRC/ONS. pp. 40–8.

GSS (1996) *Harmonised Concepts and Questions for Government Surveys*. London: ONS.

Marshall, G., Roberts, S., Burgoyne, C., Swift, A. and Routh, D. (1995) 'Class, gender and the asymmetry hypothesis', *European Sociological Review*, 11: 1–15.

Martin, J. (1995) 'Defining a Household Reference Person', *Survey Methodology Bulletin*, 37: 1–7.

Martin, J. (1998) 'A new definition for the Household Reference Person', *Survey Methodology Bulletin*, 43: 1–8.

Martin, J. and Barton, J. (1996) 'The effect of changes in the definition of the Household Reference Person', *Survey Methodology Bulletin*, 38: 1–8.

ONS (1998) *Inter Departmental Business Register: A Brief Guide*. London: ONS.

ONS (2000) *Standard Occupational Classification 2000: Volume 1. Structure and descriptions of unit groups*. London: The Stationery Office.

Prandy, K. (1990) 'The revised Cambridge Scale of Occupations', *Sociology*, 24: 629–55.

Rose, D. (1994) *The Registrar General's Class Schema: Characteristics and Criticisms. A Report to ESRC*. Colchester: ESRC Research Centre on Micro-social Change, University of Essex.

Rose, D. (1995) *A Report on Phase 1 of the ESRC Review of OPCS Social Classifications*. Swindon: ESRC; reproduced in Appendix 1 of D. Rose and K. O'Reilly (eds) *Constructing Classes: Towards a New Social Classification for the UK*. Swindon/London: ESRC/ONS. pp. 151–67.

Rose, D. and O'Reilly, K. (1998) *The ESRC Review of Government Social Classifications*. London/Swindon: ONS/ESRC.

Rose, D. and Pevalin, D.J. (with O'Reilly, K.) (2003) *The National Statistics Socio-economic Classification: Origins, Development and Use*. London: ONS.

Runciman, W.G. (1990) 'How many classes are there in contemporary British society?', *Sociology*, 24: 377–96.

Sacker, A., Firth, D., Fitzpatrick, R., Lynch, K. and Bartley, M. (2000) 'Comparing health inequality in men and women: prospective study of mortality 1986–96', *British Medical Journal*, 320: 1303–7.

Savage, M., Barlow, J., Dickens, P. and Fielding, A. (1992) *Property, Bureaucracy and Culture*. London: RKP.

Scott, J. (1996) *Stratification and Power: Structures of Class, Status and Command.* Cambridge: Polity Press.

Sørensen, A. (1994) 'Women, family and class', *Annual Review of Sociology*, 20: 27–47.

Vågerö, D. (2000) 'Health inequalities in women and men: studies of causes of death should use household criteria', *British Medical Journal*, 320: 1287–8.

2
The NS-SEC Explained

David Rose and David J. Pevalin

INTRODUCTION

Now we have described the NS-SEC, in this chapter we shall be concerned
with the central conceptual, methodological, theoretical and analytic issues
pertaining to it. We begin, however, with a brief statement about the nature of
socio-economic classifications. What are they? What form does the NS-SEC
take and why? We shall then deal with the conceptual basis of the NS-SEC.
Once this has been explained, we shall discuss certain issues that flow from the
conceptual model and that we believe analysts should take into account in their
research practice. These issues will be illustrated by reference to the study of
health inequalities.

WHAT IS A 'SOCIO-ECONOMIC CLASSIFICATION'?

We have sometimes been asked why the new government classification is
called a 'socio-economic classification'. In fact, the ONS decided upon this
appellation. However, from a social scientific viewpoint, the term 'socio-
economic' is merely a descriptive one. That is, it has no theoretical or analytic
status whatever and so there can be no single definition of the term 'socio-
economic classification'. According to Jones and McMillan (2001), 'socio-
economic' as a neologism was originally coined in 1883 by the American
sociologist, Lester Ward, as a purely descriptive way of referring to one of the
earliest concerns of sociology, namely the study of the intersection between the
social and economic spheres of life. One of the first official attempts to classify
a national population in terms of both social and economic variables is found in
the Registrar General's Social Class scheme of 1913. As we saw in the
introduction to Part I, in this scheme the 'classes' were groupings by occupation (and initially industry) – the economic level – that had (or, rather, were
supposed to have) equivalent social standing or 'culture' – the social level.
Indeed, 'culture' was more or less a reference to education, in the sense of
knowing how to avoid risks, especially in relation to health (Stevenson, 1928;
cf. Szreter, 1984). In the USA, the first similar attempt at classifying the
population, in 1917, employed the term 'social-economic groups'. Here the
groups were distinguished in terms of skill levels among 'manual' and 'non-
manual' occupations (Edwards, 1917).

In more recent times, as Ganzeboom and his colleagues (1992b) have noted, social scientists have become divided between those who favour categorical approaches to socio-economic classification (SEC) and those who prefer continuous measures. That is, some favour SECs that divide the population into a discrete number of categories or social positions. Others prefer measures that allow for 'an unlimited number of graded distinctions between occupational groups' which assume that 'differences between occupational groups can be captured in one dimension' represented by a single parameter (Ganzeboom et al., 1992b: 3–4). We shall briefly examine these two approaches, while noting that each uses occupational information for its derivation. Some of the issues discussed here are further developed in Chapter 4.

American research post-1945 led to attempts to construct quantitative socio-economic scales, scores or indices (see Jones and McMillan, 2001). These continuous or hierarchical measures might be seen as more avowedly 'socio-economic' in the sense that they combine information on occupation, education and income, that is summarise social and economic variables relating to occupations. Their primary aim is to reveal the distributive aspects of social inequality (see Egidi and Schizzerotto, 1996). For example, Duncan's (1961) 'Socioeconomic Index' or SEI brought together 'social' (in this case status or prestige) measures of occupations with educational and income measures in an attempt to predict status from information on education and income. In Duncan's view, the SEI made a link between occupation on the one hand and education and income on the other. Thus, the overall status of each occupation was simultaneously estimated in terms of both its social status and its economic status. Thereby, the correlation of status with education and income became a matter of definition. This type of approach remains the commonest explicit description of a socio-economic measure. Although differently theorised and derived, the Cambridge Scale is another example of a continuous measure of social stratification (Prandy, 1990). An internationally comparable SEI measure has also been developed (see Ganzeboom et al., 1992a).

However, many social scientists prefer to see occupation, education and income as separate dimensions relating to social stratification. In particular, they wish to explore the effects of social position as reflected through people's positions within the division of labour alone. Thus, there is another tradition in socio-economic classification that is rather different from Duncan's unitary approach. This one sees individuals in similar socio-economic situations as occupying as a consequence common positions in the social structure in terms of social power and thus concentrates on the *relational* aspects of inequality as well as the distributive ones. In other words, individuals possess certain resources as a result of their situations and consequently face a range of possibilities and constraints in terms of their behaviour. Those who share similar resources, and thus similar structural positions, will share similar possibilities and constraints in terms of 'life chances' (e.g. chances for educational attainment, health, material rewards and social mobility). Therefore, they may also hypothetically be expected to act in similar ways. Hence, in this approach, the structural base of social power provides 'a link between the *organisation of society* and the position and behaviour of individuals' (Breen and Rottman, 1995b: 455, emphasis added; see also Egidi and Schizzerotto, 1996; Goldthorpe and Marshall, 1992). Of course, there are many potential bases of social power other than those arising from the division of labour – for example, age, race, gender, social status. Nevertheless, it is generally agreed among sociologists that the most important in modern market-economy societ-ies is that of social class: that is, social power based on market or economic power (see for example Breen and Rottman, 1995a; Marshall, 1997: Ch.1; Scott, 1996). Thus, we can also see categorical social class measures as being 'socio-economic' classifications. As we saw in Chapter 1, the NS-SEC is an example of a categorical class measure, as we shall now explain.

ORIGINS OF THE NS-SEC

In its origins, the NS-SEC is a development of a sociological class schema that has been widely used in pure and applied research both in the UK and internationally. This schema was initially devised by the Nuffield College sociologist John Goldthorpe for social mobility research in the UK, and was first known as the Nuffield Class Schema. However, it is now most commonly referred to in the UK as the 'Goldthorpe schema', a convention we shall follow here (see Erikson and Goldthorpe, 1992; Goldthorpe (with Llewellyn and Payne), 1980/1987; Goldthorpe, 1997). The Goldthorpe schema has been profitably used in many ways: international studies of social mobility (Erikson and Goldthorpe, 1992); a major study of class in Britain (Marshall et al., 1988); international studies of social justice (Marshall et al., 1997) and of health inequalities (Kunst et al., 1998a; 1998b); and in British election studies (e.g. Andersen and Heath, 2002; Heath et al., 1985).

The ESRC Review team's decision to adopt the Goldthorpe schema in order to create the NS-SEC (but to adapt it through thorough *ex ante* validation procedures as discussed later) was made precisely because Goldthorpe's schema has been widely used and accepted and is conceptually clear. More-over, in a series of studies (e.g. Birkelund et al., 1996; Evans, 1992; 1996; Evans and Mills, 1998; 2000; O'Reilly and Rose, 1998), it has been reasonably validated *ex post* in criterion terms as a measure of the underlying concept of employment relations as discussed in the next section. Importantly from the viewpoint of any proposed government SEC, it has also been shown to have validity in construct terms as a good predictor of health and educational outcomes (see for example Bartley et al., 1996; Sacker et al., 2000). In terms of its conceptual basis, therefore, the NS-SEC follows that of Goldthorpe's schema, as described below. As we observed in Chapter 1, SEG spoke this theory without knowing it and was therefore already amenable to this concep-tion, capturing the essential elements of a truly social scientific SEC quite well. Thus the NS-SEC attempts to make explicit what was latent in SEG by reference to employment relations characteristics that are widely recognised as significant in the literature (such as mode of payment, career prospects and autonomy).

The Goldthorpe schema

While operationally similar to SC and particularly SEG (i.e. requiring information on occupation and employment status, and in some instances size of
establishment, in order to allocate people to class positions) class analysts
regard the Goldthorpe schema as having a far more satisfactory theoretical and
conceptual basis. The schema was originally conceived as bringing together
into classes individuals who shared similar work and market situations
(Goldthorpe (with Llewellyn and Payne), 1980/1987; also see Lockwood,
1958/1989). More recently Goldthorpe and his associates have modified this
conception. They now prefer the concept of *employment relations* in the
context of occupations, as expressed via employment contracts, in order to
emphasise the idea of a class structure of 'empty places' that individuals fill
(Erikson and Goldthorpe, 1992; cf. Mills and Evans in Chapter 4 below). The
classes themselves are thus seen as 'sets of structural positions. *Social*
relationships within *markets*, especially within *labour markets*, and within
firms define these positions. Class positions exist independently of individual
occupants of these positions. They are "empty places"' (Sørensen, 1991: 72,
emphasis added). Empirical research then addresses the issue of how structural
positions, as objectively defined in this manner, affect life chances. In other
words, we can see social class as an important mechanism through which life
chances are distributed. The analytic implications of this point are discussed
later in the chapter.

The primary conceptual distinctions made in Goldthorpe's employment
relations approach are those between: (1) *employers*, who buy the labour of
others and assume some degree of authority and control over them; (2) *self-
employed (or 'own account') workers*, who neither buy labour nor sell their
own to an employer; and (3) *employees*, who sell their labour to employers and
thus place themselves under the authority of their employer. Thus any class
schema based on employment relations, that is one that defines positions in
terms of *social relationships at work*, must include these three basic class
positions. Why these basic positions exist should be obvious for any society
based on the institutions of private property and a labour market. However, we
can immediately note that Goldthorpe's primary distinctions separately identify
the self-employed, a category that was egregiously absent from SC. Nevertheless, the three basic class positions only provide the first step in the
conceptual model. Further distinctions are required within all three positions if
we are to produce a useful classification.

Employees account for anything up to 90 per cent of the active working
population. Clearly, they do not all hold similar class positions. That is,
employers do not treat all employees alike in respect of their relations with
them as defined by the explicit and implicit terms of employment contracts.
There is differentiation in employers' relations with employees. Thus, crucial to
Goldthorpe's conception is a further level of distinction within the employment
relations of employees.

To observe that there are quite diverse employment relations and conditions
among employees is another way of saying that they occupy different *labour*

market situations and *work situations* (Lockwood, 1958/1989) as expressed through employment contracts. Labour market situation equates with issues such as source of income, economic security and prospects of economic advancement. Work situation refers primarily to location in systems of authority and control at work, although degree of autonomy at work is a secondary aspect. Hence, in this conceptual construction, variation in employment contracts provides the main basis for establishing its construct validity (see Rose and O'Reilly, 1998: Appendix 10). That is,

> membership of the classes it distinguishes, as well as having differing sources and levels of income, also have differing degrees of stability of both income and employment and differing expectations as to their economic futures that together condition both their life chances and many aspects of their attitudes and patterns of action. (Goldthorpe, 2000a: 1578–9)

The Goldthorpe schema thus distinguishes broadly different *positions* (*not* persons) as defined by social relationships in the workplace – that is, by how employees are regulated by employers through employment contracts (Goldthorpe, 2000b). Three forms of employment regulation are distinguished.

The 'service relationship'

First, there is the *'service relationship'* in which the employee renders 'service' to the employer in return for 'compensation' in terms of both immediate rewards (e.g. salary) and long-term or prospective benefits (e.g. assurances of security and career opportunities). This relationship 'is likely to be found where it is required of employees that they exercise *delegated authority or specialised knowledge and expertise* in the interests of their employing organization' (Erikson and Goldthorpe, 1992: 42, emphasis in the original). Hence, within this relationship, employers must allow a certain amount of autonomy and discretion to the employee. Hence, also, employees must be encouraged to make a moral commitment to the employing organisation. The service relationship is designed to create and sustain this type of commitment. The service relationship typifies higher professional, senior administrative and senior management occupations. This is where 'the largest responsibilities in decision-making attach and which will in turn offer the fullest range of beneficial conditions associated with the service relationship' (ibid.: 43). However, the service relationship is also found in a more restricted or attenuated form in lower professional and managerial occupations, as well as in higher technical occupations.

The 'labour contract'

In contrast with the service relationship, the *'labour contract'* entails a relatively short-term exchange of money for effort. Employees are closely supervised and give discrete amounts of labour in return for a wage (or nowadays even a 'salary' in the limited sense of a direct payment to a bank account). Payment is calculated on or related to the amount of work done or required or by the actual amount of time worked. The labour contract is typical for 'working class' occupations, but again is found in attenuated forms, for example for supervisors of 'manual' workers and for 'skilled' workers. That is, these occupations have slightly more favourable employment terms than others in the rest of the 'working class' where external controls can be fully effective.

Intermediate forms of employment regulation

Intermediate or *mixed* forms of employment regulation combine aspects from both the service relationship and the labour contract. These are typical for clerical occupations, as well as for some technical, sales and service occupations. They are especially prevalent in large, bureaucratic organisations.

Further comments

The contrast between the service relationship and the labour contract is *ideal–typical*. In the real world, actual employment relations may only approximate these types. Goldthorpe (2000b) discusses the reasons why these forms of employment regulation exist and are common across countries with developed market economies. Briefly, two factors are implicated in determining the form of employment regulation: (1) the degree to which work may be monitored by the employer (external controls) and (2) the specificity of human capital used by employees in their jobs. Thus, where employers have difficulty in monitoring the work of employees and employee human capital is high, a service relationship will exist. Where work is easily monitored and controlled and where human capital of employees is low, a labour contract will exist. Mills and Evans discuss these issues further in Chapter 4.

   Erikson and Goldthorpe (1992: 42) have also noted that the distinction between the service relationship and the labour contract is similar to some conventional distinctions made in several European countries. France, of course, distinguishes between *cadres* or *employés* and *ouvriers*; Germany between *Beamte* or *Angestellte* and *Arbeiter*; and the UK between *staff* and *workers*.

Employers and the self-employed

The Goldthorpe schema also separately identifies categories for the other two basic class positions: employers and the self-employed. Employers are divided between 'large' and 'small'. The distinction here is between employers who delegate at least some managerial tasks ('large') and those who tend to undertake these tasks themselves ('small'). The former occupations are allocated to Class I, and the latter to Class IV (Figure 2.1). Similarly, because of their different market and work situations, Goldthorpe distinguishes between

I	Higher grade professionals, administrators and managers; large proprietors
II	Lower grade professionals, administrators and managers; higher grade technicians; supervisors of non-manual employees
IIIa	Routine non-manual employees, higher grade
IIIb	Routine non-manual employees, lower grade (personal service workers)
IVa	Small proprietors, artisans, etc., with employees
IVb	Small proprietors, artisans, etc., without employees
IVc	Farmers and smallholders; other self-employed workers in primary production
V	Lower grade technicians; supervisors of manual workers
VI	Skilled manual workers
VIIa	Semi- and unskilled workers (not in agriculture etc.)
VIIb	Agricultural and other workers in primary production

Figure 2.1 *The Goldthorpe class schema*

professional and non-professional small employers, in Classes I and IV respectively. The latter consideration also applies to the self-employed.

THE DERIVATION OF THE NS-SEC

We can now examine how the NS-SEC relates to Goldthorpe's schema. Figure 2.2 offers a diagrammatic representation of the way in which the NS-SEC is derived. As with the Goldthorpe schema, the primary distinction made by the NS-SEC is between employers, employees and the self-employed. To these we have added a fourth basic position for positions that involve involuntarily exclusion from employment relations altogether. Like Goldthorpe, we then make some further distinctions among the basic class positions, as Figure 2.2 indicates.

Employers and the self-employed

Modern corporate forms of property mean that most employers are organisations rather than individuals. The individual employers who do remain are largely 'small' employers (L8), but an SEC needs to recognise both them and the tiny proportion (0.1 per cent) of larger individual employers (L1), although as we noted in Chapter 1 few of these today are 'heroic' capitalists. Similarly the self-employed without employees (L9) occupy a distinctive position and must be kept separate from employees.

Employees

The category of employees has both grown and become more differentiated within bureaucratic enterprises. As we have noted, employees occupy a very wide range of market and work situations; that is, their employment relations and conditions are sufficiently variable that we can make meaningful distinctions between them in class terms. In terms of these distinctions, we have followed the crucial line of division made by Goldthorpe, and depicted in

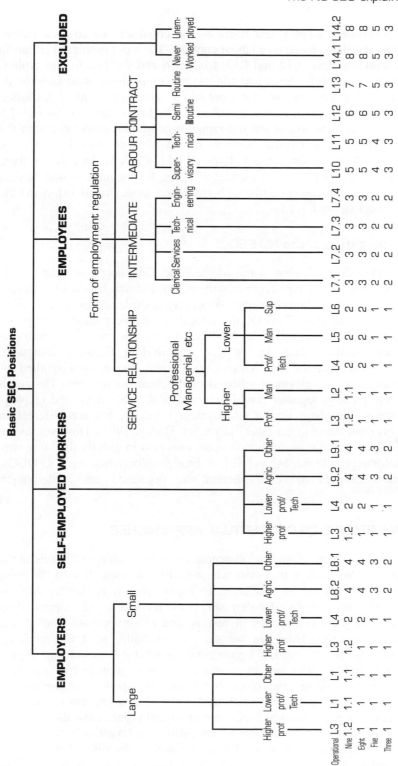

Figure 2.2 The conceptual derivation of the NS-SEC

Figure 2.2, between employment relations and conditions based on a service relationship and those based on a labour contract. The latter typifies positions in the core working class (L12 and L13, Classes 6 and 7). The former typifies higher managerial, professional and administrative positions (what Goldthorpe terms the 'service class' or '*salariat*'), notably in categories L2 and L3, Classes 1.1 and 1.2. In practice, of course, members of the lower service class (L4, L5 and L6, Class 2) have less of the full range of conditions associated with the service relationship, and some members of the working class have a more relaxed form of the labour contract (L10 and L11, Class 5). In addition, there are intermediate groups – most clerical workers, for example – who have a mixed form of employment regulation between the service relationship and the labour contract (as in L7, Class 3).

Operationalisation of the NS-SEC

Although the ESRC Review team adopted the Goldthorpe schema for its conceptual model, it did not accept its current instantiation. Unlike Goldthorpe, the team was able to validate the schema *ex ante*, as explained in more detail in the introduction to Part II. Thus, the allocation of occupational groups by employment status combinations to NS-SEC classes was created by analysing employment relations data. As we shall see in Part II, these data were especially collected on the LFS. Various other sources were also consulted for information on the employment relations of different occupations. Thus each NS-SEC class brings together combinations of SOC2000 OUGs and employment statuses that share similar employment relations, but are different in these terms from those in the other classes (cf. Bailey, 1994). However, as we saw in Chapter 1, the classification is operationalised in exactly the same way as the Goldthorpe schema, SC and SEG – through information on SOC OUGs, employment statuses and establishment size organised into a derivation matrix.

THE IMPORTANCE OF CONCEPTUAL APPROACHES

It might be asked why we were so concerned to stress conceptual issues in the ESRC Review. We believe that those who use SECs in research, even the more pragmatic users, should be concerned to know what it is that an SEC is supposed to be measuring so that they can (1) use it correctly; (2) improve their hypotheses and their explanation of results; and (3) investigate whether the classification is valid. How can we say, for example, what the mortality patterns revealed by SC *mean*, if we are not clear what it is measuring? This is no academic quibble. The lack of a clear conceptual rationale has important consequences in limiting the scope for influencing policy. If we do not understand the causal pathways which lead to the regular patterns revealed by research (i.e. the processes which generate empirical regularities) then it is not apparent how recommendations can be provided on relevant policy actions to address these persistent variations. Examples include the difficulties encountered in setting targets for reducing health variations that can be linked to achievable policies and, more generally, in developing policies to target deprived groups.

Of course, we are not suggesting that having a clear conceptual rationale for an SEC removes all the barriers to explaining what social differences mean. Not everything can be explained by what any particular SEC measures directly – employment, for example, is not the only determinant of life chances. However, a properly constructed and validated SEC removes at least one barrier to explanation. Moreover, as we saw in the introduction to Part I, some of the dissatisfaction with the old government classifications was directly related to the failure to provide a clear rationale for them and all that flows from this conceptual void, such as how and in what circumstances to use and maintain particular classifications and for what purposes.

THE EXAMPLE OF HEALTH INEQUALITIES

We can illustrate our point by reference to an example that is extremely important in the case of government SECs – that of health inequalities – an issue discussed in several of the later chapters in Part III of this volume and by ourselves in a previous paper (Rose and Pevalin, 2000). One of the major uses of SECs in the UK has been in studies of fertility, morbidity and mortality, that is as a means of obtaining a macro or societal perspective on these issues. So, for example, health inequalities are differences between classes in respect of morbidity and mortality. The study of these inequalities makes the social factors in the production of health outcomes more visible. We are therefore linking health with social organisation. This is vital for a range of public policy and monitoring issues (e.g. WHO targets for reducing social differences in health).

Of course one can use other independent variables than a class measure such as the NS-SEC to study health outcomes, for instance income, education, housing tenure, consumption (e.g. car ownership). However, none of these alternatives measures the basic structuring principles of society in the way that a social class variable such as the NS-SEC does. Thus, when we pose questions about how the social structure shapes outcomes, social class is of prime importance. Moreover, we need to keep the idea of social class analytically distinct from the possible consequences which the occupancy of a class position may give rise to, for example income or housing. This separation will allow us to examine the mechanisms that link class to outcomes. The same is true for factors that are necessary for the occupation of positions, for example education or skill level. Therefore, SECs should not be measures of either of these. Similarly, it is undesirable to use indices of socio-economic position ('SEI' or 'SES' scores) that combine occupational information on education and income (see Rose et al., 2001: Section 2; Hodge and Siegel, 1968: 319–20).

Indeed, we would argue more generally that far too little attention has been given to the causal narratives linking class to a whole range of dependent variables. And this is why we need an SEC conceived and constructed in the manner we have indicated. One of the strengths of the approach taken in the

ESRC Review, indeed its underlying principle, is that the NS-SEC offers not necessarily improved statistical associations over those SECs it has replaced, but lends itself to the possibility of *explaining* the associations we find. The NS-SEC both displays variation and has *analytic transparency*. We know what the NS-SEC is measuring – employment relations and conditions, that is aspects of the work situation and the employment contract. We can therefore construct causal or explanatory narratives that specify how the NS-SEC (and its components and correlates) link to a range of outcomes via a variety of intervening variables (see Breen and Rottman, 1995a; Marshall, 1997: Introduction; Wilkinson, 1997: 593). This is decidedly not the case for SC. Because it was not clear what it measured it did not have analytic transparency. It may have shown statistical associations with dependent variables of interest, but it did not lend itself to causal explanations (see Bartley et al., 1996). Indeed, in Raymond Illsley's phrase, it was 'a constantly changing measuring rod' which, because it lacked conceptual clarity, changed in ways that were not understood (see Rose, 1997: 170–1). Overall, therefore, we would agree with Breen and Rottman (1995a: 467) when they observe that it is necessary to 'hypothesise and test a number of different intervening variables that would represent alternative mechanisms linking class and outcome'; that is, specifying causal narratives (cf. Wilkinson, 1997).

For example, there is growing evidence that the amounts of control and autonomy a person has at work are important factors in explaining heart disease (Bosma et al., 1997). The service relationship's 'prospective perspective', associated with secure career employment among top managers and professionals, has components such as greater control and autonomy at work, more self-esteem, greater self-care with regard to factors like diet and exercise, more choice over medical treatment and so on. This we have learned, for example, from the Whitehall Studies. These show that, contrary to popular belief, it is those at the bottom of employment hierarchies who are most stressed (Bosma et al., 1997; Marmot et al., 1997; Marmot and Davey Smith, 1997; and more generally Carroll and Davey Smith, 1997).

What we require are more analyses that show how class effects are mediated via specific intervening variables. How class has its effects will vary according to what it is we wish to explain. We must thus construct and test different models designed to link the NS-SEC to a range of different outcomes. However, we must also be careful in our analyses that we do not simply set up a 'variable race' between different independent variables that do not have a common metric (Breen and Goldthorpe, 1999: 7).

ANALYTIC ISSUES

Thus, when it comes to analysis using the NS-SEC (or any similar measure) there seem to us to be three issues which must be considered. First, of course, we accept that there may be situations where, for example, the class/health relationship might reduce or disappear when other variables are introduced into a model. Equally, however, we need to be clear about what this might mean. Second, we also have to think of the basic modelling and measurement issues:

that is, are our procedures technically correct and appropriate to the problem? But third, and most important, *we have to think theoretically before we think statistically*. We need an explicit causal or explanatory narrative formed into testable hypotheses about the class/health relationship. We would argue, for instance, that variables such as housing tenure and income are themselves conditioned by class. We might even think of them as component variables that might help us to understand the mechanisms by which class and mortality are related. Indeed some have suggested that class is a kind of 'latent' variable that underpins variables such as housing tenure and income. More precisely, however, we would prefer to say that class might have direct relations with aspects of health, or it might be mediated via the life chances that derive from class position. Introducing life chance or deprivation measures into a model investigating the class/health relationship might reduce the direct effects of class, but it would be a mistake then to conclude that this reduces the contribution which class makes to our understanding of health outcomes. On the contrary, such a finding would be in line with a class causal narrative properly conceived.

Therefore we need first to think not of relations between variables, but of *social relationships* – and class is, of course, a crucial form of social relationship. Nor, in using a variable such as the NS-SEC, should we take the narrow view that class is only about the employment relations directly measured in order to create it. That is not the case. We were only able to measure a small sub-set of a potentially wider range of employment relations variables. This sub-set was used to *operationalise* the class variable, but we should not then suppose that these variables must alone explain how class relates to dependent variables of interest. And, as we have just noted, there are in any case life chances which flow from people's work and market situations (or 'employment relations'), including housing, income and other aspects of material circumstances. The real point about employment relations is that they have implications for income, economic security and prospects for both individuals and their families. Hence, also, we need to consider whether we should always use an individual measure of the NS-SEC rather than a household or family measure, a point to which we shall return in Chapter 12.

A proxy for income?

In this respect, we would also argue that the use of SECs in research is not simply to act as a proxy for income where income data themselves are unavailable. We use SECs because they are measures designed to help us identify key forms of social relations to which income is merely epiphenomenal. Hence, again, the need for thinking theoretically before thinking about appropriate forms of analysis. It is also the case that SECs are relatively more general and stable measures than income. Income is well known to fluctuate over the lifecourse; indeed panel data regularly reveal a high level of 'income churning' from year to year (for the UK case see Jarvis and Jenkins, 1997). What the NS-SEC might reasonably be expected to proxy is the lifecourse/

earnings profile, an issue currently under investigation by members of the Review team (see Goldthorpe, 1997: 45–6; Rose and O'Reilly, 1998: 40). However, absolute income is by no means a straightforward determinant of health or mortality.[1] Health inequality is linked to *relative* deprivation, *relative* income, *relative* poverty – indeed the very concept of inequality is inherently relative (see Marshall and Swift, 1996: 376).

A FINAL COMMENT ON CONCEPTUAL ISSUES

Social scientists are more often in dispute over conceptual issues than any others. It might thus be helpful at this point to make some further distinctions and comments. As Goldthorpe (1990; cf. Popper, 1960) has noted, a conceptual approach such as that proposed here is advanced as a *nominal* proposition. It proposes that the world should be viewed in a certain way. That is what the NS-SEC concept proposes, as we have tried to indicate. This is different from a *hypothesis*, which is a *real* proposition that says the world *is* a certain way. It is with hypotheses that we should ultimately be concerned. However, we need a conceptual scheme before we can hypothesise and make relevant observations. Nevertheless, concepts are tools that must be evaluated. The best way of evaluating them is in terms of how useful they are. How well do our concepts aid in the investigation of the problems that concern us? Do they allow us to pose interesting questions and obtain illuminating results? This is why construct validation is important (see Part III). Concepts must always be judged in terms of their empirical consequences. They are neither true nor false in an empirical sense.

Second, we have emphasised that the form of the NS-SEC is one of socio-economic positions as defined by employment relations – of empty places and not of persons. In this sense, the classification is a *schema*, a conceptual construction. To convert it into an empirical instrument, we need an algorithm that maps occupations and employment statuses onto the schema's categories. That is, we need a derivation matrix as we noted previously. In turn, to create this algorithm we require information on employment relations for employee occupations and status combinations within the matrix (see Goldthorpe, 1997). This information for the NS-SEC came from employment relations data especially collected in the 1996/97 LFS and discussed in Part II (also see Rose and Pevalin with O'Reilly, 2003). Only then can we allocate people, via their occupation and employment status combination, to the schema's empty places and validate the classification to ensure we have adequately measured the underlying concepts (criterion validation as discussed in Part II). Then we can see whether the classification does help us to understand the types of problem that it is designed to address (construct validation as discussed in Part III).

The next two parts of this book thus deal with the adequacy and effectiveness of the new classification as both a measure and a useful research tool for social scientists and policy analysts.

NOTES

1 For an illuminating discussion of these issues in relation to health research, see Elstad (1998) and Lynch and Kaplan (1997). For another view both on class analysis in relation to health inequalities in general and on the relationship between class and income in particular, see Higgs and Scambler (1998) and Scambler and Higgs (1999, esp. 287–8). For a more general discussion of related issues see Kunst and Mackenbach (1994: Part 2).

REFERENCES

Andersen, R. and Heath, A. (2002) 'Class matters: the persisting effects of contextual social class on individual voting in Britain, 1964–97', *European Sociological Review*, 18: 125–38.

Bailey, K.D. (1994) *Typologies and Taxonomies: An Introduction to Classification Techniques*. Thousand Oaks, CA: Sage.

Bartley, M., Carpenter, L., Dunnell, K. and Fitzpatrick, R. (1996) 'Measuring inequalities in health: an analysis of mortality patterns from two social classifications', *Sociology of Health and Illness*, 18: 455–75.

Birkelund, G.E., Goodman, L. and Rose, D. (1996) 'The latent structure of job characteristics of men and women', *American Journal of Sociology*, 102: 80–113.

Bosma, H., Marmot, M.G., Hemingway, H., Nicholson, A.C., Brunner, E. and Stansfeld, S.A. (1997) 'Low job control and risk of coronary heart disease in Whitehall II (prospective cohort) study', *British Medical Journal*, 314: 558–65.

Breen, R. and Goldthorpe, J.H. (1999) 'Class inequality and meritocracy: a critique of Saunders and an alternative analysis', *British Journal of Sociology*, 50: 1–27.

Breen, R. and Rottman, D. (1995a) *Class Stratification: A Comparative Perspective*. London: Harvester Wheatsheaf.

Breen, R. and Rottman, D. (1995b) 'Class analysis and class theory', *Sociology*, 29: 453–73.

Carroll, D. and Davey Smith, G. (1997) 'Health and socio-economic position', *Journal of Health Psychology*, 2: 275–82.

Duncan, O.D. (1961) 'A socioeconomic index for all occupations', in A.J. Reiss (ed.) *Occupations and Social Status*. New York: Free Press.

Edwards, A.M. (1917) 'Social-economic groups of the United States. Gainful workers of United States, classified by social-economic groups or strata', *Publications of the American Statistical Association*, 15: 643–61.

Egidi, V. and Schizzerotto, A. (1996) 'Social stratification and mobility. Concepts, indicators and examples of application', *Proceedings of the Siena Group Meeting, June 1996*. Paris: INSEE.

Elstad, J.I. (1998) 'The psycho-social perspective on social inequalities in health', in M. Bartley, D. Blane and G. Davey Smith (eds) *The Sociology of Health Inequalities*. Oxford: Blackwell. pp. 30–58.

Erikson, R. and Goldthorpe, J.H. (1992) *The Constant Flux*. Oxford: Clarendon Press.

Evans, G. (1992) 'Testing the validity of the Goldthorpe class schema', *European Sociological Review*, 8: 211–32.

Evans, G. (1996) 'Putting men and women into classes: an assessment of the cross-sex validity of the Goldthorpe class schema', *Sociology*, 30: 209–34.

Evans, G. and Mills, C. (1998) 'Identifying class structure. A latent class analysis of the criterion-related and construct validity of the Goldthorpe class schema', *European Sociological Review*, 14: 87–106.

Evans, G. and Mills, C. (2000) 'In search of the wage-labour/service contract: new evidence on the validity of the Goldthorpe class schema', *British Journal of Sociology*, 51: 641–61.

Ganzeboom, H., De Graaf, P. and Treiman, D. (1992a) 'A Standard International Socio-Economic Index of Occupational Status', *Social Science Research*, 21: 1–56.

Ganzeboom, H., Luijkx, R. and Treiman, D. (1992b) 'International class mobility in comparative perspective', *Research in Stratification and Mobility*, 8: 3–79.

Goldthorpe, J.H. (with Llewellyn, C. and Payne, C.) (1980/1987) *Social Mobility and Class Structure in Modern Britain*. Oxford: Clarendon Press.

Goldthorpe, J.H. (1990) 'A response', in J. Clark, C. Modgil and S. Modgil (eds) *John H. Goldthorpe: Consensus and Controversy*. London: Falmer Press.

Goldthorpe, J.H. (1997) 'The "Goldthorpe" class schema: some observations on conceptual and operational issues in relation to the ESRC Review of Government Social Classifications', in D. Rose and K. O'Reilly (eds) *Constructing Classes: Towards a New Social Classification for the UK*. Swindon/London: ESRC/ONS. pp. 40–8.

Goldthorpe, J.H. (2000a) 'Rent, class conflict, and class structure: a reply to Sørensen', *American Journal of Sociology*, 105: 1572–82.

Goldthorpe, J.H. (2000b) 'Social class and the differentiation of employment contracts', in J.H. Goldthorpe, *On Sociology: Numbers, Narratives, and the Integration of Research and Theory*. Oxford: Oxford University Press. pp. 206–29.

Goldthorpe, J.H. and Marshall, G. (1992) 'The promising future of class analysis – a response to recent critiques', *Sociology*, 26: 381–400.

Heath, A., Jowell, R. and Curtice, J. (with Field, J. and Levine, C.) (1985) *How Britain Votes*. Oxford: Pergamon.

Higgs, P. and Scambler, G. (1998) 'Explaining health inequalities: how useful are concepts of class?', in G. Scambler and P. Higgs (eds) *Modernity, Medicine and Health: Medical Sociology towards 2000*. London: Routledge. pp. 82–99.

Hodge, R.W. and Siegel, P.M. (1968) 'The measurement of social class', in D. Stills (ed.) *International Encyclopaedia of the Social Sciences*, Vol. 15. New York: Macmillan and Free Press.

Jarvis, S. and Jenkins, S.P. (1997) 'Low income dynamics in 1990s Britain', *Fiscal Studies*, 18: 123–43. Reprinted in *IDS Bulletin*, 1998, 29: 32–41 and in D. Rose (ed.) *Researching Social and Economic Change: The Uses of Household Panel Studies*. London: Routledge. pp. 188–209.

Jones, F.L. and McMillan, J. (2001) 'Scoring occupational categories for social research: a review of current practice with Australian examples', *Work, Employment and Society*, 15: 539–63.

Kunst, A., Groenhof, F., Mackenbach, J. and the EU Working Group on Socioeconomic Inequalities in Health (1998a) 'Mortality by occupational class among men 30–64 years in 11 European countries', *Social Science and Medicine*, 46: 1459–76.

Kunst, A., Groenhof, F., Mackenbach, J. and the EU Working Group on Socioeconomic Inequalities in Health (1998b) 'Occupational class and cause specific mortality in middle aged men in 11 European countries: comparison of population based studies', *British Medical Journal*, 316: 1636–41.

Kunst, A.E. and Mackenbach, J.P. (1994) *Measuring socio-economic inequalities in health*. Copenhagen: WHO Regional Office for Europe.

Lockwood, D. (1958/1989) *The Blackcoated Worker*. London: Allen and Unwin/ Oxford: Clarendon Press.

Lynch, J.W. and Kaplan, G.A. (1997) 'Understanding how inequality in the distribution of income affects health', *Journal of Health Psychology*, 2: 297–314.

Marmot, M.G., Bosma, H., Hemmingway, H., Brunner, E. and Stansfeld, S. (1997) 'Contribution of job control and other risk factors to social variations in coronary heart disease incidence', *Lancet*, 350: 235–9.

Marmot, M.G. and Davey Smith, G. (1997) 'Socio-economic differentials in health: the contribution of the Whitehall Studies', *Journal of Health Psychology*, 2: 283–96.

Marshall, G. (1997) *Repositioning Class: Social Inequality in Industrial Societies.* London: Sage.

Marshall, G., Rose, D., Newby, H. and Vogler, C. (1988) *Social Class in Modern Britain*. London: Hutchinson.

Marshall, G. and Swift, A. (1996) 'Merit and mobility: a reply to Saunders', *Sociology*, 30: 375–86.

Marshall, G., Swift, A. and Roberts, S. (1997) *Against the Odds? Social Class and Social Justice in Industrial Societies*. Oxford: Clarendon Press.

O'Reilly, K. and Rose, D. (1998) 'Changing employment relations? Plus ça change, plus c'est la même chose? Reflections arising from the ESRC Review of Government Social Classifications', *Work, Employment and Society*, 12: 713–33.

Popper, K.R. (1960) 'Essentialism versus nominalism', in K.R. Popper, *The Poverty of Historicism*. London: RKP.

Prandy, K. (1990) 'The revised Cambridge Scale of Occupations', *Sociology*, 24: 629–55.

Rose, D. (1997) 'Thinking about social classifications', in D. Rose and K. O'Reilly (eds) *Constructing Classes: Towards a New Social Classification for the UK*. Swindon/London: ESRC/ONS. pp. 168–77.

Rose, D. and O'Reilly, K. (1998) *The ESRC Review of Government Social Classifications*. London/Swindon: ONS/ESRC.

Rose, D. and Pevalin, D.J. (2000) 'Social class differences in mortality using the National Statistics Socio-economic Classification – too little, too soon: a reply to Chandola', *Social Science and Medicine*, 51: 1121–7.

Rose, D. and Pevalin, D.J. (with O'Reilly, K.) (2003) *The National Statistics Socio-economic Classification: Origins, Development and Use*. London: ONS.

Rose, D., Pevalin, D.J. and Elias, P. (with Martin, J.) (2001) *Towards a European Socio-economic Classification: Final Report to Eurostat of the Expert Group*. London/ Colchester: ONS/ISER, University of Essex. Available at: http://www.iser.essex.ac.uk/ons/ns-sec/esec_final_report.pdf

Sacker, A., Firth, D., Fitzpatrick, R., Lynch, K. and Bartley, M. (2000) 'Comparing health inequality in men and women: prospective study of mortality 1986–96', *British Medical Journal*, 320: 1303–7.

Scambler, G. and Higgs, P. (1999) 'Stratification, class and health: class relations and health inequalities in high modernity', *Sociology*, 33: 275–96.

Scott, J. (1996) *Stratification and Power: Structures of Class, Status and Command*. Cambridge: Polity Press.

Sørensen, A.B. (1991) 'On the usefulness of class analysis in research on social mobility and socioeconomic inequality', *Acta Sociologica*, 34: 71–87.

Stevenson, T.H.C. (1928) 'The vital statistics of wealth and poverty', *Journal of the Royal Statistical Society*, 91: 207–30.

Szreter, S.R.S. (1984) 'The genesis of the Registrar General's Social Classification of Occupations', *British Journal of Sociology*, 35: 522–46.

Wilkinson, R.G. (1997) 'Health inequalities: relative or absolute standards?', *British Medical Journal*, 314: 591–5.

Part II
The NS-SEC as a measure of employment relations

INTRODUCTION

The chapters in Parts II and III are essentially concerned with the validation of the NS-SEC. Here, we shall briefly consider the validation approaches taken in the Review and which form the basis for the studies discussed in the other chapters.

In terms of validation, two crucial issues need to be demonstrated. First, it must be shown that the NS-SEC is a reasonable measure of the underlying concept of employment relations, as discussed in Chapter 2 and that it has internally homogeneous categories, each as different as possible from one another. Second, we need to show that the NS-SEC adds value by offering an improved understanding of other variables (such as health variables) compared with what we would obtain if we only used the NS-SEC's component variables (say employment status or SOC2000) or other proxy variables. As O'Reilly has explained, the first issue is one of *criterion validation* and the second of *construct validation* (see Rose and O'Reilly, 1998: Appendix 10). Construct validation is tackled in Part III and is discussed in detail there.

CRITERION VALIDATION

A measuring instrument 'is valid if it does what it is intended to do. An indicator of some abstract concept is valid to the extent that it measures what it purports to measure. . . . Validity concerns the crucial relationship between concept and indicator' (Carmines and Zeller, 1979: 12). In the case of the NS-SEC, therefore, we need to know that it is a reasonably adequate index of the conceptualisation of the social structure set out in Chapter 2. There are two methods by which a classification could be constructed in order for its criterion validity to be assessed.

The first method would involve the construction of a socio-economic classification (SEC) derivation matrix by expert judgement in which each cell is assumed to be internally homogeneous in terms of employment relations. This is the method Goldthorpe was constrained to use to create his schema. In that case, the best available evidence from official and academic data on terms and conditions of employment guided the actual allocation of Goldthorpe class values to the cells of his matrix. However, as Goldthorpe (1997: 42) acknowledges, this method inevitably involved a greater degree of subjective judgement and guesswork than the direct measurement of employment relations. For this reason, once such a matrix is created, it should be subjected to *ex post* criterion validation using independent data (as in the case of Evans' pioneering validation studies of the Goldthorpe schema: see Evans, 1992; 1996; Evans and Mills, 1998; 2000). Analytic exercises of this kind are designed to see how far the Goldthorpe schema, as operationalised in his way, succeeds 'in capturing empirically the differentiation of classes that it is supposed to capture conceptually' (Goldthorpe, ibid.).

The second method would involve a special data collection exercise in which we attempted to measure the employment relations of employees at the level of SOC OUG and employment status combinations. This is what Goldthorpe (1997) has referred to as *ex ante* validation and was the method chosen by the Review team. As we have seen, it involved asking individuals about aspects of their employment contracts. Because a large sample is required for such an exercise, relevant questions were asked on the LFS. This yielded sufficient cases for analyses at the OUG level of SOC for the largest OUGs, covering by far the majority (75+ per cent) of the working population. The exercise was designed to measure the extent to which occupations may be grouped together according to the model of employment regulation and classes specified previously. Issues of adequacy were also applied to employment status categories. We investigated, for example, the adequacy of a size cut-off of twenty-five employees between large and small employers (McKnight, 1997; O'Reilly, 1997). We also examined whether a special employment status category was required for part-time employees.

In selecting appropriate LFS questions to use as indicators of employment relations and conditions among employees, the Review team was by no means working in the dark. Recent research suggested that there were three conceptually separable, although empirically correlated, respects in which employment relations might continue to be differentiated according to whether a service relationship, intermediate or labour contract form of regulation exists. These were (1) forms of remuneration; (2) promotion opportunities; and (3) autonomy, especially as regards time (see Goldthorpe, 1997). Hence the questions that were asked on the LFS.[1] So, for example, salary payments, the presence of incremental scales, longer periods of notice and high degrees of autonomy, taken together, would indicate a service relationship. The absence of these criteria would indicate a labour contract. A mixture of positive and negative values would suggest intermediate regulation.

The LFS data were analysed along lines described elsewhere (see Chapter 3; O'Reilly and Rose, 1997; 1998; Rose and O'Reilly, 1998; Rose and Pevalin with O'Reilly, 2003). Briefly, an employment regulation variable in the form of a 'service relationship score' (SRS) was calculated for all employee OUG/employment status combinations. A binary variable was created from each question to indicate the presence or absence of a service relationship. The scores on each item were then summed to produce the SRS. The reliability of the SRS scale was assessed and proven satisfactory; that is, the linear combination of the employment relations variables formed an internally consistent scale in which no item was redundant. Each item thus captured a related but different aspect of employment relations. A derivation matrix was then constructed in which each cell was as internally homogeneous as possible with respect to employment relations. The resulting NS-SEC was then 'validated' using various methods of analysis (latent class analysis, logistic regression and OLS regression, for example) described in subsequent chapters.

It should be noted, however, that only a few elements in a far wider potential set of employment relations items were covered by our LFS questions. Equally, limited space on the questionnaire meant that the questions themselves were rather crude. Moreover, there are real difficulties in producing reliable employment relations data in surveys of individuals. For example, respondents find it hard to distinguish being on an incremental scale from the receipt of an annual pay award. Better quality data could only come from employers through an analysis of the implicit and explicit terms of actual employment contracts, but this would present some real sampling difficulties if representative data were to be obtained. Consequently, for these and other reasons (including small numbers in the LFS for some OUGs), our survey data on employment relations had to be supplemented wherever possible using both data from other sources (e.g. careers databases, employee and employer organisations, reports and academic studies) and expert judgements.

So, the NS-SEC classes have been constructed on the basis of information provided by individuals on their employment relations. Each class has been designed to be as internally homogeneous in these terms as possible. Thus, criterion validation is built into the procedures we used. As Mills and Evans note in Chapter 4, it is therefore somewhat tautological to discuss analyses such as theirs and the others in Part II as being criterion validation studies equivalent to those used for *ex post* validation studies along the lines of those previously undertaken by Evans, Mills and others in relation to the Goldthorpe schema. Rather, the NS-SEC studies in Part II relate to the adequacy with which we have constructed classes in relation to the underlying employment relations concept using our LFS data and other information we collected about occupations.

THE VALIDATION STUDIES

The Review team deliberately chose to employ a variety of different methods to assess the NS-SEC and these are reflected in Chapters 3, 4 and 5. In Chapter 3, McKnight and Elias use multivariate OLS regression models to assess variations in employment relations and conditions, as measured by a five-item SRS, across the 1990 and 2000 SOCs and five measures of social class that include two versions of the NS-SEC. Mills and Evans, in Chapter 4, utilise a series of RC(M) log-multiplicative models to investigate variations in ten employment relations items across twenty-six employee groups drawn from the operational categories and sub-categories of the NS-SEC. In Chapter 5, Coxon and Fisher use cluster analysis at the individual level and correspondence analysis at the occupational unit group level to examine further the adequacy of allocations within the NS-SEC.

Chapter 6 by Fisher has a rather different focus. We have seen that the derivation matrices for all the SECs we have examined employ three pieces of information in order to determine class allocations – SOC OUG, employment status and size of establishment. Goldthorpe (1997: 47–8) recommended that the Review should focus attention on the employment status categories. In particular he suggested that we should try and find better ways to operationalise the distinction between higher and lower managerial occupations and between employees, managers and supervisors. We saw in Chapter 1 that these recommendations have been implemented so far as is possible and that the new structure of SOC has aided with this. Goldthorpe also supported the idea of a separate class for the long-term unemployed and the never worked and again this has been done. The final recommendation he made was to consider creating a special employment status category for part-time employment. This matter is further considered in Chapter 6.

NOTES

1 These data were collected in the 1996/97 winter quarter of the LFS. Questions were asked as follows:

1   Which of the following best describes how you are paid in your present job?
Monthly salary plus performance
Monthly salary only
Weekly wage
Hourly paid
Piecework
Other

2   Are you on a recognised pay scale with increments, either automatic or performance related?
Yes
No
Don't know

3   If you decided to leave your job, how much notice are you officially required to give?
Less than one week
One week but less than one month
One month but less than three months
Three months or more
Don't know

4   In your sort of work, are there opportunities for promotion, either in your current organisation or by changing employers?
Yes
No
Don't know

5   Who decides what time you start and leave work?
Flexitime system
Employer decides
I decide within certain limits
Negotiated with employer

6   Does your job require you to design and plan important aspects of your own work, or is your work largely specified for you?
I am required to design/plan my work

Work is largely specified by others
Other
7 How much influence do you personally have in deciding what tasks you are to do?
A great deal
A fair amount
Not much
None at all

In the spring 1997 quarter of the LFS the following question was asked:

8 Does your sort of work have a recognised career ladder?
Yes
No
Don't know

REFERENCES

Carmines, E.G. and Zeller, R.A. (1979) *Reliability and Validity Assessment*. Beverly Hills, CA: Sage.

Evans, G. (1992) 'Testing the validity of the Goldthorpe class schema', *European Sociological Review*, 8: 211–32.

Evans, G. (1996) 'Putting men and women into classes: an assessment of the cross-sex validity of the Goldthorpe class schema', *Sociology*, 30: 209–34.

Evans, G. and Mills, C. (1998) 'Identifying class structure. A latent class analysis of the criterion-related and construct validity of the Goldthorpe class schema', *European Sociological Review*, 14: 87–106.

Evans, G. and Mills, C. (2000) 'In search of the wage-labour/service contract: new evidence on the validity of the Goldthorpe class schema', *British Journal of Sociology*, 51: 641–61.

Goldthorpe, J.H. (1997) 'The "Goldthorpe" class schema: some observations on conceptual and operational issues in relation to the ESRC Review of Government Social Classifications', in D. Rose and K. O'Reilly (eds) *Constructing Classes: Towards a New Social Classification for the UK*. Swindon/London: ESRC/ONS. pp. 40–8.

McKnight, A. (1997) 'Social classification and employment relations and conditions: the effect of workplace size, public sector employment and non-response', *Mimeo*, Institute for Employment Research, University of Warwick, Coventry.

O'Reilly, K. (1997) 'Establishment size and the SEC', *Mimeo*, ESRC Research Centre on Micro-social Change, University of Essex, Colchester.

O'Reilly, K. and Rose, D. (1997) 'Criterion validation of the interim revised social classification', in D. Rose and K. O'Reilly (eds) *Constructing Classes: Towards a New Social Classification for the UK*. Swindon/London: ESRC/ONS. pp. 62–77.

O'Reilly, K. and Rose, D. (1998) 'Changing employment relations? Plus ça change, plus c'est la même chose? Reflections arising from the ESRC Review of Government Social Classifications', *Work, Employment and Society*, 12: 713–33.

Rose, D. and O'Reilly, K. (1998) *The ESRC Review of Government Social Classifications*. London/Swindon: ONS/ESRC.

Rose, D. and Pevalin, D.J. (with O'Reilly, K.) (2003) *The National Statistics Socio-economic Classification: Origins, Development and Use*. London: ONS.

3
Empirical Variation in Employment Relations and Conditions

Abigail McKnight and Peter Elias

INTRODUCTION

As we have now seen, terms and conditions of employment form the conceptual basis of the NS-SEC, building on a long history of classifying individuals according to, what sociologists refer to as, their employment relationship. This chapter examines the empirical evidence for distinct and identifiable social class categories according to variation in employment relations and conditions. The study compares and contrasts the ability of various classification schemes to differentiate between constituent categories in terms of employment relations and conditions by measuring the amount of heterogeneity between constituent groups. A number of schemes, which aim to identify homogeneous groups of individuals but differ in terms of their conceptual basis, are compared. Three different social classification systems and two levels of the NS-SEC are compared alongside two occupational classifications. Measures of the nature of the employment relationship based upon structure of pay, work autonomy, promotional prospects and flexibility of working time are used to quantify employment relations and conditions, drawing on the set of specially commissioned questions included in the Winter 1996/97 Labour Force Survey (LFS). The work undertaken for this chapter therefore forms part of the overall validation of the NS-SEC. Here the focus is on the adequacy of the *ex ante* validation procedures used to create the NS-SEC.

Background

Work on the development and validation of the NS-SEC began in 1994. Early work (see Rose, 1995) established the continuing need for a social classification and outlined some of the problems associated with the previous officially maintained social classifications (SC and SEG). As explained in Chapter 2, the conceptual framework for the new classification follows a well-defined sociological position that employment relations and conditions are central to delineating the structure of socio-economic positions in modern societies.

An important part of the Review team's work related to the validation of the classification. This chapter presents a methodology for exploring validity in terms of the ability of a classification scheme to differentiate between its constituent categories. Comparisons are made between versions of the NS-SEC and three other classifications that also use the Standard Occupational Classification (SOC) and employment status as basic building blocks.

The LFS data used in our analyses and already described in the introduction to Part II represent the largest body of information ever collected in the UK on employees' terms and conditions of employment providing a unique opportunity to compare individuals and groups of individuals. Five variables have been identified as those that most closely reflect the conceptual basis of the NS-SEC. These variables cover structure of pay, period of notice required, promotion prospects and flexibility in working time.

This study concentrates on employees only as variation in the employment relations and conditions as measured in the LFS does not apply to the classification of the self-employed. The NS-SEC also covers the unemployed and other economically inactive sections of the population, but as we are exploring the variations in the relations and conditions of current employment these groups are not covered here, either.

QUANTIFYING EMPLOYMENT RELATIONS AND CONDITIONS

This section provides some summary statistics from the information collected on employment relations and conditions and shows the distribution of responses to the five questions selected for this study. This is followed by a description of the recoding of the responses to produce a set of binary variables and ultimately the composite variable known as the service relationship score (SRS) discussed in the introduction to Part II. For the analysis we selected employees with responses to all five questions on employment relations and conditions. This reduced the sample size by 12 per cent. Cases were excluded when the respondent did not know the answer to a question or where no response was recorded. For example, for 2,114 individuals it was recorded that they did not know if they were on a recognised pay scale with increments and no response was recorded for a further 21 individuals. Further examination revealed that, not surprisingly, it was generally proxy respondents who did not know the answer to particular questions. For the above example this was the case for 60 per cent of the individuals. Approximately one-third of individuals in the LFS provide information through a proxy. Proxy responses were more likely to be made for individuals working in skilled manual occupations or in the armed forces. Although there was some variation in the proportion of individuals who did not know the answer to the questions on employment relations and conditions by social class categories ('response rates' were greater for individuals in higher social classes), it is difficult to judge whether the selection introduces any significant bias within social class categories. In total 46,421 out of 52,932 employees responded to all five questions. Frequencies of the question responses for employees are shown in Tables 3.1 to 3.5.

Table 3.1   *Which of the following best describes how you are paid in your present job?*

	Frequency	%	Recoding
Monthly salary plus performance	3,773	8.1	1
Monthly salary only	26,166	56.4	1
Weekly wage	12,418	26.8	0
Hourly paid	2,537	5.5	0
Piecework	280	0.6	0
Other	1,247	2.7	0
Total	46,421	100	

Table 3.2   *Are you on a recognised pay scale with increments, either automatic or performance related?*

	Frequency	%	Recoding
Yes	24,386	52.5	1
No	22,035	47.5	0
Total	46,421	100	

Table 3.3   *If you decide to leave your job, how much notice are you officially required to give?*

	Frequency	%	Recoding
Less than 1 week	2,007	4.3	0
1 week or over but less than 1 month	17,498	37.7	0
1 month or over but less than 3 months	22,904	49.3	1
3 months or more	4,012	8.6	1
Total	46,421	100	

Table 3.4   *In your sort of work, are there opportunities for promotion, either in your current organisation or by changing employers?*

	Frequency	%	Recoding
Yes	32,419	69.8	1
No	14,002	30.2	0
Total	46,421	100	

Table 3.5   *Who decides what time you start and leave work?*

	Frequency	%	Recoding
Flexitime system	2,984	6.4	1
Employer decides	31,861	68.6	0
I decide within certain limits	9,842	21.2	1
Negotiated with employer	1,734	3.7	1
Total	46,421	100	

The responses show that employees were most likely to receive a monthly salary (56 per cent), be on a recognised pay scale, either automatic or performance related (52 per cent), required to give between one and three months' notice (49 per cent), have opportunities for promotion (70 per cent) and for the employer to decide the time they start and leave work (69 per cent).

Construction of the index of employment relations and conditions: the SRS

While it is possible to examine the responses to the five questions individually, in the absence of a composite variable it is difficult to assess the overall position of individuals or groups of individuals. The creation of an index can capture all of the measured dimensions of employment relations and conditions summarised into one variable. This composite variable can then be used to examine the variation between class categories within various schema. As outlined above and in the introduction to Part II, the five employment relations and conditions questions included in the LFS were each designed to inform on an important aspect of employment relations and conditions which forms part of the conceptual basis of the NS-SEC.

If the LFS employment relations variables, or a linear combination of them, are a reliable measure of the conceptual basis of the NS-SEC then they can play an important role in providing empirical evidence of variance by social class categories. We summarise the information from all the variables by constructing an additive scale from the binary values assigned to the variables according to whether the response indicated the presence (1) or absence (0) of a service relationship.

In Tables 3.1 to 3.5 the last column shows the recoding of the responses used to produce the binary variables. The SRS is then created by summing the binary variables for each individual. The higher the value of the SRS the better are the employment relations and conditions of the survey respondent. The SRS ranges from 0 to a maximum of 5. Across all employees the mean value for the SRS is 2.76.

While there are clearly a variety of different indices that could be constructed, from a statistical perspective an additive scale created from a set of variables used in this way should display a number of important features:

- It should be constructed on the basis of content validity.
- It should be reliable (it must be free from error and therefore yield consistent results).
- Each component (item) of the scale should be correlated with the other items but also add an important dimension to the scale.

As the five questions were individually designed to capture an important aspect of employment relations and conditions it is assumed that content validity is met, that is to say that they directly measure some important aspect of employment relations and conditions. This rests on the assumption that the variables form a representative collection of employment relations and conditions.

To test the reliability of the SRS we turn to techniques more commonly used in other disciplines than our own. In psychometric analysis much attention is paid to the reliability of test scores in their ability to measure aspects of competence in a subject. An additive scale can be formed from results from a series of tests that cover different areas of a subject. Each test (item) must be in the same broad area (subject) but test a different dimension to add to the overall assessment. In this sense they need to be correlated with one another but not be measuring the same thing. We need to carry out a similar analysis on the additive scale of employment relations and conditions. For this purpose a reliability coefficient is estimated which is based on the average correlation of items within the scale (responses to the five questions). This coefficient sets an upper limit to the reliability. If it is very low then there are either not enough items or they have very little in common. It is easy to spot the parallels between our scale items and test scores as we have assigned a one to indicate better terms and conditions of employment and a zero for less favourable terms and conditions of employment.[1]

The most commonly used reliability coefficient is Cronbach's coefficient alpha[2] (Cronbach, 1951), which is an estimator of internal consistency of a multi-item scale. The coefficient alpha is defined as:

$$\alpha = \left(\frac{k}{k-1} \right) \left(1 - \sum_{i=1}^{k} \frac{\sigma_i}{\sigma_s} \right)$$

where: k = number of items in the scale
σ_i = variance of item i
σ_s = variance of the scale

The alpha coefficient for the SRS is 0.698 which is within the bounds of acceptable reliability for a five-item scale (Peterson, 1994). No one item appears to be dominating the scale and each item adds to the variability measured by the scale. The incremental pay variable has the lowest effect on the alpha coefficient if deleted but adds to the scale variance and appears to be an important component of the scale. These results indicate that the linear combination of employment relations and conditions variables forms an internally consistent scale. Correlation between the variables shows that the items are interrelated but no item is redundant, that is to say that each item captures a related but different measure of employment relations and conditions.

Analytical framework

A simple way to assess the ability of different classification schemes to differentiate between a variable of interest is to compare averages within each category. This methodology, although simple, can lead to spurious results as some of the variation found will not be directly related to the social class categories under consideration. Employment relations and conditions vary across a range of factors not necessarily related to social class. The extent to which individuals classified to social class categories have these characteristics in any particular data set will affect the average relations and conditions of employment within any particular class. These include age, gender, job tenure and full-time/part-time working. Through the estimation of individual-level ordinary least squares (OLS) regressions it is possible to control for variation associated with these factors and estimate the effect of belonging to a particular class category independent of these other influences. In the following analysis, the SRS is the dependent variable and is regressed on a number of control variables and a set of binary variables indicating membership to a category within a classification scheme. Separate regressions of the following form are estimated for a range of classifications:

$$y = \beta_0 + \sum_{k_1=1}^{k_1} \beta_{k_1} x_{k_1} + \sum_{k_2=1}^{k_2} \beta_{k_2} x_{k_2} + \varepsilon$$

where: k_1 relates to the control variables: age, job tenure, gender, full-time/part-time employment
k_2 is a set of binary variables representing categories within a classification
ε is an error term, $\varepsilon \sim N(0, 1)$

The variables denoting membership to class categories are included as a set of dichotomous variables and therefore we compare class categories relative to a reference category. To aid comparison across classification schemes we have selected a common category; this group comprises individuals working in unskilled or routine occupations. This group generally occupies the 'lowest' position in all the classification schemes considered.

DIFFERENTIATING EMPLOYMENT RELATIONS AND CONDITIONS BY SOCIO-ECONOMIC AND OCCUPATIONAL CLASSIFICATIONS

This section provides a visual representation of the results obtained from the regression analysis (the regression results can be found in the Appendix). Each figure plots the coefficients from an ordinary least squares regression for the classification groups identified on the horizontal axis. The coefficients represent average point differences in the SRS from the reference category. The reference categories are age 16–19 years, female, part-time, less than three months' job tenure, workers employed in unskilled or routine occupations. For example, the coefficient on the variable for males can be interpreted as the average point difference in the SRS for males relative to females. Statistically insignificant coefficients (fail to reject hypothesis of no significant difference from the reference category at the 5 per cent level) are shown as grey bars. In the figures showing the results for the different classification schemes we also include the

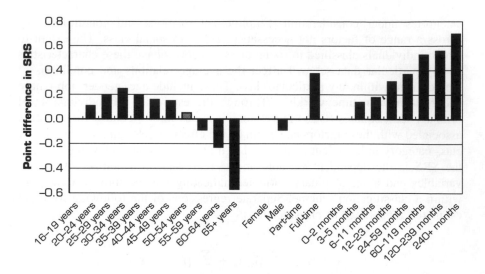

Figure 3.1 *Point differences in the SRS from reference categories – control variables*

'unadjusted' differences in the SRS for class categories relative to the reference group. This allows the reader to assess the effect of the control variables and allows those who prefer the unadjusted results to use these.

We start by considering the influence of the control variables. Figure 3.1 shows the coefficients for the control variables from the regression for the operational version of the NS-SEC. A complete set of control variables was included in all the regressions and although the results vary slightly according to which classification scheme is being considered, they broadly follow the same pattern (results from the other regressions are included in the Appendix). Any variation is due to the ability of different classification schemes to pick up the variation in these control variables.

It can be seen that the effects of age, sex, job tenure and working time are strong and well defined. Age has a quadratic relationship with the SRS increasing up to 30–34 years and then declining. Male employees have a slightly lower average SRS relative to female employees. Full-time employees have better relations and conditions of employment, scoring, on average, an additional 0.36 points in the SRS than otherwise identical part-time employees. Relations and conditions of employment increase monotonically with job tenure.

All of the social classification schemes we consider use the most detailed level of the Standard Occupational Classification (SOC) combined with employment status and workplace size as building blocks. It is therefore instructive to explore the relationship between the SRS and the SOC. The SOC's conceptual basis is skill rather than employment relations and conditions so there is no a priori reason why we should expect to find a strong gradient in the SRS. A variant of the SOC (SOC90) has been in use as the common standard across official UK statistical sources (and most survey data sets) since 1991. As we saw in Part I, a revised version of the SOC (SOC2000) was completed in 2000 in preparation for the 2001 Census and is being gradually introduced across a range of statistical data sources.[3] Part of the process of revision (and the development of the NS-SEC) involved the reclassification of the Winter 1996/97 LFS providing a large sample of employees whose occupations were coded according to both versions of SOC. This information was exploited to re-base the NS-SEC using SOC2000 and will prove to be invaluable in any studies of continuity and change.

Following the SOC we show the results from three other socio-economic classifications. Socio-economic Groups (SEG) were introduced in 1951, extensively amended in 1961 and then periodically revised with the introduction of new occupational classifications. After SEG we look at Social Class based on Occupation (SC). As we saw in the introduction to Part I, this classification scheme was first used for the 1911 Census but has since undergone a number of significant revisions. SC is now generally thought to be a classification of occupational skill but was originally a classification of 'cultural' categories. For more information on, and the derivation of, both of these socio-economic classifications see OPCS (1991) and Rose and O'Reilly (1997).

The third social classification that we include in our empirical analysis is an operationalisation of the Goldthorpe class schema using SOC90 unit groups (Goldthorpe and Heath, 1992). The Goldthorpe schema has a strong sociological conceptual basis, stratifying groups according to employment relations and conditions as discussed in the previous chapter (Erikson and Goldthorpe, 1992). Finally, we turn to the NS-SEC. Two versions of the NS-SEC are examined: the operational version with thirteen categories and the 'official' version with seven classes.

At the beginning of each sub-section we provide the detailed breakdown of the classification under analysis. Not all of the categories feature in the empirical analysis owing to the restriction of them concerning employees only.

SOC90 major groups

Figure 3.2 shows the adjusted and unadjusted differences in average SRS between SOC90 major groups (see Table 3.6). The black bars show the

Table 3.6 *SOC90 major groups*

1	Managers and administrators
2	Professional occupations
3	Associate professional and technical occupations
4	Clerical and secretarial occupations
5	Craft and related occupations
6	Personal and protective service occupations
7	Sales occupations
8	Plant and machine operatives
9	Other occupations

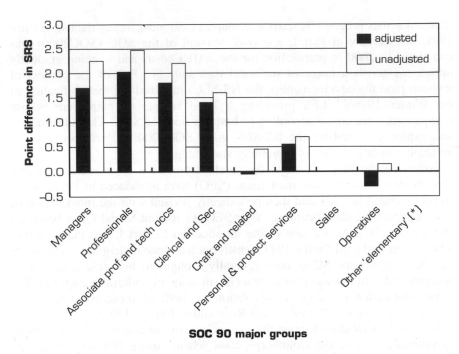

SOC 90 major groups

Figure 3.2 *Point differences in the SRS from reference category – SOC90 major groups*

coefficients from the regressions which include the control variables, labelled 'adjusted'. The white bars show the relative variation between social class categories that are found in the raw data, labelled 'unadjusted'. Comparison between these two series reveals the effect of controlling for other factors. The results from the adjusted series show variation in the SRS that can be ascribed to membership of an SOC major group relative to the reference category denoted by (*). The first thing to note is the absence of a monotonic relationship between the SRS and SOC90 major groups in either the unadjusted or adjusted series. This means that occupations classified at a higher level in the skill hierarchy do not necessarily have better relations and conditions of employment (i.e. are not more likely to have a service relationship). For example, craft and related occupations (SOC90 major group 5) have lower relations and conditions of employment than personal and protective service occupations (major group 6) and sales occupations (major group 7) in the adjusted and unadjusted SRS.

Many occupations included in SOC90 major group 5 have undergone deskilling over the last decade owing to technological developments and structural change. These occupations have been repositioned in SOC2000 further down the skill hierarchy. In addition, higher skilled protective service occupations in major group 6 have been promoted to major group 3 in SOC2000. Overall, the SOC90 major groups can at most be partitioned into two groups. The group at the top with high average relations and conditions of employment – most likely to have a service relationship – includes major groups 1 to 4 (managers and administrators through to clerical and secretarial occupations) and the bottom group with low average relations and conditions of employment – more likely to have a labour contract – includes major groups 5 to 9 (craft and related occupations through to other 'elementary' occupations). The adjustment process reduces the variation between SOC90 major groups with the exception of major group 7 (sales occupations).

SOC2000 major groups

Table 3.7   *SOC2000 major groups*

1	Managers and senior officials
2	Professional occupations
3	Associate professional and technical occupations
4	Administrative and secretarial occupations
5	Skilled trades occupations
6	Personal service occupations
7	Sales and customer service occupations
8	Process, plant and machine operatives
9	Elementary occupations

A comparison with SOC2000 major groups (Figure 3.3) reveals a similar overall pattern to that found for SOC90 major groups. The move between SOC90 major groups and SOC2000 major groups (Table 3.7) does not change

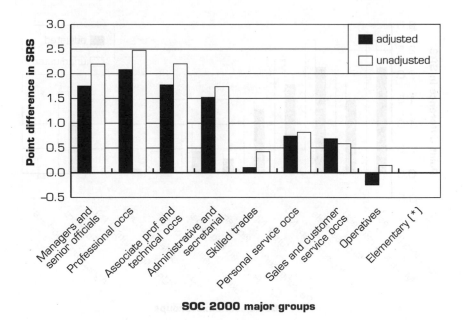

Figure 3.3 *Point differences in the SRS from reference category – SOC2000 major groups*

the rank position of major groups according to average SRSs (unadjusted and adjusted). The differences are: a small increase in the average SRS for major group 2 (professional occupations) and major group 5 (skilled trades occupations); larger increases for major group 4 (probably as a result of the inclusion of administrative occupations and a reclassification of elementary clerical occupations to major group 9), major group 6 (due to the removal of low-level service occupations to major group 9). Major group 7 (sales and customer service occupations) has a lower average SRS, which is likely to be due to the reclassification of high-level sales occupations up to major group 3.

The next set of figures shows the coefficients for the social class schemes from five different regressions, each including the set of control variables shown in Figure 3.1.

Socio-economic groups

Figure 3.4 shows the results from the regression that distinguishes between SEGs. Comparing the unadjusted and the adjusted variation in the relative SRS by SEG reveals that adjusting for the control variables decreases the SRS for all groups relative to unskilled manual workers, although there is very little difference between personal service workers' unadjusted and adjusted SRS. This implies that a significant part of the lower SRS for unskilled manual

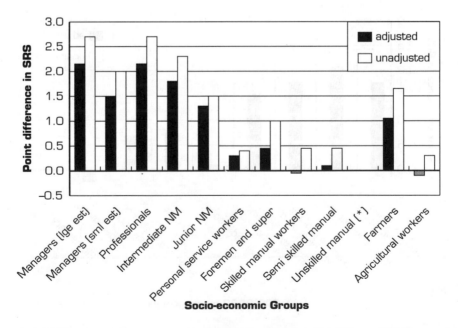

Figure 3.4 *Point differences in the SRS from reference category – Socio-economic Groups*

workers can be explained by the control variables – they are more likely to be any or all of the following: at the beginning or end of their working life, male, working part time and with little experience in their current job. The category of unskilled manual workers ranks the lowest in terms of the SRS in the unadjusted series. In the adjusted series these workers share the lowest position with agricultural workers and skilled manual workers. Overall, this classification scheme proves not to discriminate well in terms of employment relations and conditions with a number of pairs of categories being virtually indistinguishable on this basis. For example, there is no statistically significant difference between unskilled manual workers, skilled manual workers and agricultural workers or between professional workers (employees) and managers (large establishments). However, we should recall that collapsed versions of SEG might combine the latter two into one class similar to NS-SEC Class 1.

Social Class based on Occupation

The regression results obtained when distinguishing between categories in SC (Figure 3.5) show a fairly strong gradient in SRS. Three main groups can be identified with professional, managerial and technical (and the armed forces[4]) occupying the highest position; skilled non-manual occupations, the middle and skilled manual, partly skilled and unskilled occupations the lowest position.

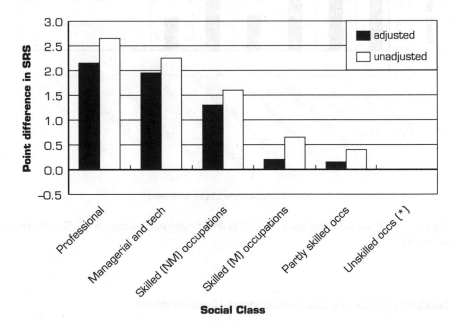

Figure 3.5 *Point differences in the SRS from reference category – Social Class based on Occupation*

The Goldthorpe class schema

In Figure 3.6, the Goldthorpe class schema, for which the conceptual basis is the same as the NS-SEC, shows a fairly well-defined gradient between service class (higher grade), service class (lower grade), routine non-manual employees, and farmers and smallholders. However, the Goldthorpe class schema shows very little differentiation between foremen and technicians, and personal service workers and three other categories (skilled manual workers, semi- and unskilled manual workers, and agricultural workers[5]) in terms of employment relations and conditions, measured by the SRS. However, it is important to note that the reference category in Goldthorpe's class schema includes semi-skilled manual workers as this classification does not separately identify unskilled manual workers. This may partly explain the insignificant difference between skilled manual and agricultural workers and the reference category in the adjusted series. It is also worth noting that the Goldthorpe class schema is not designed to be strictly hierarchical.

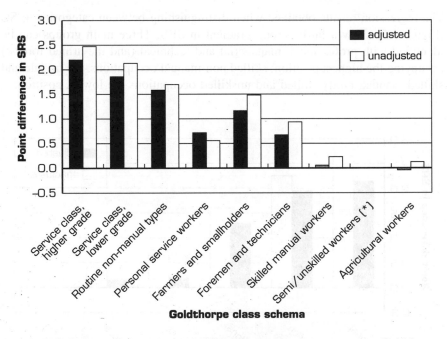

Figure 3.6 *Point differences in the SRS from reference category – Goldthorpe class schema*

National Statistics Socio-economic Classification

Figures 3.7 and 3.8 show the results for two versions of the National Statistics Socio-economic Classification (NS-SEC). The operational version has thirteen

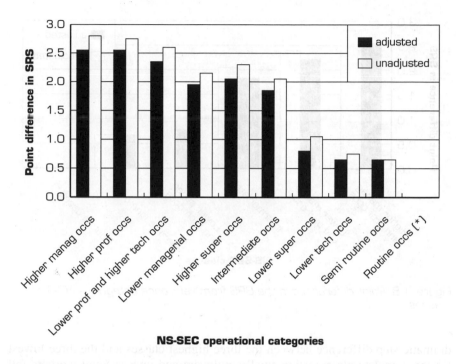

NS-SEC operational categories

Figure 3.7 *Point differences in the SRS from reference category – NS-SEC operational categories*

categories (plus an additional category for the never worked and long-term unemployed). This operational version can be collapsed into seven classes (plus an additional class for the never worked and long-term unemployed) as seen in Chapter 1. In this chapter we analyse results from the thirteen operational categories and seven-class version.

The operational version of the NS-SEC (Figure 3.7) shows a gradient in the SRS but as there are a large number of categories the difference between some categories is small. Two categories (lower managerial occupations and semi-routine occupations) look a little out of line (only lower managerial in the unadjusted series). Four tiers can be identified with higher managerial, higher professional and lower professional and higher technical occupations at the top, followed by lower managerial, higher supervisory and intermediate occupations and then lower supervisory and lower technical and semi-routine occupations and finally routine occupations with the lowest average SRS. Controlling for age, gender, full-time/part-time status and job tenure reduces the variance in the SRS across operational categories relative to the reference category (routine occupations) with the exception of semi-routine occupations. This suggests that employees in semi-routine occupations share other characteristics with employees in routine occupations that are associated with lower average SRSs.

The seven-class version of the NS-SEC shows a clearly defined gradient (Figure 3.8) in the unadjusted and adjusted series. The results show a fairly

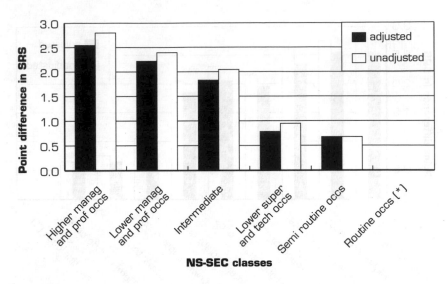

Figure 3.8 *Point differences in the SRS from reference category – NS-SEC classes*

dramatic step difference between the three highest classes and the three lowest (in the complete classification small employers and own account workers fall between these two groups). Employees in intermediate occupations score on average an additional two points in the SRS compared with employees in lower supervisory and technical occupations. Once again semi-routine occupations' average SRS relative to routine occupations is unaffected by the control variables. Two classes – lower supervisory and technical occupations and semi-routine occupations – cannot be separately identified in the adjusted series. These issues are further explored by Mills and Evans in the next chapter.

In the Appendix we also include the regression results from models where the NS-SEC has been constructed using SOC90 OUGs (Tables 3.A8 and 3.A9). Comparison between the coefficients from these models and the models for NS-SEC using SOC2000 reveals very little difference. This is an important finding for the purposes of continuity because it means that a consistent time series can be constructed bridging between data series which have classified occupations using SOC90 (including retrospective occupation histories) and data series from 2000 onwards where occupations will be classified according to SOC2000.

SUMMARY

In this chapter we have contrasted a number of classification schemes in terms of their ability to distinguish between their constituent categories in terms of the employment relations and conditions of employees allocated to them. Employment relations and conditions form the conceptual basis of the National Statistics Socio-economic Classification (NS-SEC), building largely on the work of Goldthorpe. The two officially maintained social classifications that preceded the NS-SEC (SC and SEG) lacked clearly defined conceptual frameworks. This weakness limited their use and hampered interpretation of empirical findings. We have not attempted to test the validity of the NS-SEC in terms of its ability to identify differentials in life chances, instead we have demonstrated the criterion validity of the new NS-SEC, or at any rate the adequacy of its *ex ante* validation (for further discussion on this point see Mills and Evans in the next chapter).

In this chapter we assess the ability of the SOC (SOC90 and SOC2000), three social classifications (SEG, SC and Goldthorpe's class schema), and the operational categories and seven-class version of the NS-SEC, to differentiate between constituent categories on the basis of the service relationship score (SRS).

To identify the 'net' effect of membership to a social class (or occupation) category we regressed the SRS on a set of control variables in addition to the categories of the different classification schemes. In relation to the control variables we found that relations and conditions of employment rise with age up to 30–34 years and then decline, male employees have slightly lower average relations and conditions of employment than female employees, full-time employees have higher average relations and conditions of employment than part-time employees, employment relations and conditions increase with job tenure.

The separate regressions for the different classification schemes showed that although the control variables were well defined, there were *much* larger differences between categories within the classification schemes. To aid comparisons between the classification schemes we chose unskilled or routine occupations as the reference category for all schemes. The control variables, with a few exceptions, reduced the variation between the reference category and all other categories in the classification schemes. This suggests that employees in unskilled or routine occupations have additional characteristics associated with a low SRS.

The SOC is not a social classification and its conceptual basis is skill, but the unit groups of the SOC form one of the building blocks for all of the socio-economic classifications considered so we started by examining the variation in the SRS across SOC major groups. SOC90 and SOC2000 major groups are not characterised by a well-defined gradient in the SRS. At best the four major groups at the top of the skill hierarchy can be characterised as having high average SRSs and the five major groups at the bottom of the skill hierarchy having low average SRSs.

Of the two previous government social classifications, SEG appears not to have an ordinal structure with regards to the SRS. Not all groups can be separately distinguished using this measure of employment relations and conditions. SC has a clear gradient in the SRS between the top three classes but the bottom three, all of which have significantly lower average SRSs, are virtually indistinguishable (particularly skilled manual occupations and partly skilled occupations).

A classification scheme that does have relations and conditions of employ-ment at the heart of its conceptual basis is the Goldthorpe class schema. An operationalisation of this schema using SOC90 unit groups shows a fairly clearly defined relationship with the SRS. One category, personal service workers (IIIb), has a noticeably low average SRS given its apparent position in the classification (see Chapter 12). The reference category for the classification includes semi-skilled manual workers and this is likely to contribute to the fact that the 'lowest' three categories have statistically insignificant differences in average SRSs. It is also worth noting that the Goldthorpe class schema is not designed to be strictly hierarchical. For some purposes Goldthorpe advocates collapsing some of the categories to create more aggregated classes. There may also be an argument for separately identifying these categories because, although some of the classes are indistinguishable in terms of the SRS, they may be characterised by different life chances.

The operational version of the NS-SEC has a number of pairs of categories that cannot be distinguished in terms of average SRSs. For example, higher managerial occupations and higher professional occupations; lower managerial occupations and higher supervisory; lower technical occupations and semi-routine occupations. However, with the exception of the latter two, these categories collapse together in the seven-class version. This version is charac-terised by a strong gradient in the SRS. Nevertheless, two classes (lower supervisory and technical occupations and semi-routine occupations) cannot be distinguished in terms of average adjusted SRSs.

Having examined the 'validity' of the NS-SEC against other classifications, we shall see in the next chapter how Mills and Evans turn to a more detailed examination of the adequacy with which the NS-SEC categories measure the underlying concept of employment relations.

APPENDIX

Table 3.A1   *SOC90 major groups – OLS regression results, dependent variable SRS*

Variables	Coeff.	SE	Sig.
Constant	0.506	0.039	0.000
Age (ref. 16–19 years)			
20–24 years	0.257	0.032	0.000
25–29 years	0.410	0.031	0.000
30–34 years	0.476	0.031	0.000
35–39 years	0.425	0.031	0.000
40–44 years	0.342	0.032	0.000
45–49 years	0.286	0.032	0.000
50–54 years	0.197	0.033	0.000
55–59 years	0.014	0.035	0.691
60–64 years	–0.143	0.041	0.001
65+ years	–0.487	0.061	0.000
Sex (ref. female)			
Male	0.024	0.013	0.074
Working time status (ref. part-time)			
Full-time	0.562	0.016	0.000
Job tenure (ref. less than 3 months)			
3–5 months	0.167	0.035	0.000
6–11 months	0.248	0.034	0.000
12–23 months	0.370	0.032	0.000
24–59 months	0.454	0.030	0.000
60–119 months	0.641	0.030	0.000
120–239 months	0.734	0.031	0.000
240+ months	0.900	0.034	0.000
SOC90 major groups (ref. other occupations)			
Managers	1.719.	0.026	0.000
Professionals	2.027	0.027	0.000
Associate professional & technical occupations	1.822	0.027	0.000
Clerical and secretarial occupations	1.351	0.025	0.000
Craft & related occupations	–0.012	0.028	0.679
Personal & protective services occupations	0.587	0.026	0.000
Sales occupations	0.786	0.028	0.000
Operatives	–0.277	0.028	0.000
Number of observations	46,420		
Model R-squared	0.389		

Table 3.A2   *SOC2000 major groups – OLS regression results, dependent variable SRS*

Variables	Coeff.	SE	Sig.
Constant	0.671	0.036	0.000
Age (ref. 16–19 years)			
20–24 years	0.180	0.031	0.000
25–29 years	0.308	0.030	0.000
30–34 years	0.368	0.030	0.000
35–39 years	0.325	0.030	0.000
40–44 years	0.264	0.031	0.000
45–49 years	0.208	0.031	0.000
50–54 years	0.127	0.032	0.000
55–59 years	−0.020	0.034	0.560
60–64 years	−0.202	0.040	0.000
65+ years	−0.545	0.060	0.000
Sex (ref. female)			
Male	0.028	0.013	0.033
Working time status (ref. part-time)			
Full-time	0.490	0.015	0.000
Job tenure (ref. less than 3 months)			
3–5 months	0.143	0.034	0.000
6–11 months	0.216	0.033	0.000
12–23 months	0.336	0.031	0.000
24–59 months	0.413	0.029	0.000
60–119 months	0.579	0.030	0.000
120–239 months	0.654	0.030	0.000
240+ months	0.808	0.033	0.000
SOC2000 major groups (ref. elementary occupations)			
Managers & senior officials	1.734	0.023	0.000
Professional occupations	2.076	0.023	0.000
Associate professional & technical occupations	1.809	0.022	0.000
Administrative & secretarial	1.528	0.021	0.000
Skilled trades	0.065	0.025	0.009
Personal service occupations	0.768	0.026	0.000
Sales & customer service occupations	0.660	0.025	0.000
Operatives	−0.242	0.024	0.000
Number of observations	46,420		
Model R-squared	0.413		

Table 3.A3   *Socio-economic Groups – OLS regression results, dependent variable SRS*

Variables	Coeff.	SE	Sig.
Constant	0.383	0.042	0.000
Age (ref. 16–19 years)			
20–24 years	0.315	0.032	0.000
25–29 years	0.453	0.031	0.000
30–34 years	0.504	0.030	0.000
35–39 years	0.475	0.031	0.000
40–44 years	0.415	0.031	0.000
45–49 years	0.366	0.031	0.000
50–54 years	0.285	0.032	0.000
55–59 years	0.131	0.035	0.000
60–64 years	0.002	0.041	0.953
65+ years	–0.301	0.061	0.000
Sex (ref. female)			
Male	–0.029	0.013	0.030
Working time status (ref. part-time)			
Full-time	0.575	0.015	0.000
Job tenure (ref. less than 3 months)			
3–5 months	0.174	0.035	0.000
6–11 months	0.240	0.033	0.000
12–23 months	0.346	0.031	0.000
24–59 months	0.426	0.030	0.000
60–119 months	0.595	0.030	0.000
120–239 months	0.650	0.030	0.000
240+ months	0.774	0.033	0.000
Socio-economic Groups (ref. unskilled manual)			
Managers (large establishments)	2.104	0.032	0.000
Managers (small establishments)	1.495	0.036	0.000
Professionals	2.121	0.036	0.000
Intermediate non-manual	1.842	0.030	0.000
Junior non-manual	1.297	0.029	0.000
Personal service workers	0.349	0.035	0.000
Foremen & supervisors	0.442	0.037	0.000
Skilled manual workers	–0.054	0.033	0.098
Semi-skilled manual	0.089	0.032	0.005
Farmers	1.037	0.193	0.000
Agricultural workers	–0.080	0.078	0.306
Armed forces	1.971	0.087	0.000
Number of observations	46,420		
Model R-squared	0.399		

Table 3.A4   *Social Class based on Occupation – OLS regression results, dependent variable SRS*

Variables	Coeff.	SE	Sig.
Constant	0.430	0.043	0.000
Age (ref. 16–19 years)			
20–24 years	0.288	0.032	0.000
25–29 years	0.420	0.031	0.000
30–34 years	0.468	0.031	0.000
35–39 years	0.442	0.031	0.000
40–44 years	0.375	0.031	0.000
45–49 years	0.317	0.032	0.000
50–54 years	0.234	0.032	0.000
55–59 years	0.059	0.035	0.091
60–64 years	–0.079	0.041	0.055
65+ years	–0.409	0.061	0.000
Sex (ref. female)			
Male	–0.061	0.013	0.000
Working time status (ref. part-time)			
Full-time	0.555	0.015	0.000
Job tenure (ref. less than 3 months)			
3–5 months	0.170	0.035	0.000
6–11 months	0.249	0.034	0.000
12–23 months	0.353	0.032	0.000
24–59 months	0.439	0.030	0.000
60–119 months	0.620	0.030	0.000
120–239 months	0.686	0.031	0.000
240+ months	0.830	0.034	0.000
Social Class (ref. unskilled occupations)			
Professional	2.137	0.037	0.000
Managerial & technical	1.929	0.029	0.000
Skilled (non-manual) occupations	1.322	0.029	0.000
Skilled (manual) occupations	0.180	0.031	0.000
Partly skilled occupations	0.172	0.030	0.000
Armed forces	1.973	0.087	0.000
Number of observations	46,420		
Model R-squared	0.387		

Table 3.A5   *Goldthorpe class schema – OLS regression results, dependent variable SRS*

Variables	Coeff.	SE	Sig.
Constant	0.708	0.036	0.000
Age (ref. 16–19 years)			
20–24 years	0.168	0.031	0.000
25–29 years	0.264	0.030	0.000
30–34 years	0.298	0.030	0.000
35–39 years	0.262	0.030	0.000
40–44 years	0.197	0.031	0.000
45–49 years	0.151	0.031	0.000
50–54 years	0.077	0.032	0.016
55–59 years	–0.091	0.034	0.008
60–64 years	–0.238	0.040	0.000
65+ years	–0.605	0.060	0.000
Sex (ref. female)			
Male	–0.034	0.013	0.009
Working time status (ref. part-time)			
Full-time	0.402	0.015	0.000
Job tenure (ref. less than 3 months)			
3–5 months	0.151	0.034	0.000
6–11 months	0.223	0.033	0.000
12–23 months	0.328	0.031	0.000
24–59 months	0.396	0.029	0.000
60–119 months	0.563	0.030	0.000
120–239 months	0.628	0.030	0.000
240+ months	0.755	0.033	0.000
Goldthorpe class schema (ref. semi/unskilled manual)			
Service class, higher grade	2.217	0.019	0.000
Service class, lower grade	1.848	0.018	0.000
Routine non-manual employees	1.574	0.019	0.000
Personal service workers	0.683	0.022	0.000
Farmers & smallholders	1.162	0.164	0.000
Foremen & technicians	0.689	0.023	0.000
Skilled manual workers	0.044	0.024	0.065
Agricultural workers	–0.048	0.073	0.508
Number of observations	46,420		
Model R-squared	0.418		

Table 3.A6   *NS-SEC (operational categories) using SOC2000 – OLS regression results, dependent variable SRS*

Variables	Coeff.	SE	Sig.
Constant	0.599	0.036	0.000
Age (ref. 16–19 years)			
20–24 years	0.120	0.031	0.000
25–29 years	0.203	0.030	0.000
30–34 years	0.248	0.029	0.000
35–39 years	0.208	0.030	0.000
40–44 years	0.158	0.030	0.000
45–49 years	0.131	0.030	0.000
50–54 years	0.046	0.031	0.142
55–59 years	−0.084	0.034	0.012
60–64 years	−0.228	0.040	0.000
65+ years	−0.562	0.059	0.000
Sex (ref. female)			
Male	−0.085	0.013	0.000
Working time status (ref. part-time)			
Full-time	0.355	0.015	0.000
Job tenure (ref. less than 3 months)			
3–5 months	0.136	0.034	0.000
6–11 months	0.182	0.032	0.000
12–23 months	0.302	0.030	0.000
24–59 months	0.364	0.029	0.000
60–119 months	0.514	0.029	0.000
120–239 months	0.566	0.029	0.000
240+ months	0.684	0.032	0.000
NS-SEC using SOC2000 (ref. routine occupations)			
Higher managerial occupations	2.543	0.029	0.000
Higher professional occupations	2.531	0.026	0.000
Lower professional & higher technical occupations	2.357	0.021	0.000
Lower managerial occupations	1.951	0.025	0.000
Higher supervisory occupations	2.020	0.034	0.000
Intermediate occupations	1.855	0.020	0.000
Lower supervisory occupations	0.815	0.025	0.000
Lower technical occupations	0.603	0.031	0.000
Semi-routine occupations	0.655	0.019	0.000
Number of observations	46,420		
Model R-squared	0.437		

Table 3.A7   *NS-SEC (classes) using SOC2000 – OLS regression results, dependent variable SRS*

Variables	Coeff.	SE	Sig.
Constant	0.613	0.036	0.000
Age (ref. 16–19 years)			
20–24 years	0.127	0.031	0.000
25–29 years	0.209	0.030	0.000
30–34 years	0.254	0.029	0.000
35–39 years	0.213	0.030	0.000
40–44 years	0.169	0.030	0.000
45–49 years	0.140	0.030	0.000
50–54 years	0.054	0.031	0.086
55–59 years	–0.078	0.034	0.021
60–64 years	–0.225	0.040	0.000
65+ years	–0.569	0.059	0.000
Sex (ref. female)			
Male	–0.106	0.012	0.000
Working time status (ref. part-time)			
Full-time	0.343	0.015	0.000
Job tenure (ref. less than 3 months)			
3–5 months	0.141	0.034	0.000
6–11 months	0.182	0.032	0.000
12–23 months	0.303	0.030	0.000
24–59 months	0.360	0.029	0.000
60–119 months	0.513	0.029	0.000
120–239 months	0.564	0.030	0.000
240+ months	0.688	0.033	0.000
NS-SEC using SOC2000 (ref. routine occupations)			
Higher managerial & professional occupations	2.544	0.022	0.000
Lower managerial & professional occupations	2.201	0.019	0.000
Intermediate occupations	1.850	0.020	0.000
Lower supervisory & technical occupations	0.743	0.022	0.000
Semi-routine occupations	0.651	0.019	0.000
Number of observations	46,420		
Model R-squared	0.433		

Table 3.A8   *NS-SEC (operational categories) using SOC90 – OLS regression results, dependent variable SRS*

Variables	Coeff.	SE	Sig.
Constant	0.616	0.036	0.000
Age (ref. 16–19 years)			
20–24 years	0.138	0.031	0.000
25–29 years	0.217	0.030	0.000
30–34 years	0.255	0.029	0.000
35–39 years	0.224	0.030	0.000
40–44 years	0.166	0.030	0.000
45–49 years	0.131	0.030	0.000
50–54 years	0.054	0.031	0.082
55–59 years	–0.096	0.034	0.004
60–64 years	–0.230	0.040	0.000
65+ years	–0.577	0.059	0.000
Sex (ref. female)			
Male	–0.082	0.013	0.000
Working time status (ref. part-time)			
Full-time	0.356	0.015	0.000
Job tenure (ref. less than 3 months)			
3–5 months	0.140	0.034	0.000
6–11 months	0.202	0.032	0.000
12–23 months	0.311	0.030	0.000
24–59 months	0.371	0.029	0.000
60–119 months	0.527	0.029	0.000
120–239 months	0.582	0.030	0.000
240+ months	0.699	0.033	0.000
NS-SEC using SOC90 (ref. routine occupations)			
Higher managerial occupations	2.463	0.028	0.000
Higher professional occupations	2.481	0.026	0.000
Lower professional & higher technical occupations	2.330	0.021	0.000
Lower managerial occupations	1.955	0.025	0.000
Higher supervisory occupations	1.918	0.032	0.000
Intermediate occupations	1.784	0.020	0.000
Lower supervisory occupations	0.792	0.025	0.000
Lower technical occupations	0.585	0.030	0.000
Semi-routine occupations	0.594	0.019	0.000
Number of observations	46,420		
Model R-squared	0.433		

Table 3.A9   *NS-SEC (classes) using SOC90 – OLS regression results, dependent variable SRS*

Variables	Coeff.	SE	Sig.
Constant	0.626	0.036	0.000
Age (ref. 16–19 years)			
20–24 years	0.142	0.031	0.000
25–29 years	0.222	0.030	0.000
30–34 years	0.265	0.030	0.000
35–39 years	0.233	0.030	0.000
40–44 years	0.180	0.030	0.000
45–49 years	0.146	0.030	0.000
50–54 years	0.065	0.031	0.038
55–59 years	−0.086	0.034	0.011
60–64 years	−0.223	0.040	0.000
65+ years	−0.575	0.059	0.000
Sex (ref. female)			
Male	−0.099	0.013	0.000
Working time status (ref. part-time)			
Full-time	0.342	0.015	0.000
Job tenure (ref. less than 3 months)			
3–5 months	0.144	0.034	0.000
6–11 months	0.199	0.032	0.000
12–23 months	0.312	0.031	0.000
24–59 months	0.368	0.029	0.000
60–119 months	0.524	0.029	0.000
120–239 months	0.580	0.030	0.000
240+ months	0.701	0.033	0.000
NS-SEC using SOC90 (ref. routine occupations)			
Higher managerial & professional occupations	2.480	0.022	0.000
Lower managerial & professional occupations	2.162	0.019	0.000
Intermediate occupations	1.781	0.020	0.000
Lower supervisory & technical occupations	0.718	0.022	0.000
Semi-routine occupations	0.590	0.019	0.000
Number of observations	46,420		
Model R-squared	0.428		

NOTES

1 In a similar way to weights assigned to questions (harder questions being assigned higher weights) we have also experimented with weighting the responses to the question, although the analyses shown here use the unweighted SRS. The results arising from various weighting schemes are available from the authors on request.

2 We are grateful to Jean Martin for suggestions and advice on the use and interpretation of this statistic.

3 For an introduction to SOC2000 see ONS (2000), Elias and McKnight (2001) and Elias et al. (2000).

4 Employees working in the armed forces are not classified to an SEG or SC category owing to the limited information collected on precise occupations for employees in the armed forces. Instead they are kept as a separate category and the coefficient for this group is not shown in the charts but can be found in the Appendix.

5 This class would normally be dominated by the self-employed but our sample is restricted to employees only. For employees, two SOC90 unit groups are classified to this class comprising managers in farming, horticulture, forestry and fishing (SOC90 unit groups 160 and 169). This explains the relatively high average employment relations and conditions for this class (based on fifty-two individuals).

REFERENCES

Cronbach, L.J. (1951) 'Coefficient alpha and the internal structure of tests', *Psychometrika*, 16: 297–334.

Elias, P. and McKnight, A. (2001) 'Skill measurement in official statistics: recent developments in the UK and the rest of Europe', *Oxford Economic Papers*, 3: 508–40.

Elias, P., McKnight, A., Davies, R. and Kinshott, G. (2000) 'Occupational change: revision of the Standard Occupational Classification', *Labour Market Trends*, 108: 563–72.

Erikson, R. and Goldthorpe, J.H. (1992) *The Constant Flux: A Study of Class Mobility in Industrialised Societies*. Oxford: Clarendon Press.

Goldthorpe, J.H. and Heath, A. (1992) 'Revised class schema, 1992', *JUSST Working Paper 13*. Oxford: Nuffield College.

Office for National Statistics (ONS) (2000) *Standard Occupational Classification 2000*. London: The Stationery Office.

Office of Population Census and Surveys (OPCS) (1991) *Standard Occupational Classification, Volume 3*. London: HMSO.

Peterson, R.A. (1994) 'A meta-analysis of Cronbach's coefficient alpha', *Journal of Consumer Research*, 21: 381–91.

Rose, D. (1995) *A Report on Phase 1 of the ESRC Review of OPCS Social Classifications*. Swindon: ESRC.

Rose, D. and O'Reilly, K. (1997) *The ESRC Review of Government Social Classifications: Report on Phase 2*. Colchester: ESRC Research Centre on Micro-Social Change, University of Essex.

4
Employment Relations, Employment Conditions and the NS-SEC

Colin Mills and Geoffrey Evans

He knew, too, that the problem was one of classification. He had to break the interlinked stories into separate threads, and work from those. At the moment, he was guilty of trying to weave them all into a pattern, a pattern that might not be there. By separating them all, maybe he'd be in with a chance of solving each. (Ian Rankin, *Hide and Seek*)

INTRODUCTION

Our original brief for this chapter was to investigate the criterion-related validity of the National Statistics Socio-economic Classification (NS-SEC). To do this properly would have entailed:

1   The taking of measurements on independently validated indicators of the construct or constructs underlying the NS-SEC.
2   Examining the pattern and strength of association between these indicators and the NS-SEC itself.

Normally the tighter the structure of the correlation between the indicators and the NS-SEC the more confidence we would have in the classification's validity and the more entitled we would feel to claim that the NS-SEC does its intended job well.

Unfortunately, as noted in the introduction to Part II, there is a snag that prevents us from carrying out a simple validation exercise. For the most part we have data and indicators that have already been used in the original construction of the NS-SEC. In these circumstances, to present what we do in the language of validation would be a pointless exercise in circular reasoning. What we present below is therefore not another attempt to show that the NS-SEC is valid, but simply an exposition of how the various aspects of employment relations and conditions (hereafter ERC) vary between NS-SEC categories. In the course of doing this we also:

1   Suggest a novel way of combining information about different aspects of ERC.
2   Make some suggestions about ways to combine categories of the NS-SEC that are consistent with the conceptualisation of social class that underlies it.

SOCIAL CLASS AND THE NS-SEC

In what follows we restrict our attention to those NS-SEC groups that contain employees.[1] We have nothing to say about the status of large employers, owners of small businesses, farmers, 'own account' workers and so forth, other than that the criteria for allocating them to positions in the NS-SEC can have nothing to do with variation in their ERC. In so far as NS-SEC categories, or aggregations thereof, can be identified with distinct social classes, the self-employed and farmers occupy class positions that must be defined with reference to different organising principles.[2] We are concerned solely with ERC distinctions within the mass of wage and salary earners and follow a line of sociological investigation that owes more to Lockwood (1958/1989) than to Marx or Weber. The central question in this tradition concerns the kinds of fault lines that can usefully be regarded as distinctions of class in the wage-earning population. These must be distinctions that, though correlated with education, status, prestige, income, earnings and myriad other features of the stratification order, are not themselves described in these terms. Nothing of sociological importance is to be gained by labelling as differences in social class, say, differences in levels of educational attainment.

As we have seen already, the underlying idea behind the NS-SEC is that occupational groups are to be differentiated in terms of ERC. Social classes can then be identified by virtue of the proximity of particular occupational groups to each other within a 'space' with axes that are defined by the relevant relations/conditions.[3] These axes allow us to define polar types or ways in which employment can be regulated and employees motivated, namely a 'service' relation and a 'wage–labour' relation (Goldthorpe, 2000). In addition there will be a number of mixed or 'intermediate' types combining, in varying proportions, the features of the ERC of both poles. The principal types are hypothesised to emerge because employers find them to be efficient ways of regulating the effort–reward bargain given the constraints imposed by technology, the practicalities of effort monitoring and the frictional costs incurred in hiring and firing employees.

In developing the argument from Chapter 2, therefore, the style of regulation adopted by employers is the result of two features of the organisation of work. The first is the degree of difficulty experienced by employers in monitoring employee job performance. The second is the degree of specificity of the skills and knowledge employees routinely make use of in the performance of their work. The first factor determines whether or not it is useful to tie payment directly to productivity. This depends on the tangibility of what is produced and on the extent that it is possible to measure the separate contributions to joint production. The second factor determines whether it is necessary to provide incentives to encourage employees to develop and utilise organisation-specific skills and know-how. In the standard human-capital model it is the firm that must bear most of the costs of firm-specific skill investment while the employee bears the costs of generally utilisable skills. From the employee's point of view, time invested in the acquisition of organisation-specific skills is time lost in the acquisition of more generally marketable skills (unless there are complementarities). The logic of the situation suggests that employees need incentives to acquire organisation-specific human capital. In this model the risks of the investment are spread between employer and employee. The employee develops skills that are mostly of use to one employer. However, unless the organisation-specific skills can be acquired costlessly and instantly the employer has an interest in retaining the employee and in the event of the contract being severed, of retaining the employee's services until such times as an adequate replacement can be found. Work that is difficult to monitor and requires high levels of organisation-specific skill is likely to require a so-called 'service class' contractual package. The explicit part of this will consist of a monthly salary, a long notice period, incremental salary increases, and discretion over time use. The more implicit part (the so-called psychological contract) will emphasise future promotion opportunities and flexibility in the sense that the employer will expect the employee to put in (unpaid) hours beyond the limits of the normal working day in order to get particular jobs done.

The polar opposite of the service relationship is the wage–labour contract. In its purest form, say a spot market for manual labour, there is a discrete exchange of money for effort. Performance is easy to measure because of the tangibility either of what is produced or of the service rendered. The skills that are required are widely available and the employer has little incentive to enter into an enduring relationship with the employee. Where the job task allows some discretion in the amount of effort expended, then payment by the piece can be expected. Where the technology allows rather little discretion (Goldthorpe uses the example of the production line) then hourly rates or weekly wages are more likely.

As well as the service and labour contract types there are grounds for expecting to find more or less well-defined intermediate or mixed arrangements. Situations where skill specificity is low and the difficulty of monitoring relatively high are typical of routine clerical work. Accordingly contracts tend to mix features of both the service and the labour contract. Typically such jobs are salaried, and some flexibility in time keeping is allowed. However, promotion opportunities are limited, notice periods are measured in weeks rather than months and employees are not expected to work more than their contracted number of hours without additional payment. Given the wide availability of skills it is not surprising that, as Goldthorpe points out, organisations frequently resort to the use of agency staff to fill secretarial, receptionist and other soft-skill positions.

Goldthorpe also sees the supervisors of manual workers and lower grade technicians as occupying intermediate positions. Here it may be necessary to motivate the acquisition of organisation-specific skills, but the evaluation of job performance is more straightforward. Though such employees may not attain salaried 'staff' status and can therefore expect to be paid for any extra hours they work, they are likely to have their feet on the rungs of an internal promotion ladder, albeit one that may be structured by seniority rather than performance. In the NS-SEC, however, these groups are not seen as intermediate but as having more in common with Classes 6 and 7.

CLASSIFYING OCCUPATIONS

Sensible taxonomies can rarely be judged true or false, only more or less useful for a given purpose.[4] The NS-SEC is intended to perform a number of roles, and though more thoroughly based on systematic sociological thinking than previous official classifications, its function is in social audit as well as basic social scientific research. Therefore in its construction, considerations other than simply the optimal way to group occupations for a single explanatory purpose have necessarily been given some weight. An obvious requirement that follows from this is the need to maintain a degree of continuity with previous official classifications. Another is that the NS-SEC should remain a classification of occupations rather than of jobs or individuals. This latter condition is especially restrictive because it is the individual employee who holds a job in an organisation and it is the person–position pair that has work duties and obligations and is ascribed rights, rewards and perquisites whether by formal contract, by 'custom and practice' or by collective bargaining. However, in the typical social survey it will usually be too costly to collect sufficient information to classify jobs (in the sense of person–position pairs). Nevertheless, for the purposes of social audit, and for scientific studies where occupation is of interest only as a control variable, it is still useful to classify individuals, not in terms of the actual ERC associated with their particular job, but in terms of ERC averaged over occupations.

Classifying occupations rather than jobs is the obvious pragmatic strategy. However, it should be noted that taking the unit of analysis to be the occupation is not intrinsic to the conceptualisation of social class advanced by Goldthorpe. In our view, many 'class analysts' have taken Parkin (1971: 18) too literally when he claims that: 'The backbone of the class structure . . . is the occupational order.' Leaving aside ossicular similes it makes more sense to say that the basic unit of analysis should be the ERC pertaining to a person–job pair.[5]

Another issue raised in Chapter 2 that has troubled stratification researchers and thus deserves comment is whether, in the abstract, it is better to represent the 'stratification order' by means of a taxonomy, such as a class schema, or by a metrical variable representing the distribution of an attribute in a continuous sample space.[6] Our view on this is that there can, in fact, be no answer to this question *in the abstract*. To some degree what we do must be the result of a pragmatic decision rather than a matter of principle and will depend on the precise role that the taxonomy/variable is asked to perform. If we are merely interested in a rough and ready control for unmeasured factors that might have a confounding effect on the relationships of interest, then a simple continuous metrical representation may be adequate. If we are interested in explaining, or generating hypotheses about, the way in which combinations of employment conditions impact on social behaviour, social attitudes or health, then there are advantages (given the current state of development of social measurement) in using a taxonomy.

Where, in our opinion, the case for metrical representation is weakest is when a single dimension of the 'stratification order' is extracted from the analysis of occupational data that includes alike employees, the self-employed and agricultural occupations. Such analyses invariably suggest that the latter two categories are not well represented in one dimension and that their location in the hierarchy of scale values can vary significantly depending on what exactly is being scaled. Important differences can be observed depending on whether the analysis is of social status (via friendship or spare-time association data), prestige (via ranking exercises), or socio-economic status (via index construction). These differences are particularly apparent in cross-national perspective, especially in comparison with the high level of cross-national agreement in the ranking of occupational categories pertaining to employees. Representing all occupations on a single dimension predisposes the evidence in favour of finding no distinct breaks between particular groupings of occupations and leads the 'one dimensionalists' to believe that what is essentially a methodological artefact is actually a feature of the underlying reality they are attempting to represent.[7]

The case for a metrical representation has greater face validity when, as in this chapter, attention is restricted to employees alone. One can reasonably make the argument that 'service' and 'wage–labour' relationships are poles of a continuum and that intermediate forms lie at various distances between them. Thus person–job pairs, and, if need be, occupations, can reasonably be given scale scores to reflect their mutual distances. A more sophisticated version might distinguish different dimensions of the relationship and hence separate scale scores for degree of 'serviceness', opportunity for career advancement and promotion, amount of autonomy and so forth (Evans, 1992). For a social scientist, replacing the names of things with the names of variables is surely desirable but one should also retain a sense of the manner in which the variables are interrelated.[8] If one is making a representation of a world in which the dimensions of interest are correlated and where the distribution of values along each dimension is not unimodal, smooth or continuous, then a taxonomy rather than a scale score is likely to give the most insight into the processes that generated the joint distribution.[9]

Conditions of employment tend to come as contractual 'package deals' and this implies strong correlations between the presence or absence of particular job attributes as well as a multimodal joint probability distribution. The package deals are local saddle or focal points towards which employer–employee bargaining tends to move. One reason for expecting equilibria or focal points to emerge is the common-sense observation that both employers and employees create social institutions (personnel departments, trade unions) which amongst other things monitor the working conditions on offer within competing organisations or to comparable types of employees. In other words, certain focal outcomes of the effort–reward bargaining process will tend to diffuse throughout the labour market. Viewed in cross-section the system will not be in global equilibrium and this will give the impression of variation around the multiple local equilibria. Some of this variation will simply reflect movement towards equilibrium. Some, however, will reflect adaptation to local conditions or niches. These niches may reflect special or atypical features of the organisation, its environment or its technology. Often these peculiarities will be reflected in the labour process itself or in the occupational environment and hence will be captured by occupational taxonomies.[10] Almost inevitably this leads us to ask whether particular modal categories are 'close to' or 'distant from' each other and whether observations that lie close to modal categories are sufficiently similar as to be regarded, for all practical purposes, as being assimilable to that modal category.

The choice between taxonomic and metrical representations of the structure of employment relations depends then, ultimately, on three things. First, it depends on how we think the real world actually is. Second, it depends on whether the particular representation we use is good enough for the purpose we have in mind.[11] Third, it depends on the fertility of the representation in terms of its power to give answers to existing questions and in enabling us to formulate new questions. Common sense suggests that a definitive view on the first of these will be difficult to arrive at because, inevitably, what we directly observe are highly error-prone indicators of a somewhat messy reality. However, we can say without fear of contradiction that the joint probability density over all the elements of ERC will look neither like a Manhattan cityscape with tall towers separated by flat planes nor like the gently rolling Sussex Downs. Reality will be something in between, a small number of relatively steep hills and valleys with some summits in close proximity to each other and other summits quite distant. The answers to the second and third questions cannot be determined a priori and the proof of the pudding must be in the eating, as the chapters in Part III demonstrate.

DATA

In Table 4.1 we list the twenty-six employee categories and sub-categories of the operational version of the NS-SEC that we use as our elementary building blocks. Next to each is the label we use to identify individual NS-SEC categories in the figures presented below. We make use of ten ERC criterion variables taken from the 1997 UK Quarterly Labour Force Survey (LFS). The responses to nine questions are taken from the first quarter and to the tenth from the third quarter. As we saw in Chapter 2, eight of the questions were added specially to the LFS for the Economic and Social Research Council's Review of Government Social Classifications: one, on overtime working, is a composite of regular LFS items; another on variability of working hours is a standard LFS question. The question rubrics and response categories are presented in Table 4.2 along with the variable names we have assigned.

All of the questions have face validity as indicators of important aspects of ERC. The selection of indicators, the specific question wordings and the response formats are, of course, matters of judgement. We ourselves had no input into the process that led to their selection and we rely on the opinions of a panel of experts. It is, however, reassuring to note that in the course of writing

Table 4.1   *NS-SEC categories used in the analysis*

Occupational title and label
L2   Higher managerial **(hm)**
L3.1   Higher professional (traditional) **(hp1)**
L3.2   Higher professional (new) **(hp2)**
L4.1   Lower professional and higher technical (traditional) **(lp1)**
L4.2   Lower professional and higher technical (new) **(lp2)**
L5   Lower managerial **(lm)**
L6   Higher supervisory **(hs)**
L7.1   Intermediate (clerical and administrative) **(io1)**
L7.2   Intermediate (service) **(io2)**
L7.3   Intermediate (technical and auxiliary) **(io3)**
L7.4   Intermediate (engineering) **(io4)**
L10   Lower supervisory **(ls)**
L11.1 Lower technical (craft) **(lt1)**
L11.2 Lower technical (process operative) **(lt2)**
L12.1 Semi-routine (sales) **(sr1)**
L12.2 Semi-routine (service) **(sr2)**
L12.3 Semi-routine (technical) **(sr3)**
L12.4 Semi-routine (operative) **(sr4)**
L12.5 Semi-routine (agricultural) **(sr5)**
L12.6 Semi-routine (clerical) **(sr6)**
L12.7 Semi-routine (childcare) **(sr7)**
L13.1 Routine (sales and service) **(r1)**
L13.2 Routine (production) **(r2)**
L13.3 Routine (technical) **(r3)**
L13.4 Routine (operative) **(r4)**
L13.5 Routine (agricultural) **(r5)**

this chapter we found that our results stood up to reasonable variation both in the combination of indicators employed and in their coding.

METHOD OF ANALYSIS

Our first step is to find a simple way of representing the association between the categories of the NS-SEC and the criterion variables. We do this in the following way. To each r by c cross-tabulation (where r indexes the twenty-six rows corresponding to the occupational groups of the operational version and c varies depending on the number of response categories for the criterion variable being considered) we fit an RC(M) log-multiplicative model (Clogg and Shihadeh, 1994; Goodman, 1991). The model has the following form:

$$\log(F_{ij}) = \mu + \lambda_i^o + \lambda_j^c + \sum_{m=1}^{M} \varphi_m u_{im} v_{jm}$$

The λ terms are to be understood as 'main effects' for the occupation (o) and criterion (c) variables as in a conventional log-linear model (Gilbert, 1994); the φ are 'uniform association' parameters; the u_{im} are row scores; and the v_{jm} are

Table 4.2   *Criterion items and response categories*

Question	Response categories
NLFSQ1. Which of the following best describes how you are paid in your present job? **JOBPAY**	Monthly salary plus performance Monthly salary only Weekly wage Hourly paid Piecework Other Don't know
NLFSQ1. Are you on a recognised pay scale with increments, either automatic or performance related? **PAYINC**	Yes No Don't know
NLFSQ1.If you decided to leave your job, how much notice are you officially required to give? **NOTICE**	Less than one week One week but less than one month One month but less than three months Three months or more Don't know
LFSQ1. Composite from replies to several questions about whether the respondent ever works overtime. **OTIME**	Never works overtime Yes, unpaid Yes, paid
LFSQ1. Does the total number of hours you work tend to vary from week to week? **HRSVARY**	Yes No
NLFSQ1. Who decides what time you start and leave work? **STLVE**	Flexitime system Employer decides I decide within certain limits Negotiated with employer Don't know
NLFSQ1. In your sort of work, are there opportunities for promotion, either in your current organisation or by changing employers? **PROM**	Yes No Don't know
NLFSQ3. Does your sort of work have a recognised career or promotion ladder, even if it means changing employers to go up it? **LADDER**	Yes No
NLFSQ1. Does your job require you to design and plan important aspects of your own work, or is your work largely specified for you? **PLANWK**	I am required to design/plan my work Work is largely specified by others Other Don't know
NLFSQ1. How much influence do you personally have in deciding what tasks you are to do? **TASKS**	A great deal A fair amount Not much None at all Don't know

LFS, standard LFS question; NLFS, new LFS question; Q1, first quarter; Q3, third quarter.

column scores to be estimated. There can be more than one dimension of association for a given table, hence the summation over the M dimensions. This means that we estimate a set of row and column scores for each table as well as the M association parameters to go with them. Score parameters are identified by imposing zero mean and unit variance restrictions on them and in effect are chosen to maximise the association parameters subject to the restriction that the M dimensions must be orthogonal.[12] The maximum M for a given table is Min$(I,J) - 1$; thus one for a 26×2 table, two for a 26×3 table, three for a 26×4 table and so forth. This way of modelling the data has the advantage that we can represent parsimoniously the relationship between the twenty-six occupational groups and each criterion variable whilst retaining all of the information contained in the original response categories. We can also include missing data on a criterion variable as a response category.[13] For presentational purposes we base our interpretation mainly on the adjusted row scores which combine the occupational scores on a particular dimension with the relevant association parameter. These adjusted row scores are defined as:

$$u^*_{im} = \overline{\varphi_m u_{im}}$$

In effect they scale the occupational scores up or down depending on whether the φ coefficient indicates relatively strong row/column association in a particular dimension. This has the effect of reducing interoccupational 'distance' if the association is weak and increasing it if it is strong. It also gets around a presentational difficulty inherent to this type of model that information about association is contained both in row/column scores and in the association parameters. Adjusted column scores are defined in a similar way *mutatis mutandis*.

Fit statistics for the modelling exercise are contained in Table 4.3. These are probably of little interest to the general reader and can be skipped without loss of continuity. In all but two cases sample sizes are in excess of 49,000 observations and we were guided in model selection by consideration of the proportion of cases misclassified and the Bayesian Information Criterion (BIC) (Raftery, 1986; 1995) rather than by likelihood-ratio chi-square values. After finding good-fitting low-dimensional models we make use of score information on up to three dimensions.

THE NS-SEC AND THE CRITERION VARIABLES

Table 4.4 shows the adjusted row scores for each occupational group for tables that required only an RC(1) structure to capture the occupation by criterion variable association. The polarities of the dimensions are arbitrary: all that matters for our purposes are the distances between occupational categories.[14]

For tables that require models with two or more dimensions to capture the row/column association (RC(2) and RC(3)), interpretation is aided by the inspection of plots. Figures 4.1a to 4.4b below plot the adjusted column and row scores.

Table 4.3   *Fit statistics for Goodman RC(M) models*

	G^2	df	Δ	BIC
JOBPAY n = 49,403				
1.1 Independence	20,360.9	150	26.5	18,739.7
1.2 RC(1)	2,274.5	120	6.3	977.6
1.3 RC(2)	615.3	92	2.0	–379.1
1.4 RC(3)	313.9	66	1.4	–399.4
PAYINC n = 49,395				
2.1 Independence	5,542.4	50	14.4	5,002.0
2.2 RC(1)	48.7	24	0.6	–210.7
NOTICE n = 49,383				
3.1 Independence	17,993.7	100	25.8	16,913.0
3.2 RC(1)	1,141.6	72	4.6	363.5
3.3 RC(2)	365.6	46	1.8	–131.6
3.4 RC(3)	45.6	22	0.5	–191.9
OTIME n = 49,859				
4.1 Independence	8,940.7	50	17.4	8,399.8
4.2 RC(1)	1,896.6	24	7.6	1,637.0
4.3 RC(2)	0.0	0	0.0	0.0
STLVE n = 49,403				
5.1 Independence	1,1293.3	100	18.1	10,212.5
5.2 RC(1)	1,881.0	72	3.9	1,102.8
5.3 RC(2)	103.5	46	0.5	–393.7
PROM n = 49,401				
6.1 Independence	5,161.0	50	12.2	4,620.6
6.2 RC(1)	45.8	24	0.3	–213.6
LADDER n = 23,495				
7.1 Independence	3,019.2	25	13.6	2,767.6
7.2 RC(1)	0.0	0	0.0	0.0
PLANWK n = 49,406				
7.1 Independence	16,471.0	75	24.4	15,660.5
7.2 RC(1)	105.0	48	0.5	–413.8
TASKS n = 49,403				
8.1 Independence	15,694.5	100	22.1	14,613.7
8.2 RC(1)	277.2	72	2.6	–500.9
HRSVARY n = 41,699				
9.1 Independence	2,229.5	25	10.0	1,963.6
9.2 RC(1)	0.0	0	0.0	0.0

As an additional visual guide to interpretation we have indicated in Table 4.4 plausible divisions between service, mixed and wage–labour groupings of occupations. The reader is invited to mentally impose equivalent divisions onto the figures. It should be noted that these divisions have been drawn a priori, the point being to see how well they correspond to the empirical reality captured in our models. General rules for interpreting the tables and figures are as follows:

Table 4.4   Parameter estimates (adjusted row scale scores) from RC(1) models

		PAYINC	PROM	LADDER	PLANWK	TASKS	HRSVARY
L2	Higher managerial	-0.30	-0.46	-0.39	-0.90	-1.24	-0.44
L3.1	Higher professional (traditional)	-0.41	-0.47	-0.53	-0.72	-0.68	-0.38
L3.2	Higher professional (new)	-0.41	-0.69	-0.49	-0.66	-0.51	-0.24
L4.1	Lower professional (traditional)	-0.76	-0.50	-0.58	-0.56	-0.59	-0.17
L4.2	Lower professional (new)	-0.16	-0.31	-0.27	-0.63	-0.84	-0.33
L5	Lower managerial	-0.03	-0.15	-0.15	-0.64	-1.02	-0.23
L6	Higher supervisory	-0.38	-0.39	-0.31	-0.23	-0.33	-0.02
L7.1	Intermediate clerical and admin	-0.28	-0.08	-0.06	0.02	0.06	0.29
L7.2	Intermediate service	-0.29	-0.24	-0.23	-0.04	0.02	0.19
L7.3	Intermediate technical & auxiliary	-0.26	0.14	-0.13	-0.05	-0.04	0.09
L7.4	Intermediate engineering	-0.24	-0.32	-0.43	-0.14	0.06	-0.25
L10	Lower supervisory	0.06	-0.14	-0.09	-0.12	-0.25	-0.08
L11.1	Lower technical craft	0.10	0.01	0.01	0.07	0.21	0.00
L11.2	Lower technical process	0.03	-0.14	-0.02	0.35	0.42	-0.05
L12.1	Semi-routine sales	0.24	0.06	0.03	0.44	0.49	0.27
L12.2	Semi-routine service	0.18	0.14	0.04	0.29	0.31	0.07
L12.3	Semi-routine technical	0.23	0.18	0.26	0.46	0.49	0.02
L12.4	Semi-routine operative	0.27	0.15	0.25	0.50	0.66	0.16
L12.5	Semi-routine agricultural	0.27	0.55	0.51	0.13	0.17	-0.27
L12.6	Semi-routine clerical	0.00	0.02	0.14	0.20	0.16	0.40
L12.7	Semi-routine childcare	-0.15	0.57	0.45	-0.04	-0.08	0.55
L13.1	Routine sales and service	0.49	0.42	0.28	0.27	0.30	0.19
L13.2	Routine production	0.37	0.46	0.51	0.76	0.91	0.34
L13.3	Routine technical	0.32	0.44	0.42	0.30	0.53	-0.13
L13.4	Routine operative	0.40	0.44	0.50	0.46	0.40	0.38
L13.5	Routine agricultural	0.67	0.30	0.28	0.40	0.39	-0.34

1   In Table 4.4 negative scores always indicate more 'service'-like ERC arrangements.
2   The wider the range of scores the stronger the association evidenced in the originating table.
3   Scores are not constrained to be monotonic in row order.

Special rules for interpreting the figures are as follows:

1   Plots of the row (occupation) points should be understood as being in the space defined by the plot of the column (criterion) points.
2   Two-/three-dimensional plots of the column points are provided (Figures 4.1a, 4.2a, 4.3a, 4.4a) and where appropriate rotated to give the reader the best view of the relative position of each point.
3   Row points are plotted in only two dimensions (three-dimensional plots are too crowded to be of much use).
4   To interpret a row plot refer it to the corresponding plane of the column plot. Sometimes it will be necessary to reflect the former around the y axis to achieve the correct orientation – that is, flip the figure over as though you were looking through the reverse side of it.
5   Row points that appear in the direction of specific column points indicate departures from independence in that direction.
6   It is not legitimate to interpret the proximity, in the sense of Euclidean distance, between a row point and a column point (i.e. the joint plotting of rows and columns is misleading).[15]
7   The orientation of the axes of the plots is arbitrary in the sense that it is chosen to satisfy a convenient mathematical criterion; therefore axes may be rotated around the origin in any way that aids substantive interpretability (and maintains orthogonality).
8   It is legitimate to interpret the proximity, in the sense of Euclidean distance, between row points, and the interpretation of the figures in terms of clusters of row points will often be the most convenient.

We start our discussion with some general comments on the patterns revealed by the RC(1) models. We then turn to the interpretation of the figures that report the results from the RC(2) and RC(3) models.

   The first question to address is whether, on the assumption that the NS-SEC measures variations in ERC, the criterion variables discriminate the occupational categories in ways that are reasonable. For those tables where there is only one dimension of association we can evaluate this by direct inspection of Table 4.4. For annual pay increments, promotion opportunities, the existence of career ladders, the necessity to design/plan work and control over work tasks there is a rough and ready 'top to bottom' hierarchy with white-collar jobs tending to have negative scores and blue-collar jobs positive scores. This pattern is repeated for the extent to which hours of work vary, though with noticeably more inversions of order. However, non-monotonicity and lack of agreement across items in the rank order do not per se constitute evidence against the validity of the occupational groupings. The fact that the two agricultural groups (L12.5 and L13.5) have negative scores on HRSVARY and thus appear similar in this respect to white-collar occupations is an aspect of reality that we would expect to see represented in any reasonable taxonomy.[16] What would constitute evidence of invalidity is an absence of any differences between groups, not inversions of order. The criteria measure different aspects of ERC and there is no reason to believe that an occupation should have the same relative position with regard to each one. There is in fact a reasonable amount of agreement across the first dimension of all items. Though the inter-item Pearson product-moment correlations range between 0.23 and 0.96, 90 per cent of the coefficients lie between 0.56 and 0.96 and 62 per cent between 0.75 and 0.96. Further inspection of Table 4.4 reveals that the discriminatory power of each criterion is rather similar. The strength of the association in each occupation by criterion table is captured in the range of the occupational scale scores. This is widest for TASKS and narrowest for HRSVARY. Judging the overall strength of association for the remaining four items is more difficult because that association is spread over two or three dimensions; therefore we now turn our attention to the interpretation of Figures 4.1a to 4.4b.

Figure 4.1a represents the JOBPAY space within which we plot, in terms of their departures from independence, the NS-SEC categories in Figures 4.1b and 4.1c. The first dimension of Figure 4.1a (JP1) contrasts piecework arrange-ments with payment of a monthly salary either with or without a performance-

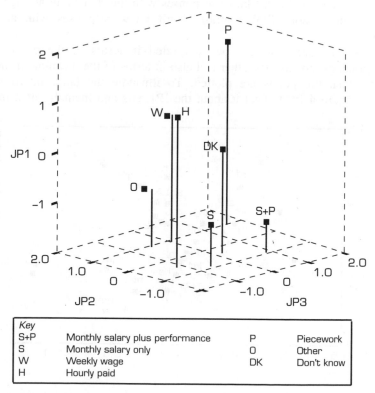

Key			
S+P	Monthly salary plus performance	P	Piecework
S	Monthly salary only	O	Other
W	Weekly wage	DK	Don't know
H	Hourly paid		

Figure 4.1a *Three-dimensional solution for JOBPAY: columns*

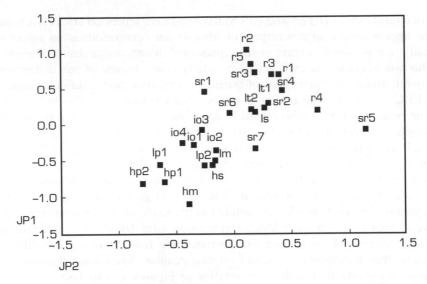

Figure 4.1b *Three-dimensional solution for JOBPAY: rows JPI by JP2*

related component. The other categories fall between these two polar types. The second dimension (JP2) contrasts weekly wages, miscellaneous other payment systems and don't know responses with the remaining arrangements. The third dimension (JP3) contrasts don't know responses with all other responses.

Figures 4.1b and 4.1c can be interpreted in terms of the proximity of occupational groups to each other and also in terms of the meaning of the axes against which the points are plotted. To illustrate the latter interpretation, consider Figure 4.1b. Reflect it about the JP1 axis and mentally fit it into the

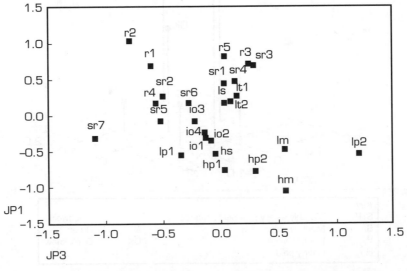

Figure 4.1c *Three-dimensional solution for JOBPAY: rows JPI by JP3*

JP1/JP2 plane of Figure 4.1a. In terms of the configuration before you in Figure 4.1b, there is a main axis of differentiation going from southwest to northeast defined by a weekly wages versus salary distinction. Some occupations are clearly attracted by the 'gravitational effects' of other column categories. For example routine production (r2) and routine agricultural (r5) occupations have some affinity with piecework payment while semi-routine agricultural occupations (sr5) are attracted to the 'other' category – perhaps payment in produce or in housing.[17] In Figure 4.1c there is a northwest to southeast axis defined by an hourly versus salary plus performance pay distinction. There are, however, several other sources of attraction. Semi-routine childcare occupations (sr7) show some affinity for the 'other' category. Presumably a proportion of these are live-in nannies, au pairs and suchlike that receive board and lodgings and a small allowance. Piecework systems attract routine agricultural occupations (r5), routine and semi-routine technical occupations (sr3, r3) as well as a number of other occupations (sr1, sr4, ls, lt1, lt2). Salary plus performance pay has an affinity with managerial occupations (hm, lm), but especially 'new' lower professionals (lp2). The latter attraction may seem curious until one realises that this occupational group includes technical and wholesale representatives whose remuneration will typically depend upon how much of the product they sell.

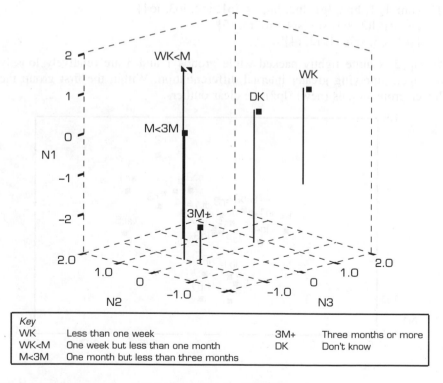

Key			
WK	Less than one week	3M+	Three months or more
WK<M	One week but less than one month	DK	Don't know
M<3M	One month but less than three months		

Figure 4.2a *Three-dimensional solution for NOTICE: columns*

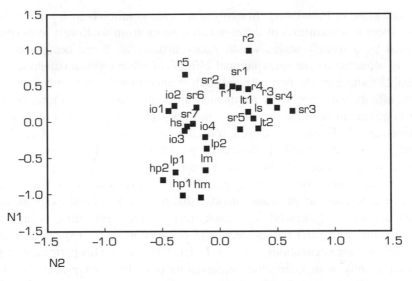

Figure 4.2b *Three-dimensional solution for NOTICE: rows N1 by N2*

The two-dimensional plots in Figures 4.1b and 4.1c only partially enable the viewer to envisage the full three-dimensional configuration. This reveals three groupings of occupations:

1   {hm, hp1, hp2, lp1, lp2, lm, hs, io1, io2, io3, io4}
2   {ls, lt1, lt2, sr1, sr3, sr4, sr6, r3, r5}
3   {sr2, sr5, sr7, r1, r2, r4}

Group 2 is quite tightly packed while groups 1 and 3 are relatively loosely arranged, implying greater internal differentiation. Within the first group the lower professionals (new) (lp2) are clear outliers.

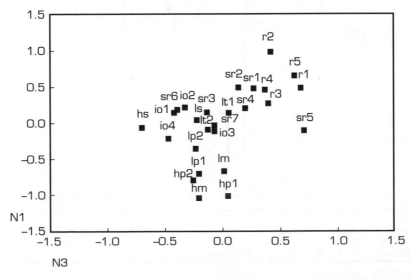

Figure 4.2c *Three-dimensional solution for NOTICE: rows N1 by N3*

Figure 4.2a represents the NOTICE space within which we plot, in terms of their departures from independence, the NS-SEC categories in Figures 4.2b and 4.2c. The first dimension of Figure 4.2a (N1) contrasts long notice periods (greater than three months) with all periods shorter than one month. The other categories fall between these two polar types. The second dimension (N2) contrasts one week's notice with durations greater than a week but less than a month. The third dimension (N3) contrasts one week's notice with durations greater than one month. The configurations of NS-SEC categories in Figures 4.2b and 4.2c are less clear cut than in the corresponding configurations for JOBPAY. There is an unambiguous group of white-collar occupations {hm, hp1, hp2, lp1, lm} which is more likely than average to be required to give three or more months of notice. The rest of the NS-SEC categories are, roughly speaking, strung out in the plane of the second and third dimensions at a 45 degree angle to the origin. The most noticeable feature of this pattern is the strong attraction to notice periods of one week or less of the agricultural (sr5, r5) and semi-routine sales occupations (sr1).

Figures 4.3a and 4.3b show the results for OTIME and could be used as a textbook example of the utility of the RC(M) model. Figure 4.3a reveals a roughly sidelong equilateral triangle representing two substantively meaningful contrasts: the first dimension (OT1) between unpaid overtime and other arrangements and the second dimension (OT2) between paid overtime and other arrangements. The NS-SEC categories in Figure 4.3b lie in continua along the sides of the triangle. The lower side contains the white-collar occupations and moving from left to right there is a shift in favour of the probability of paid over unpaid overtime. The top side contains the blue-collar occupations and moving from left to right there is a shift in favour of the probability of paid overtime over no overtime. We could well imagine an

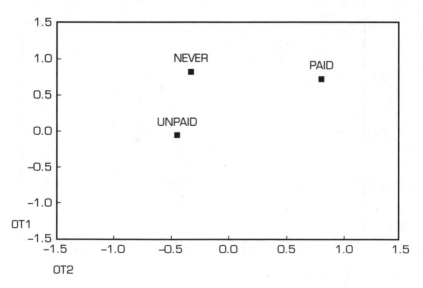

Figure 4.3a *Two-dimensional solution for OTIME: columns OT1 by OT2*

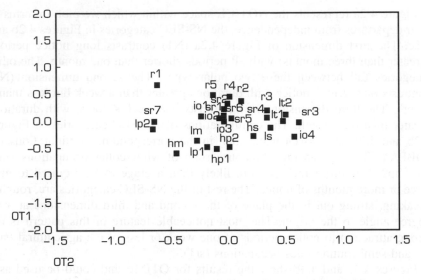

Figure 4.3b *Two-dimensional solution for OTIME: rows OT1 by OT2*

occupational continuum that has been snapped and bent back upon itself. Two groups of occupations do not fit neatly into this pattern. First, along with the lower professionals (new) (lp2) the semi-routine childcare occupations (sr7) share higher than expected probabilities of either never working overtime or working unpaid overtime. Second, a number of intermediate occupations {io1, io2, io3, sr5, sr6} seem equidistant from all vertices.

Figure 4.4a reveals the basic contrasts for STLVE to be between arrangements that give the employee considerable choice and those that are relatively

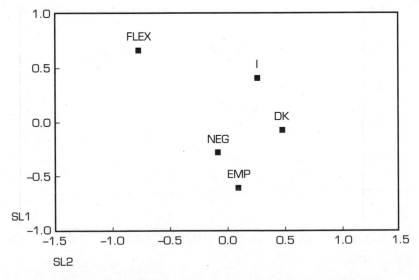

Figure 4.4a *Two-dimensional solution for STLVE: columns SL1 by SL2*

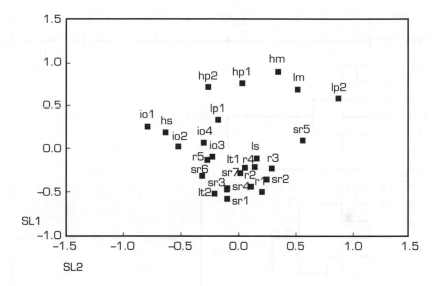

Figure 4.4b *Two-dimensional solution for STLVE: rows SL1 by SL2*

rigid (SL1) and between specifically flexitime systems and all other possibil-ities (SL2). Strung out in a line from flexitime arrangements to self-determination is a set of white-collar occupations. Strung out in a second line from flexitime to 'employer decides' are most of the rest of the occupations. Not quite fitting into the pattern are the 'traditional' lower professionals (lp1) and the semi-routine agricultural occupations (sr5). The former could be read as an outlier of the white-collar group that is subject to slightly more constraint on its hours of work. Presumably the nature of outdoors agricultural work gives some employees a certain amount of autonomy in deciding their starting and finishing times.

PUTTING IT ALL TOGETHER

So far all we have demonstrated is that each item, taken separately, is associated with the NS-SEC. It is natural to go on to ask: in what way are all the items taken together related? A convenient way to answer this question is to take the adjusted NS-SEC scores from each of the log-multiplicative models and use them to define the axes of a k-dimensional space. Each NS-SEC category is then located as a point in the space and distances between points can be defined in any convenient way. In what follows we use simple Euclidean distance with the distance between point x and point y given by: $[\Sigma (x_k - y_k)^2]$ with the summation being over the k dimensions. This gives us a distance matrix that can be explored using standard data reduction techniques.[18] In Figure 4.5 we display the dendrogram from a hierarchical cluster analysis of the distance matrix.[19]

Read from left to right it shows the progress of an algorithm acting on the NS-SEC categories, causing the evolution of a taxonomy by joining together

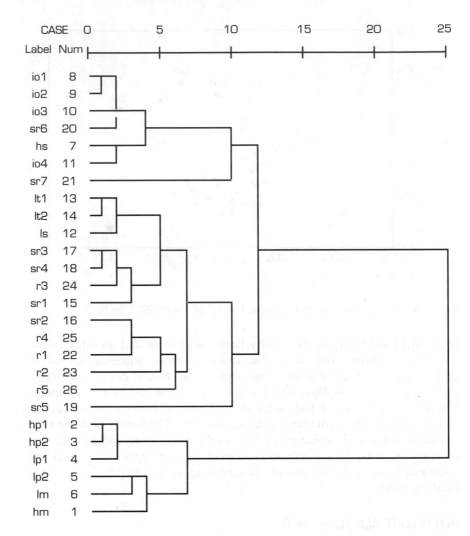

Figure 4.5 *Hierarchical cluster analysis: dendrogram using average linkage (between groups)*

proximate categories, and then agglomerations of categories. Normally this type of display is intended to suggest a meaningful typology of the objects and this is how we use it.

A reasonable expectation is that all NS-SEC categories that are conventionally grouped together should be joined to the same clusters early in the clustering process. This expectation is, however, only partially met. The 'service class' occupations (L2, L3.1, L3.2, L4.1, L4.2, L5) fall into two groups, one consisting of managerial, co-ordinating and regulating occupations (hm, lm, lp2) and the second consisting of various types of professionals (hp1, hp2, lp1). This result is interesting because, at least superficially, it lends some modest support to the views of those who would wish to recognise a distinction between managerial and professional occupations, as discussed in Chapter 1.

Clearly distinct from the service class occupations are the L7 intermediate employees (io1, io2, io3, io4), though these are also mixed with L6 higher supervisors (hs) and L12.6 semi-routine clerical occupations (sr6). Forming a separate group are L10 lower supervisory (ls), L11.1 lower technical craft (lt1) and L11.2 lower technical process (lt2) occupations. These, in the now outmoded parlance of the twentieth century, are the skilled manual workers and their supervisors. They are linked quite closely to a cluster of semi-routine and routine occupations comprising semi-routine sales (sr1), semi-routine technical (sr3), semi-routine operative (sr4) and routine operative (r4). Finally we find a very loosely aggregated cluster of routine and semi-routine occupations: routine sales, service and production (r1, r2), routine operative and agricultural (r4, r5) and semi-routine service (sr2).

In summary, the taxonomic structure revealed by the dendrogram takes the following form:

1   A white-collar cluster divided into managers and professionals.
2   An intermediate cluster consisting of higher supervisors, clerical, admin-istrative, service and technical occupations.
3   Skilled manual occupations and their supervisors.
4   Mainly semi-routine occupations.
5   Mainly routine occupations.

Two NS-SEC categories do not fit easily into this classification. First, the semi-routine agricultural occupations (sr5) are a distant outlier of both the semi-routine and the routine manual clusters. Second, the semi-routine childcare occupations (sr7) are an outlier of the intermediate cluster.

We can look at the clustering of the NS-SEC groups in an alternative way by using the distance matrix as input to a multidimensional scaling (MDS) routine. The idea is to make a low-dimensional representation that preserves the rank order of the inter-point distances. In this case three dimensions are sufficient and the resulting plot of NS-SEC points in this space is displayed in Figure 4.6.[20]

MDS plots can be interpreted by inferring a meaning to the dimensions, but also in terms of the proximity of points to each other, and it is the latter that seems most relevant to our concerns.[21] In all respects the cluster analysis dendrogram and the MDS map are congruent. In addition we can see that some groups are much more loosely clustered (i.e. more heterogeneous) than others. For instance, the managerial group displays greater internal variety than the professional group. At the other end of the class structure the mainly semi-routine group is more tightly packed than the mainly routine group. We can clearly see that the semi-routine childcare occupations (sr7) inhabit a space that is almost equidistant between the intermediate cluster and the mainly routine cluster. As the clustering algorithm proceeds sr7 is eventually linked to the intermediate occupations (see Figure 4.5). However, we should not read too much into this. In fact, changing to a different clustering algorithm links sr7 to the mainly routine occupations cluster and it is likely that clustering different data sets may give it equally dissimilar fates. Rose and Pevalin comment further on this in Chapter 12.

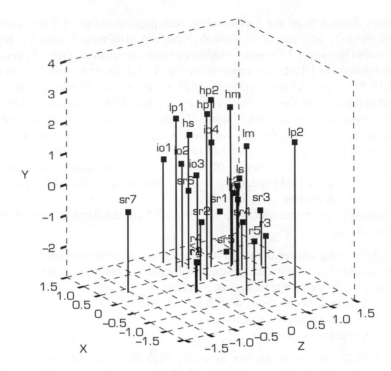

Figure 4.6 *Three-dimensional MDS configuration for NS-SEC categories*

It is one thing to describe clusters of occupations, but it is entirely another to say in what ways the clusters differ from each other, and whether the differences are such as to warrant use of the vocabulary of class. With this thought in mind we turn to how the ERC attributes are combined in some parts of our taxonomic representation.

To begin let us take up the issue of the relative lack of homogeneity among the professional and managerial white-collar employees, Goldthorpe's service class (Goldthorpe, 1982). Above we identified two loose clusters consisting on the one hand of higher and lower managers along with the 'new' lower professionals and on the other the remaining professional occupations. Superficially it would seem that this is not a simple split between managers and professionals. However, close examination of the occupations labelled 'new lower professionals' reveals that these include *inter alia*: technical and wholesale representatives, importers and exporters. The assignment of either professional or managerial status to these occupations is somewhat arbitrary. Despite the pretensions of their members to professional status, these occupations could equally well be seen as auxiliary to management.

In terms of Figure 4.6 all the professional and managerial occupations share roughly the same co-ordinates on the first and third dimensions of the configuration and differ markedly on the second: why? What distinguishes the managerial cluster from the professionals is an affinity among the former group for a salary system with a performance-related element. It would seem that attempts to tie rewards in a transparent way to job performance have made relatively little headway amongst the professions, but are more advanced among managerial occupations. However, although the prevalence of performance-related portions of the managerial reward package has increased, the significance of this, in terms of the fraction of earnings accounted for, is, as yet, tiny.[22] This raises an important issue for any attempt to produce a taxonomy by purely inductive methods. To put it simply, what comes out of it depends upon what goes into it.

In terms of the ERC measures available to us, professionals and managerial occupations differ in some respects: but are the differences so large that they should be designated separate classes? In so far as this is more than a sterile point about the use of labels, the answer must depend upon the empirical utility of making the distinction. A difference is only a relevant difference if it matters for something we care about. To make progress here we must test whether, net of confounding predictors, the distinction accounts for important amounts of variation in the things that both social scientists and the public authorities care about – for instance, social attitudes, political behaviour, morbidity, mortality and so forth. This is beyond the scope of this chapter, but it is a question that could and should be investigated by others. Here we simply reinforce the points already made in Chapter 2 concerning conceptual and analytic issues.

Turning to the opposite end of the class structure, the NS-SEC categories from lt1 down to r5 have the characteristics of the wage–labour contract. The lower supervisors and the lower technical workers are somewhat distinct being slightly more likely to be paid for their overtime hours, have a greater likelihood of being on an incremental pay scale and have better promotion opportunities. However it is very difficult from Table 4.4 to detect any clear-cut qualitative differences between the semi-routine and routine manual occupations. Figure 4.5 clearly indicates that these occupations are very heterogeneous and the best that can be said is that in so far as any distinction between groupings can be maintained it is more a matter of the degree of favourability of ERC. Again this is a matter already discussed in Chapter 1.

OCCUPATION OR JOB?

Before we began the empirical sections of this chapter we raised the issue of whether jobs rather than occupations should be the appropriate objects to classify. Given our preference for jobs, but the reliance of the NS-SEC on occupations, a reasonable question to ask is: what is the degree of correspondence between the NS-SEC classification and a categorisation based directly on the ERC measurements recorded for each individual? In other words, what is the correlation between a categorisation of individuals based on the similarity of their occupational characteristics and one based purely on the characteristics of the job actually held by the individual? If an important function of the NS-SEC is to proxy the latter in circumstances where detailed information on ERC is not available then we should hope for a relatively high degree of association between the two.

In order to investigate the level of correspondence we carried out the following exercise. First, in a similar manner to procedures discussed in Chapter 3, we dichotomised all of the employment relationship variables, giving the value 1 to conditions that unambiguously indicated the presence of a 'service' relationship and 0 to all other conditions.[23] We drew ten simple random samples of 1,000 cases from the LFS and clustered each sample using the *k*-means algorithm using nine similarity indicators and a pre-specified three-cluster solution.[24] The algorithm maximises within-group similarity and between-group heterogeneity. We then cross-classified the individuals in each sample by their three-cluster solution group and a three-class NS-SEC coding and quantified the degree of association in the resulting tables using the Goodman–Kruskal tau coefficient (a proportional reduction in error measure) and Cramers *V* (a chi-square-based measure). Both coefficients have 0–1 limits. From the ten replications the range of tau with the cluster solution group 'dependent' was 0.13–0.22 and the range of *V* was 0.36–0.46. The range of tau indicates that, with realistic sample survey sizes, assuming three classes, we can expect to reduce the amount of error in predicting cluster group membership by something of the order of magnitude of between 13 and 22 per cent by conditioning the prediction on NS-SEC coding. By the standards of correlation between sociological variables based on individual-level data these associations are quite strong: by the standards of correlation between parallel indicators of the same underlying construct they are less impressive.[25]

We can further examine the strengths and weaknesses of the NS-SEC coding by directly examining the best and worst case cross-classifications. Their implications for the evaluation of the quality of the NS-SEC classification can be best communicated by employing some concepts regularly used by epidemiologists to quantify the diagnostic value of medical tests and screening procedures. We assume:

1   That the classification of an individual into one of the three groups represents a 'gold-standard' test for the presence or absence of 'service', 'mixed' and 'wage–labour' status;
2   That the threefold NS-SEC classification is a second (and inferior) diagnostic test.

We can now talk about a number of different features of the NS-SEC classification:

1   *Sensitivity* – the percentage of true positives; that is, those who truly have 'service' employment relations and are classified by NS-SEC as such.
2   *Specificity* – the percentage of true negatives; that is, those who truly do not have 'service' employment relations and are classified by NS-SEC as not having them.
3   *Positive predictive value* – the percentage of those tested positive who have the condition; that is, the percentage of those classified by NS-SEC as having 'service' employment relations who actually have them.
4   *Accuracy* – the proportion of all tests that give the correct result; that is, the percentage of agreements between the 'gold standard' and NS-SEC.

5   *Likelihood ratio of a positive test* – more commonly called the 'disparity' ratio in sociological discussions; that is, given that a person has a 'service' employment relationship the multiple by which their probability of being classified in the appropriate NS-SEC is increased.

Table 4.5   *Performance of the three-class NS-SEC as a predictor of individual-level cluster allocation: worst and best performance*

	Service	Mixed	Wage-labour
Sensitivity	54–70%	49–70%	33–36%
Specificity	73–86%	47–57%	94–95%
Positive predictive value	42–71%	39–42%	74–81%
Accuracy	68–81%	48–61%	74–74%
Likelihood ratio	2.0–4.9	0.9–1.6	5.8–7.4

These quantities are displayed in Table 4.5. It is clear that performance is poorest for diagnosing the 'mixed' cases – low accuracy, low positive predictive value and in the worst case a likelihood ratio that actually indicates a greater chance of a positive identification for individuals who are not truly 'mixed'! Performance for the 'service' category is rather better. Accuracy is high, in addition over half of true positives are always detected and in the best trial over three-quarters are correctly diagnosed. Positive predictive value can also be good, though in the worst case it is poor. Sensitivity for the 'wage–labour' condition is poor, at best only one-third of true positives are identified (the others tend to be classified as 'mixed'). However, overall accuracy is good and the positive predictive value indicates that three-quarters of those allocated to the 'wage–labour' NS-SEC are true members of this group.

A fair summary of the foregoing would be to say that the NS-SEC tends to do a good job of distinguishing between those with 'service' and 'wage–labour' employment relationships. It does less well at distinguishing both of these from 'mixed' types. The distinction of 'wage–labour' from the 'mixed' type is particularly error prone. On two counts this conclusion is rather unsurprising. First, the 'mixed' forms mix together elements of the 'service' and 'wage–labour' relationship and in consequence are likely to be confounded with the true types. Second, as alluded to in note 22, the method we use to establish our 'gold standard' is not well calibrated for the identification of 'mixed' types. We cannot rule out the possibility that a closer investigation of typical values taken by combinations of the criterion variables could well help to identify a small set of distinct 'mixed' positions that are indeed mirrored in the NS-SEC. Nevertheless, we should also recall that the creation of the NS-SEC was never driven by statistical analyses alone and for good reasons (see Rose and O'Reilly, 1998: 34).

CONCLUSIONS AND PROSPECTS

We began this chapter by stating that we were not carrying out a validation exercise in the conventional sense. Validation was ruled out because the data at our disposal were already contaminated in a way that loads the dice in favour of endorsing the validity of the NS-SEC. Nevertheless, in the course of our exposition of the relationship between the indicators of social class and the final NS-SEC, we showed it to have a certain prima facie plausibility. This is, of course, a rather weak claim amounting to the observation that we cannot find any serious evidence that the constructors of the NS-SEC have misused or misinterpreted the indicator data available to them. Given the side constraint of maintaining continuity with previous official classifications, the constructors of the NS-SEC seem to have done a reasonable job of allocating occupations to NS-SEC categories so as to minimise within-group variation. Nobody should get terribly excited about this finding. Of greater interest is that the occupationally based NS-SEC also seems to do a reasonable job of proxying for measurements of class position based on the attributes of job–person pairs. Beyond this there are a number of issues that suggest themselves as worthy of further investigation. The first of these concerns the out of sample validation of the distance maps produced by our cluster analysis and by our MDS exercise. Inductive inferences from one data set can be suggestive, but are always to be treated with scepticism. It is important that they should be replicated using completely independent data. To our knowledge there is at least one other data set, derived from a sequence of Office for National Statistics monthly omnibus surveys, that could be used for this purpose. The second prospect is the extension of the use of RC(M) models to more disaggregated occupational units. With very large data sets, such as the LFS, it should be possible to derive criterion-based occupational scores for very disaggregated occupation/ employment status combinations and to use these scores as the basic building blocks of future NS-SEC-type classifications. If this were to be pursued there might be some computational advantages in substituting correspondence analysis (see the next chapter) for the Goodman model where large and inevitably quite sparse tables are to be analysed. Third, putting to one side the form the NS-SEC is constrained to take because of its anticipated role in social auditing, the logic of our implicit argument is that stratification researchers should think less about occupations and more about jobs as the appropriate units of class analysis. This would require them to think much more deeply about how the rather ad hoc assemblage of indicators used in this chapter should be supplemented and, more importantly, how these indicators map onto the distinct (but presumably correlated) dimensions of social class. If we were able to do this, we should be in a position to replace the names of classes with the names of variables. This would bring us somewhat nearer to the social scientific goal of providing accounts of the actual mechanisms by which social class has a causal impact on behaviour, attitudes and health and somewhat further away from being just social taxonomists.

NOTES

1 In an earlier version of this chapter based on the interim version of the NS-SEC we included some formally self-employed individuals whose *de facto* conditions of work seemed likely to be similar to employees in similar occupations (e.g. some types of

professionals). In the final version of the NS-SEC these groups (L3.3, L3.4, L4.3, L4.4) are distinguished and excluded by us from further consideration.

2 As explained in Chapter 2, a separate dimension of the social class relationship distinguishes these groups. For a cautionary note on the interpretation of occupation classifications in terms of dimensions Macdonald (1972) can still be read with profit.

3 To simplify our exposition we use the term 'occupation' where strictly speaking we should say 'occupation and employment status combination'.

4 The pragmatic nature of taxonomy is just as evident in the classification of the natural world. In the past decisions were made, which at the time reasonable people could disagree about, concerning the structural features of flora and fauna that should count as denoting similarity or dissimilarity. For example, an important marker of species similarity is ability to interbreed. However, domestic dogs and wolves can interbreed but are not classified in the same species. Wolves differ from dogs in terms of other characteristics; for instance, they do not bark or wag their tails. One of the remarkable facts about the Linnaean system is that many of its apparently arbitrary features still seem sensible in the light of modern genetics which has put species distinctions on much firmer grounds. Domestic dogs are descendants of wolves and genetics provides the building blocks for an evolutionary causal account of the diversity of phenotypes captured by earlier, apparently arbitrary, taxanomical decisions.

5 This does not imply any particular view on whether the individual or the family is the most appropriate unit over which to define social classes. As we saw in Chapter 1 we could also construct so-called dominance orderings (Erikson, 1984).

6 See, for example, O'Reilly and Rose (1998) with comments from Blackburn (1998) and Prandy (1998) and reply from Rose (1998).

7 Another artefact of data and method that tends to bolster the one-dimensionalists' confidence in continuity is the blurring of focus due to the large amounts of error typical of social measurements. This can only serve to disguise discontinuities should they exist. We might also add here that one-dimensionalists frequently fail to acknowledge other difficulties. Often they are unclear about whether their techniques are meant to describe social distance or similarity in a given sample or in the population from which that sample has been drawn. This leads them to ignore issues of model fit, to capitalise on chance variation, and to omit the estimation of the uncertainty surrounding individual scale scores. A convenient discussion of these issues can be found in the exchange between Rytina, Hauser and Logan (Hauser and Logan, 1992; Rytina, 1992). If all this were not bad enough we could go on to mention the essentially arbitrary choice of axes or 'dimensions' to interpret (on this see Macdonald, 1972).

8 In the typical piece of sociological data analysis there is a response variable and a set of predictor variables whose covariances are removed from view. It is easy to forget that one can also be interested in the structure of the joint probability distribution over all variables. Incidentally, we are, by and large, not terribly impressed by the now almost ritualistic denouncement of 'variable-centred' social science in favour of more narrative or case-oriented explanatory strategies. Nobody can deny that for some purposes a narrative can give a perfectly reasonable account of the aetiology of a single event. But it does not follow from this that the aims of the historian and the social scientist are or should be the same. If history is about chaps, then geography, as a social science, is definitely about maps.

9 The taxonomy of course needs to be validated 'out of sample'.

10 More qualitative studies of particular occupations and their milieux could greatly enlarge our understanding of why some departures from the 'package deals' are relatively stable. The rationale would be similar to the detailed investigation of outliers from a statistical model and should be carried out only after the main contours of the

model have been established. This strategy might be even more profitable if a large number of studies could be considered simultaneously. For an example of work carried out in something of this spirit see Hodson (1998; 1999).

11 After all, Newtonian mechanics works perfectly well for most practical terrestrial applications even though it is not strictly speaking correct.

12 Although the model is different the results obtained from it are somewhat similar to those that would be produced by correspondence analysis (Goodman, 1991). It is interesting that the latter technique, or close relatives of it, has been used for over thirty years to analyse cross-classified occupational data from pairs of individuals (Duncan Jones, 1972; Hope, 1972; Klatsky and Hodge, 1971). Today's enthusiastic producers of scales seem to be unaware of this literature.

13 Previous analysis of these data have resorted to dichotomising the responses according to a priori notions of 'favourable' versus 'unfavourable' relations or conditions as in Chapter 3 (and also see Evans and Mills, 1998; Rose and O'Reilly, 1997; 1998).

14 The sample sizes are so large that there is no need to worry about estimates of uncertainty. Any differences that look as though they are worth talking about are significant at conventional levels.

15 The closely related technique of correspondence analysis has been taken up with some enthusiasm in corners of the UK sociological world previously hostile to any form of quantification. The proximate cause of this seems to be the endorsement of the technique by no less a luminary than Pierre Bourdieu (Bourdieu, 1989: 340). The irony is that not only does Bourdieu make use of joint row and column plots, but they contain so many points that they can only be intended to bamboozle rather than enlighten the reader.

16 Agricultural workers, like some white-collar workers, really do have to adjust their working hours to accommodate whatever tasks have to be done. The fact that for the former this is seasonally dependent is neither here nor there.

17 It is important to realise that these apparently peculiar arrangements can be extremely atypical even for the categories with an affinity for them. All that matters is that the practice in question is more common in a particular occupation than it is amongst occupations in general.

18 At this point the reader would do well to recall that in this application we use the data reduction techniques merely as ways of summarising and displaying a complex set of information. The indicator items have already been used, to aggregate more basic occupational units into the NS-SEC, and therefore it would be absurdly circular to claim that the structure we uncover can in itself validate either the use of the items, or indeed the NS-SEC itself.

19 We use the method of between-group linkage.

20 The stress coefficient is 0.05 and R^2 is 0.99.

21 The logic of our argument would not exclude using the co-ordinates on the three dimensions as continuous measures of an occupation's position in the 'stratification order'.

22 The best evidence available suggests that individual performance-related pay is not uncommon (around 40 per cent of organisations covered in an Institute of Personnel and Development survey said that such schemes applied to its managerial employees) but the contribution to the wage packet is small (the median is 4–5 per cent of base pay for senior and middle managers; IPD, 1999). We are grateful to Dr Ray Richardson for bringing this information to our attention.

23 Dichotomising the variables throws away some information about variation. However, in this exercise our unit of analysis is not the occupation but the individual

and his/her job, and we could find no satisfactory alternative method of combining the metrical and qualitative distinctions embodied in the different variables whilst working at the individual level. It should be kept in mind that we have constructed an indicator that is intended to function as a 'gold standard' for the identification of the 'service' relationship. We should not expect it to be optimal for the identification of 'wage–labour' or mixed forms.

24 In what follows we use data only from LFSQ1 and therefore exclude the LFSQ3 career ladder indicator. The choice of how many clusters to specify is not obvious. Clearly it is asking a lot of the method to expect it to identify a large number of clusters corresponding to the NS-SEC groups from a composite distance measure. Somewhat analogously a social attitude researcher would not expect to reconstruct individual response patterns to a set of Likert scale items from the summated ratings scale value. The best we can realistically hope for is to identify those with employment relationship than can be unambiguously described as having 'service', 'wage–labour' and mixed characteristics. Thus we settle for three clusters to be predicted by the NS-SEC collapsed to three categories: 1, L2 to L5; 2, L6 to L7; 3, L10 to L13.

25 Recall, however, that these are not correlations between true parallel measures because the NS-SEC classification is based on a classification of occupations not individuals.

REFERENCES

Blackburn, R.M. (1998) 'A new system of classes: but what are they and do we need them?', *Work, Employment and Society*, 12: 735–41.

Bourdieu, P. (1989) *Distinction*. London: Routledge.

Clogg, C. and Shihadeh, E. (1994) *Statistical Models for Ordinal Variables*. Thousand Oaks, CA: Sage.

Duncan-Jones, P. (1972) 'Social mobility, canonical scoring and occupational classification', in K. Hope (ed.) *The Analysis of Social Mobility*. Oxford: Oxford University Press.

Erikson, R. (1984) 'Social class of men, women and families', *Sociology*, 18: 500–14.

Evans, G. (1992) 'Testing the validity of the Goldthorpe class schema', *European Sociological Review*, 8: 211–32.

Evans, G. and Mills, C. (1998) 'A validation of the new NS-SEC', *Mimeo*, Nuffield College, Oxford.

Gilbert, N. (1994) *Analysing Tabular Data*. London: UCL Press.

Goldthorpe, J.H. (1982) 'On the service class, its formation and future', in A. Giddens and G. Mackenzie (eds) *Social Class and the Division of Labour: Essays in honour of Ilya Neustadt*. Cambridge: Cambridge University Press.

Goldthorpe, J.H. (2000) *On Sociology*. Oxford: Oxford University Press.

Goodman, L. (1991) 'Models, measures and graphical displays in the analysis of contingency tables (with discussion)', *Journal of the American Statistical Association*, 86: 1085–138.

Hauser, R. and Logan, J.A. (1992) 'How not to measure intergenerational occupational persistence', *American Journal of Sociology*, 97: 1689–711.

Hodson, R. (1998) 'Organizational ethnographies: an underutilized resource in the sociology of work', *Social Forces*, 76: 1173–208.

Hodson, R. (1999) 'Organisational anomie and worker consent', *Work and Occupations*, 26: 292–323.

Hope, K. (1972) 'Quantifying constraints on social mobility: the latent hierarchies of a contingency table', in K. Hope (ed.) *The Analysis of Social Mobility*. Oxford: Oxford University Press.

IPD (1999) *Performance pay trends in the UK*. London: Institute of Personnel and Development.

Klatsky, S. and Hodge, R.W. (1971) 'A canonical correlation analysis of occupational mobility', *Journal of the American Statistical Association*, 66: 16–22.

Lockwood, D. (1958/1989) *The Blackcoated Worker*. London: Allen and Unwin.

Macdonald, K. (1972) 'MDSCAL and distances between socio-economic groups', in K. Hope (ed.) *The Analysis of Social Mobility*. Oxford: Oxford University Press.

O'Reilly, K. and Rose, D. (1998) 'Changing employment relations? Plus ça change, plus c'est la même chose? Reflections arising from the ESRC Review of Government Social Classifications', *Work, Employment and Society*, 12: 713–33.

Parkin, F. (1971) *Class Inequality and Political Order*. London: McGibbon and Kee.

Prandy, K. (1998) 'Deconstructing classes: critical comments on the revised social classification', *Work, Employment and Society*, 12: 743–53.

Raftery, A.E. (1986) 'Choosing models for cross-classifications', *American Sociological Review*, 51: 145–6.

Raftery, A.E. (1995) 'Bayesian model selection in social research (with discussion by Andrew Gelman, Donald B. Rubin and Robert M. Hauser)', in P.V. Marsden (ed.) *Sociological Methodology*. Oxford: Blackwell. pp. 111–96.

Rankin, I. (1988) *Hide and Seek*. London: Orion Paperbacks.

Rose, D. (1998) 'Once more unto the breach: in defence of class analysis yet again', *Work, Employment and Society*, 12: 755–67.

Rose, D. and O'Reilly, K. (eds) (1997) *Constructing Classes: Towards a New Social Classification for the UK*. Swindon/London: ESRC/ONS.

Rose, D. and O'Reilly, K. (1998) *The ESRC Review of Government Social Classifications*. London/Swindon: ONS/ESRC.

Rytina, S. (1992) 'Scaling intergenerational continuity: is occupational inheritance ascriptive after all?', *American Journal of Sociology*, 97: 1658–88.

5

Criterion Validity and Occupational Classification

The seven economic employment relations measures and the NS-SEC

Anthony P.M. Coxon and Kimberly Fisher

INTRODUCTION

To summarise what we have seen so far in previous chapters, the NS-SEC assigns people of varying employment statuses in each of the Occupational Unit Groups (OUGs) defined in the SOC2000 classification to socio-economic classes. One dimension of the testing of the 'criterion validity' of the NS-SEC entailed comparison of the working conditions faced by people assigned to each new category. Initially, this testing examined the seven employment relations questions asked of respondents to the first quarter of the 1996/97 Labour Force Survey (LFS). The original LFS questions were condensed into binary *favourable* (coded as 1) and *unfavourable* (coded as 0) categories (repeated in brief in Table 5.1, and discussed in more detail in the introduction to Part II). These seven questions, referred to hereafter as employment relations and conditions, or ERC, form the focus of this chapter.

In this chapter we pursue a similar line of enquiry to that in the previous one, but using different methods.

Table 5.1   *Favourable status for the seven employment relations questions*

1 Receives monthly payments (vs. weekly, hourly, by the piece) (*jobpay*)
2 Has regular pay increments (*payinc*)
3 Has to give a minimum of a month's notice to quit (*notice*)
4 Has influence over starting and leaving time (*stlve*)
5 Has opportunities for promotion (*prom*)
6 Has influence over planning in the workplace (*planwk*)
7 Has influence over the daily employment tasks (*tasks*)

CRITERION VALIDITY

Using the useful shorthand terminology of Carmines and Zeller (1980), we saw in the introduction to Part II that criterion validity 'concerns the correlation between a measure and some criterion variable of interest' (O'Reilly and Rose, 1997: 63). The final purpose of the validation exercise is to test whether it is the case that OUGs allocated to the same socio-economic category have a homogeneous pattern of employment relationships (the OUG homogeneity hypothesis). To put it in the general language of classification, the purpose of any good classification is to ensure that categories (clusters) have minimum variance (or dissimilarity) with respect to the defining attributes and are maximally separated from (dissimilar to) other groups. It became clear that before such a task could be undertaken, preliminary analysis was necessary to assess the interrelations between the seven criteria at the individual level and at the occupational level before the OUG homogeneity hypothesis could be addressed.

If the NS-SEC scheme were simply a proxy for the range of ERC, then the process of criterion validation would become a simple methodological problem of producing the best corresponding classification – however technically complex that process might be; but, given the history of social classifications, the relationship must necessarily be more complex and grounded, not least because particular forms of ERC change and constituent OUGs exhibit changing economic relationships over time. Moreover, because the NS-SEC is criteria-based and the ERC are only indicative, it becomes an open question as to what particular variables do the best job of generating the classification. We have seen previously that the questions included in the LFS are only a sub-set of the employment relations one might potentially choose to examine. Though this issue lies outside the concern of this chapter, the general relation between the ERC and the NS-SEC is central here.

There are a number of ways in which the relationship between the NS-SEC and the ERC could be construed:

1   *The classification itself forms the criterion* (however constructed and independent of any issues of its validity), and the ERC, either singly or together, are simply viewed as useful predictors of classification membership. They act as surrogates for (or indicators of) the NS-SEC itself.
2   *The ERC are the criteria* for the construction or validation of the NS-SEC (which then acts as a surrogate for the complex of ERC), and the NS-SEC can be modified to produce greater conformity to the state of affairs represented by the ERC.
3   *The ERC can be constitutive* of the NS-SEC, though not identical with it, rather as empirical variables can be measures of an underlying latent structure – in this case a classification.

Whilst these are methodologically distinct, they are often run together in the current conceptualisation of the NS-SEC, and in any final form of the classification they will need to be carefully distinguished and one will have to emerge as victor. At present, however, a certain indulgence can be allowed as a heuristic antidote to premature specification. But such indulgence cannot run to fudging the issue of the type of relationship between the ERC themselves and their representation. It is important to remember the distinction between the internal coherence and consistency of the ERC, on the one hand, and how one or some combination of the ERC may predict or generate the NS-SEC.

In order to make this distinction clear, it is useful to make some assumptions explicit:

1   The ultimate unit (at the risk of multiplying entities (or acronyms!) the operational taxonomic unit (OTU in the language of numerical taxonomy)) of the classification is the OUG (or in a finer version[1] of the classification, the occupational title itself) rather than the individual.
2   The structure of the NS-SEC is a partition,[2] rather than a set of overlapping categories, a taxonomic tree or a ranked categorisation, any of which *could* feature as alternative representations for occupational categories.
3   The ERC are considered as dichotomous, presence/absence variables.

Each of these needs brief comment.

The unit is the entity that features as the element of the classification and which constitutes the socio-economic classification. Actual properties of the OUG itself rarely feature in such schemes; more usually, it is properties *derived from individuals* who feature in analyses. And whilst the most usual use of the NS-SEC will be to allocate an individual to a socio-economic category, the category itself is comprised of occupational titles or groups, and it is by dint of membership of an occupation and employment status that an individual is thus allocated.

The representation of a classification is the nominal scale: an exclusive and exhaustive set of categories, that is a partition. By definition it excludes multiple allocation (by exclusivity), and makes no use of any rank-ordering information that the categories may have or be given. The issue of nested or hierarchical schemes – in effect a family of partitions related upwards by sub-set inclusion – is excluded as a *representation of the classification*, though we shall see that its use is almost mandatory in comparing classifications.

The ERC are conveniently considered as dichotomous. The question of whether they are most usefully thus considered is left open; extension (or reversion) to a multi-state category (or even ordinal- or interval-level) status does not change the logic of the methodology.

PROSPECTUS OF INVESTIGATION

The present investigation is a preliminary exercise, exploratory and simplified in form and only suggestive in conclusions. It is also bound to have a transitory nature, for it is still the case, as O.D. Duncan rather gloomily stated (cited in Breiger, 1981), that 'there is no final solution to the problem of the breadth and heterogeneity of categories in a classification of occupations'. As one of the authors has argued elsewhere (Coxon et al., 1986), the transitoriness of both social classifications and their criteria (as well as the often unspecified rule system underlying allocation of elements to categories) makes the estab-lishment of its validity a hazardous enterprise. Nevertheless, given the demise of the useful, if long acknowledged as flawed (Bland, 1979), Registrar

General's Classification, a more sophisticated replacement needs to be validly established.

The two givens, then, are the current NS-SEC and the LFS data on the seven ERC. In assessing the validity of the NS-SEC, we pursued two main aims:

1   To see how patterns of ERC relate at the *individual level* the ERC are examined two at a time and how they allocate the individuals. From the co-occurrence, measures of proximity[3] are calculated, and (given the preference for categorical or non-continuous representation) the pair-wise measures between the ERC are analysed using a scaling and a hierarchical clustering scheme.
2   Two joint mapping procedures (correspondence analysis and multidimensional preference analysis) are used to examine how the ERC profiles vary between occupations in the OUGs.

THE APPROPRIATE DATA

To see clearly what the interaction is between the classification and the criteria, the appropriate data are, first, the observed probabilities, and then the response patterns (RPs) (or 'structuples' in Guttman's terminology) of the combinations of the criteria.

The observed probabilities and associated variances are – perhaps surprisingly – fairly similar. This same pattern remains even when one considers responses of full-time and part-time employees separately (see Table 5.2). A somewhat different story emerges when one examines the cumulated RPs across all seven conditions, though, again, the differences arise in the same general directions for both full-time and part-time employees. More details of the conditions of full-time and part-time workers are given in the next chapter. As subsequent analysis found that examination of full-time and part-time employees separately did not alter the general conclusions for this preliminary exploration of the criterion validity of the NS-SEC, the remainder of this chapter thus focuses on all employees who answered all seven ERC questions in the LFS.

The RPs specify the patterns of binary co-occurrence of criteria that can and do occur. Every one of the 128 possible RPs actually appear, indicating that the range and complexity of combinations of the criteria are truly large, though the frequencies range between three respondents (for the unusual combination 0110110[4]) and 4,406 respondents (the 7.3 per cent of the sample with the combination of 1111111, meaning that they enjoy favourable status on all seven conditions[5]). Although we would not expect statistical independence to hold for such data, it turns out to be a useful yardstick for looking at the similarity and dissimilarity of the combinations; the difference in the last case between the actual percentage (7.3 per cent) and the expected percentage (1.6 per cent) alerts us to this. The frequencies of the RPs are shown in the Appendix.

In the normal methodological context, the appropriate models for the analysis of these data (in classic Coombsian terminology: single-stimulus

Table 5.2 Employees with favourable and unfavourable employment relations statuses

	jobpay		payinc		notice		stlvt		prom		planwk		tasks	
	n	%	n	%	n	%	n	%	n	%	n	%	n	%
For all employees														
NO	19,782	37.3	26,948	50.8	25,042	47.2	36,555	68.9	17,457	32.9	32,594	61.5	20,770	39.2
YES	33,253	62.7	26,077	49.2	27,969	52.8	16,479	31.1	35,576	67.1	20,444	38.5	32,264	60.8
For full-time employees														
NO	12,564	32.3	18,266	47.0	15,741	40.5	25,745	66.2	10,486	27.0	21,326	54.8	13,328	34.0
YES	26,344	67.7	20,634	53.0	23,149	59.5	13,164	59.5	28,421	73.0	17,585	45.2	25,670	66.0
For part-time employees														
NO	7,218	51.1	8,682	61.5	9,301	65.9	10,810	76.5	6,971	49.3	11,268	79.8	7,532	53.3
YES	6,909	48.9	5,443	38.5	4,820	34.1	3,315	23.5	7,155	50.7	2,859	20.2	6,594	46.7

dominance data) would be inclusive sub-set models, such as Guttman scalo-gram analysis, in order to achieve a dual ordinal mapping of 'individuals' (RPs) and of variables (here, the seven ERC criteria). Such a method is empirically intractable for these data, and the fact that the data include more than half of the possible RPs rules out their applicability a priori. Even probabilistic variants such as multiple unfolding or homogeneity analysis would yield solutions of dubious relevance.

More appropriate would be probabilistic models, and preferably latent probabilistic models, such as Lazarsfeld's Latent Class Analysis (LCA) (Lazarsfeld and Henry, 1968; McCutcheon, 1987), but here the objection would be that these models, like the comparable Rasch models, rely on the principle of local independence, which is excluded theoretically by the assumptions of the constructors of the NS-SEC.

A more appealing and more cautious approach is therefore to examine the detailed interrelations between the ERC *before* proceeding to find a suitable representational model, and this is best done comparatively by using fourfold tables to disentangle the interrelationships. The crucial information yielded by the response patterns is the co-occurrence of individuals – though it could equally well be OUGs – in the combinations of the criteria states. In effect, this reduces to a familiar classification issue in combinatorial analysis (Arabie and Hubert, 1992), well known also in systematic biology as the presence/absence problem, characterised by the familiar 2×2 dichotomous table which gives the co-occurrence of the (1,0) states of the two dichotomies, with cells labelled as a, b, c, d for (++), (+ –), (– +) and (– –) for the combinations. There exist a truly large number of measures for assessing the overall (dis)similarity of such a frequency table (see Hubalek, 1982; Snijders et al., 1990) and the choice of an appropriate measure is of some consequence. Of particular relevance in the present case, when the criteria are being compared on a pair-wise basis, is the difference between the simplest measure using all the data in Table 5.3 (known as the simple matching coefficient[6]):

$$a/(a + b + c + d)$$

and the Jaccard measure:

$$a/(a + b + c)$$

which differs in excluding negative matches from assessment of similarity. Both measures assess similarity between two OTUs (Operational Taxonomic Units) as higher to the extent that they share a common attribute, and both are bounded between 0 and 1. Jaccard treats the absence of an attribute in both OTUs as being irrelevant in the calculation of relative similarity. The reason is intuitively obvious: if a property appears in neither case, then it is irrelevant and may actually introduce distortion if included.[7] Table 5.3 shows the results when applied to these data.

As a result of excluding the negative matches, the Jaccard (J) coefficient values are generally higher than the Russell and Rao (RR) values (an average

Table 5.3 *Presence/absence similarity coefficients for seven criteria (Russell and Rao: upper triangle; Jaccard: lower triangle)*

	jobpay	payinc	notice	stlve	prom	planwk	tasks
Payment timing	–	0.569	0.759	0.343	0.615	0.473	0.596
Pay increment	0.436	–	0.551	0.291	0.558	0.381	0.468
Notice period	0.541	0.402	–	0.051	0.570	0.476	0.556
Start/end time	0.246	0.190	0.232	–	0.303	0.406	0.369
Promote	0.512	0.438	0.464	0.229	–	0.422	0.552
Plan work	0.343	0.262	0.323	0.205	0.324	–	0.584
Task control	0.480	0.370	0.434	0.249	0.464	0.380	–

of 0.485 vs. 0.358) and the overall similarity between them is obviously high, which indicates that the problems which can arise from negative matches are not generally likely to be important in the interrelations between the criteria.

But neither are the measures identical, either ordinally ($\tau = 0.807$, 95 per cent CI 0.575–0.919) or linearly ($r = 0.934$, 95 per cent CI 0.843–0.973). Significantly, all the main discrepancies (inversions in rank order) occur with respect to the control over tasks criterion:

(6,7)	Tasks and planning work	(J > RR)
(2,7)	Tasks and pay increment	(J > RR)
(5,7)	Tasks and promotion	(RR > J)

This alerts us to the fact that the control over tasks criterion may show a different pattern of interrelations with the other criteria when the respondents *do not* have influence in designing their employment tasks.

How, then, may the interrelationships be portrayed? The most straightforward representation is a scaling ('smallest space') analysis,[8] which will interpret high similarities as proximity and low similarities as separation (see Figure 5.1). Once again inspection of the data values reveals some salient characteristics.

The measures agree entirely on which data pairs have the highest similarity values, and all of them involve control over tasks. Consequently, that criterion will be located centrally. The measures also agree in involving control over starting and leaving time in the biggest distances, pointing to its marginality from (or difference to) the other criteria. Once again, we need to be sensitive to the question of whether negative matches have a systematic influence on the relative positioning of the points in the solution, and therefore make a separate scaling analysis for each measure. Adopting a conservative strategy of choosing a non-metric (ordinal) transformation produces the multidimensional scaling solutions which are also presented in the Appendix. On any account, these solutions give an excellent fit to the data,[9] and they are very similar to each other, at least in their main structure (see Figure 5.2). The Shepard diagram indicates that the monotone transformation is strongly linear, and therefore a linear (metric) solution was also sought. Once again, the solution is an excellent fit and the pattern of points in the final configurations shows the same structure as the monotone solutions.[10] Given the preference for the Jaccard measure and

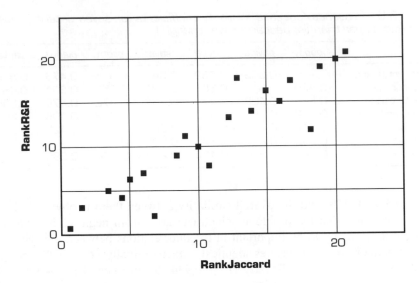

Figure 5.1 *Rank discrepancies in (0,1) measures*

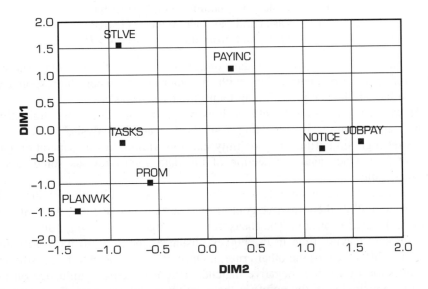

Figure 5.2 *Two-dimensional correspondence analysis: occupations by criteria data*

the superiority of a metric solution, the two-dimensional scaling solution presented in Figure 5.3, together with the minimum and maximum hierarchical clustering scheme solutions (Johnson, 1967), are derived from Jaccard measures.

The structure is manifestly not linear, though neither is it highly clustered (see Figure 5.4). In either event, the period of notice (*notice*) and timing of

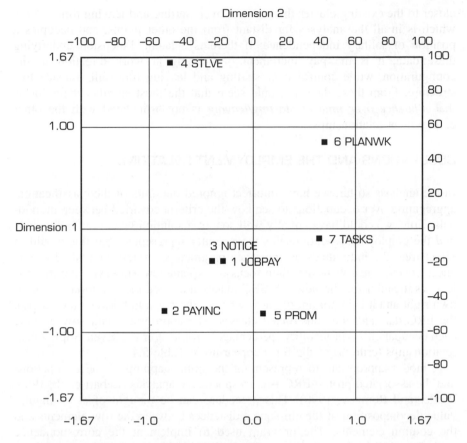

Figure 5.3 *Jaccard similarity measure of the seven criteria: two-dimensional metric solution (coefficient alienation = 0.085)*

payment (*jobpay*) form the tight core of a larger cluster which also includes promotion prospects (*prom*), control over tasks (*tasks*) and contribution to planning at work (*planwk*). The remaining two criteria are not part of this system, although the presence of regular pay increments (*payinc*) is marginally

Min (Connectedness) method								Max (Diameter) method							
0.76	4	2	6	1	3	5	7	0.76	4	2	1	3	5	6	7
0.62	.	.	.	X	X	X	. .	0.58	.	.	X X X		.	. .		
0.60	.	.	.	X X X X X			.	0.57	.	.	X X X		.	X X X		
0.58	.	.	.	X X X X X X X				0.57	.	.	X X X X X			X X X	
0.57	.	.	X X X X X X X X X					0.55	.	X X X X X X X				X X X	
0.40	X X X X X X X X X X X X X							0.38	.	X X X X X X X X X				X X X	
								0.29	X X X X X X X X X X X X X						

Figure 5.4 *Associated hierarchical clustering*

closer to the existing cluster than control over starting and leaving time (*stlve*), which is in all the analyses far distant from the other points, and occupies a position of solitary independence. If there is a latent dimension underlying these data, it is the pay increment – planning at work direction in the configuration, while control over starting and leaving time falls outside this structure. From these data, it would seem that the most significant finding is that *influence over time of starting/leaving* is not articulated with the other employment relationships.

OCCUPATIONS AND THE EMPLOYMENT RELATIONS

In the analysis so far, we have in effect ignored the units of the classification, aggregating over occupations to see how the criteria covaried between individuals. True, we could have equally well sought a solution where the individuals *and* the employment relationships were jointly represented, but this would in effect treat the individuals as 'nuisance parameters', unless individual differences *stricto sensu* were the main focus of explanation. However, the theoretical justification for the new NS-SEC makes the categories important in their own right and it is important to know whether there is a fit between the criteria, the ERC data and the constructed classes. The appropriate data now become each occupation's[11] probability (percentage) profile over the seven employment relationships (criteria) of the form appearing in Table 5.4.

A model appropriate to representing the joint mapping of the occupations and the associated profile ERC is correspondence analysis (Lebart et al., 1984; Weller and Romney, 1990). This procedure can be thought of as a singular value decomposition of the chi-square distances between the row elements and the column elements. The program used to implement the correspondence analysis (CA) is Carroll–Green–Schaffer's (1986) modification that allows unconditional comparison (i.e. between row and column categories). The two-dimensional (2-D) solution[12] of the column (ERC) points is presented in Figure 5.2.

Table 5.4 *Employment relations/criteria (for employees answering all conditions)*

SOC2000 Code	Occupation title	jobpay	payinc	notice	prom	stlve	planwk	tasks
1151	Financial managers	94.7	79.1	87.2	88.8	63.9	68.8	87.5
2132	Software professionals	94.6	61.9	85.8	92.9	57.3	75.6	78.4
3199	Scientists & engineers	82.4	64.3	70.6	75.6	33.2	44.1	64.3
4136	Database assistants	69.5	53.5	58.7	68.4	30.5	18.6	42.0
5434	Chefs, cooks	39.1	29.4	27.6	64.2	19.5	38.5	65.8
6121	Nursery nurses	76.9	59.1	65.3	58.2	06.2	60.4	83.1
7111	Sales assistants	44.6	32.1	22.3	57.9	09.1	12.0	39.6
8214	Taxi drivers	35.4	21.5	27.8	15.2	20.3	11.4	25.3
9251	Shelf fillers	62.5	43.5	22.8	73.8	06.8	04.5	26.0

Although there are similarities with the (0,1) data solution, the differences in the configurations are considerable. Control over starting and leaving time (*stlve*) remains peripheral (but is now much closer to the main cluster); likewise, notice period (*notice*) and timing of payment (*jobpay*) remain close together and are the most proximate pair. On the other hand, regular pay increments (*payinc*) and promotion opportunities (*prom*) are now more distant. Thus, when two-mode data are considered – in effect, considering occupational profiles rather than pair-wise aggregate similarity measures – the biggest differences change (promotion and starting/leaving time control in the similarities data but contribution to planning at work and timing of payment in the profiles). For a CA solution, the positioning of the column points is determined to a large degree by the simultaneous need to satisfy the constraints of the row (occupations) points, and therefore the CA column-point configuration is rightly considered as an occupation-dependent positioning – unlike the similarities (one-mode) solution. The corresponding point configuration for the occupations is presented next (each labelled by its row position in the data table).

Although the row and column points can be presented in a joint overlay, embedded in the same space,[13] this option is not taken here. The variation in (and dispersion of) the point locations is the next issue, and we would now wish to inspect the clustering evidenced here and then compare it with the OUG membership categorisation. If they turn out to be similar (or in some sense compatible), this could count as a form of empirical validation. If they turn out to be different, then a choice will need to be made between considering the employment relationships as *criteria* or as *independent information*. That is a topic for later research, and not of this chapter.

If both the rows and columns of a rectangular matrix are to be represented in a two-way two-mode scaling, then two appropriate models are simple correspondence analysis (SCA; Lebart et al., 1984: 184) and multidimensional scaling of preferences (MDPREF; Chang and Carroll, 1969). The two models are intimately related (Weller and Romney, 1990)[14] and differ primarily in terms of how the row elements are represented – as points for SCA and as vectors for MDPREF. We now choose MDPREF for this analysis because inter-set comparisons are hazardous (see below), and by projecting the row-element vectors onto the unit circle, MDPREF thus emphasises their distinctness compared with the column elements.

The MDPREF procedure consists of the singular value decomposition of a rectangular matrix. The relevant data are given in Table 5.5, where the seven employment relations (ER) criteria (*columns*) define the percentage profiles of the ninety most frequently occurring OUGs (*rows*). The model provides a joint scaling in a common space of the rows (as vectors) and the columns (points).

The data were scaled twice – first using the raw data profiles given in Table 5.5, and second using standardised profile scores, formed by extracting the 'consensus profile' (given by the column sums of the data matrix) and equalising variance within the ERC distributions, thus reducing the data to standard scores. This is tantamount to removing the 'general factor' of

Table 5.5   OUGs in sector sequence around MDPREF row vector circle

OUG order	MDPREF order	OUG ID No.	OUG description	Percentage satisfying ER criterion						
				ER 1	ER 2	ER 3	ER 4	ER 5	ER 6	ER 7
1	1	1112	Directors, chief executives major organisations	94.8	44.8	79.1	70.4	83.9	94.3	97.4
9	2	1161	Transport and distribution managers	81.8	44.3	70.5	72.7	71.6	75.6	94.9
10	3	1163	Retail and wholesale managers	75.2	42.5	62.8	72.4	46.2	67.8	91.6
11	4	1223	Restaurant and catering managers	60.8	42.5	61.9	75.1	54.1	68.5	91.2
12	5	1224	Publicans and managers of licensed premises	54.9	45.1	68.9	69.7	66.4	70.5	93.4
15	6	1239	Managers and proprietors in other services n.e.c.	82.9	36.5	63.1	63.5	65.8	73.0	92.3
2	7	1121	Production, works and maintenance managers	79.3	35.2	70.9	67.0	67.3	83.3	94.6
3	8	1122	Managers in building and contracting	72.4	34.1	60.9	56.3	74.3	80.5	96.2
22	9	2319	Teaching professionals n.e.c.	61.2	46.9	49.0	49.0	46.9	67.3	91.8
44	10	5111	Farmers	44.4	37.0	51.9	55.6	66.7	70.4	92.6
14	11	1234	Shopkeepers	68.4	21.1	47.4	50.9	59.6	66.7	75.4
61	12	6122	Childminders and related occupations	30.3	14.7	42.2	19.3	16.5	46.8	84.4
55	13	5319	Construction trades n.e.c.	30.4	23.2	39.1	58.0	27.5	40.6	75.4
63	14	6221	Hairdressers, barbers	12.3	22.3	11.8	48.3	31.3	42.2	64.0
78	15	9111	Farm workers	24.5	32.1	23.9	34.6	30.8	27.7	57.2
45	16	5113	Gardeners and groundsmen/groundswomen	39.8	36.0	35.4	47.8	26.1	37.9	57.8
57	17	5434	Chefs, cooks	39.1	29.4	27.6	64.2	19.5	38.5	65.8
87	18	9233	Cleaners, domestics	26.5	20.7	15.5	28.3	24.6	11.7	46.2
79	19	9121	Labourers in building and woodworking trades	22.6	26.2	16.7	32.1	12.2	16.7	37.6
76	20	8214	Taxi, cab drivers and chauffeurs	35.4	21.5	27.8	15.2	20.3	11.4	25.3
74	21	8212	Van drivers	35.9	22.9	24.6	39.3	15.4	16.6	33.5
73	22	8211	Heavy goods vehicle drivers	18.6	28.9	17.1	36.2	25.5	14.9	29.2
86	23	9225	Bar staff	4.9	18.5	7.5	51.4	8.9	7.5	37.1
54	24	5315	Carpenters and joiners	13.9	34.6	18.2	49.8	12.1	22.1	45.9
53	25	5314	Plumbers, heating and ventilating engineers	30.4	44.7	31.1	61.5	22.4	31.7	61.5
52	26	5312	Bricklayers, masons	10.1	31.9	15.9	43.5	17.4	14.5	34.8
89	27	9244	School mid-day assistants	45.3	35.5	22.9	18.4	0.4	2.0	38.4
85	28	9224	Waiters, waitresses	12.6	19.3	9.1	51.3	5.0	5.0	28.2
56	29	5323	Painters and decorators	15.9	37.2	23.9	46.0	14.2	16.8	39.8
47	30	5221	Metal machining setters and setter-operators	21.4	29.8	21.9	56.7	13.5	16.7	40.9

Table 5.5   *continued*

OUG order	MDPREF order	OUG ID No.	OUG description	Percentage satisfying ER criterion						
				ER 1	ER 2	ER 3	ER 4	ER 5	ER 6	ER 7
81	31	9139	Labourers in process and plant operations n.e.c.	25.1	27.7	19.9	47.2	10.8	6.1	28.1
80	32	9134	Packers, bottlers, canners, fillers	16.1	26.0	12.0	45.0	10.0	3.6	14.0
72	33	8137	Sewing machinists	4.4	34.2	5.1	37.9	15.4	2.9	18.0
77	34	8222	Fork lift truck drivers	19.0	31.2	19.0	59.0	5.4	7.3	36.6
75	35	8213	Bus and coach drivers	12.4	32.5	16.3	44.5	5.7	3.8	13.9
59	36	6115	Care assistants and home carers	52.7	38.7	40.8	61.6	17.4	23.5	62.0
46	37	5215	Welding trades	12.9	35.6	20.8	53.5	8.4	11.9	36.6
84	38	9223	Kitchen and catering assistants	33.1	34.1	20.2	53.2	7.1	8.8	32.2
69	39	8125	Metal working machine operatives	29.5	36.6	29.3	59.3	11.2	17.6	36.3
64	40	7111	Sales and retail assistants	44.6	32.1	22.3	57.9	9.1	12.0	39.6
82	41	9149	Other goods handling, storage occupations n.e.c.	39.8	35.4	29.4	64.8	9.0	14.4	40.1
67	42	8111	Food, drink and tobacco process operatives	16.8	32.5	18.0	65.5	7.8	9.8	27.0
49	43	5231	Motor mechanics, auto engineers	35.4	38.0	29.8	71.0	16.2	20.7	51.1
70	44	8131	Assemblers (electrical products)	37.9	36.0	24.9	63.4	6.3	7.9	27.8
71	45	8133	Routine inspectors and testers	37.8	39.5	33.1	67.2	8.8	14.5	48.0
83	46	9211	Postal workers, messengers, couriers	15.0	45.5	23.3	65.6	17.7	6.4	21.6
88	47	9241	Security guards and related occupations	50.8	39.0	38.4	64.6	7.2	14.4	46.9
48	48	5223	Metal working production, maintenance fitters	42.3	45.2	37.7	70.4	15.7	31.7	55.0
65	49	7112	Retail cashiers and check-out operators	54.7	39.5	22.4	71.0	8.8	4.2	21.7
50	50	5241	Electricians, electrical fitters	35.2	49.2	34.9	73.2	14.2	34.6	57.0
62	51	6124	Educational assistants	82.6	61.8	59.7	28.2	8.2	19.1	54.4
90	52	9251	Shelf fillers	62.5	43.5	22.8	73.8	6.8	4.5	26.0
68	53	8114	Chemical and related process operatives	54.6	45.4	49.3	71.0	9.7	20.8	46.9
43	54	4216	Receptionists	72.2	43.6	59.6	59.2	11.7	12.7	48.3
58	55	6111	Nursing auxiliaries and assistants	78.3	73.0	67.8	47.0	7.6	10.6	51.5
40	56	4136	Database assistants/clerks	69.5	53.5	58.7	68.4	30.5	18.6	42.0
36	57	4123	Counter clerks	85.3	77.2	72.9	83.0	17.0	16.0	38.5
39	58	4133	Stock control clerks	65.4	44.3	55.7	74.8	20.5	34.9	65.4
41	59	4150	General office assistants/clerks	75.3	47.6	59.4	69.6	32.5	26.2	55.3
66	60	7212	Customer service occupations	78.0	62.9	62.3	84.6	28.0	28.9	55.0

Table 5.5   continued

OUG order	MDPREF order	OUG ID No.	OUG description	ER 1	ER 2	ER 3	ER 4	ER 5	ER 6	ER 7
						Percentage satisfying ER criterion				
37	61	4131	Filing and other records assistants/clerks	86.2	57.4	66.8	73.0	28.0	30.4	57.1
38	62	4132	Pensions and insurance clerks	93.1	69.6	76.0	84.3	48.8	29.0	53.0
34	63	4113	Local government clerical officers/assistants	90.6	88.1	79.4	80.5	61.1	24.4	54.4
28	64	3312	Police officers (sergeant and below)	88.5	92.3	78.0	98.8	18.3	53.3	77.7
33	65	4112	Civil Service administrative officers/assistants	94.2	88.7	78.0	82.4	81.5	24.2	53.1
25	66	3119	Science and engineering	82.4	64.3	70.6	75.6	33.2	44.1	64.3
26	67	3211	Nurses	89.9	82.1	80.5	87.3	20.8	53.3	82.6
20	68	2314	Secondary education teaching professionals	95.2	92.8	86.8	89.2	20.4	78.0	84.2
32	69	4111	Civil Service executive officers	99.5	97.1	87.1	87.1	88.6	47.1	74.8
21	70	2315	Primary, nursery education, teaching profession	95.6	92.0	85.6	89.1	34.4	81.4	91.3
17	71	2211	Medical practitioners	95.1	86.4	82.6	70.7	45.1	58.2	79.9
60	72	6121	Nursery nurses	76.9	59.1	65.3	58.2	6.2	60.4	83.1
51	73	5249	Electrical/electronics engineers n.e.c.	75.2	46.1	62.6	80.6	43.2	42.7	67.0
27	74	3232	Housing and welfare officers	88.7	73.8	75.1	81.7	51.2	62.5	84.4
7	75	1151	Financial institution managers	94.7	79.1	87.2	88.8	63.9	68.8	87.5
35	76	4122	Accounts/wages clerks, book-keepers, financial	78.8	46.1	67.0	68.7	43.1	32.4	67.1
16	77	2132	Software professionals	94.6	61.9	85.8	92.9	57.3	75.6	78.4
31	78	3563	Vocational, industrial trainers and instructors	87.6	65.6	77.6	81.6	44.0	75.2	89.2
24	79	2421	Chartered and certified accountants	95.3	57.6	88.0	88.3	53.8	69.9	77.5
19	80	2312	Further education teaching professionals	90.8	69.3	75.1	76.6	29.9	85.8	88.9
29	81	3534	Finance and investment analysts/advisers	87.9	64.9	77.6	90.8	71.3	73.6	85.6
18	82	2311	Higher education teaching professionals	92.6	81.9	83.1	83.1	72.4	90.5	93.8
30	83	3542	Sales representatives	87.5	49.5	71.8	83.3	45.2	66.7	85.4
23	84	2411	Solicitors and lawyers, judges and coroners	96.4	47.4	87.6	80.3	60.6	70.8	81.8
6	85	1136	Information, communication technology managers	96.8	59.3	86.8	87.1	71.1	92.5	93.2
42	86	4215	Personal assistants and other secretaries	79.6	44.8	69.2	57.9	39.4	37.1	64.6
4	87	1131	Financial managers and chartered secretaries	94.1	50.3	85.4	78.5	75.7	88.2	96.5
5	88	1132	Marketing and sales managers	94.7	49.4	84.4	85.3	74.3	92.7	97.8
8	89	1152	Office managers	87.4	44.7	81.8	72.9	53.4	67.6	92.9
13	90	1231	Property, housing and land managers	90.8	56.9	84.6	62.3	73.8	80.8	96.2

employment relations and concentrating attention on the specifics of occupational characteristics. In both cases, a two-dimensional MDPREF solution was highly acceptable (97 per cent and 93 per cent variance accounted for, respectively).

In the MDPREF solution configurations, each ERC is represented as a single point, and each individual (OUG) profile is represented as a single vector[15] pointing in the direction of increasing 'preference', which in this context is interpreted as being the higher percentage values among the seven ERC criteria which form the profile. The angular separation between two OUG profiles represents the correlation between their vectors. Thus variation in the profiles is represented by the spread of the vector ends around the unit circle. The two sets of column points (ERC) and row vectors (OUGs) are defined by reference to each other and (strictly speaking) inter-set comparisons are not possible, except by the device of projection. This means that the ERC column points are positioned in the space by reference to the stimulus OUG vectors so that, when the ERC points are projected onto a given OUG vector, their values maximally reproduce the original OUG profile values. The MDPREF solution for this data set is given in Figure 5.5, which gives the solution for the standardised scores data.

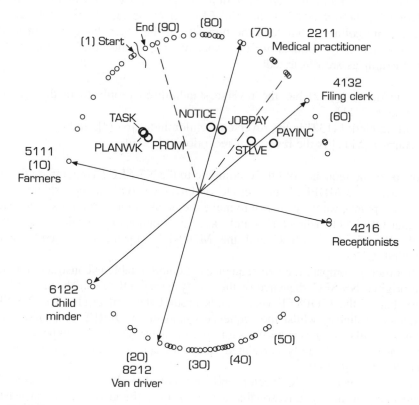

Figure 5.5 *OUGs in sector sequence around the MDPREF row vector circle*

For interpreting the configuration, we concentrate first on the pattern which the column stimuli (ERC) make in the joint space. (The configuration of ERC points is virtually the same for both data sets.) The main differentiation is between the two main clusters {5,6,7} vs. {1,2,3,4} (which might be interpreted as a job-conditions vs. job-control contrast) and this indicates that one of the two clusters tends to dominate a given OUG profile. Within this contrast, there is a further one between *stlve* and *payinc* vs. *notice* and *jobpay*.

We turn now to interpreting the 'subject (OUG) space', which is the main point of the exercise. The positioning of the OUG (row) vectors is very different indeed in the two scalings. The original data produce a 'sheaf' of OUG vectors (denoted by dashed lines in the figure) restricted to the 56 degree ('11 o'clock to 2 o'clock') sector. But this relatively small amount of variation masks considerably more underlying variation, which is revealed by scaling the standardised data. The difference is immediate and dramatic; in the case of standardised data, the vector ends are distributed round the entire circle. Moreover, the distribution of vector ends is not equally spaced – there are gaps (such as between farmers [5111] and childminders [6122], and between receptionists [4216] and stock control clerks [4133]), which would normally signal separation of distinct categories.

The MDPREF circular representation also gives novel information about the relationship between OUGs and the ERC. Because any two vectors at 180 degrees are collinear, but each the opposite of the other, there is information about which OUG profiles are the exact reverse of the other. In Figure 5.5, three examples are illustrated:

1   van driver [8212] has the reverse standardised profile to medical practitioner [2211];
2   filing clerk [4132] is the reverse of childminder [6122]; and
3   farmer [5111] is the reverse of receptionist [4216].

How does the sequence of OUGs compare to the NS-SEC? To compare the two sequences, the MDPREF unit circle of OUG vectors can be broken (at an arbitrary point); we have chosen to make the break at the point marked START, so that OUG 1112 (directors, chief executives major organisations) is first in both the original NS-SEC and the MDPREF sequences.[16] It ends at the ninetieth OUG.

In order to compare the two sequences in detail, a table is constructed, where the original NS-SEC sequence of the ninety largest OUGs has been reordered into that of the MDPREF vector ends around the unit circle. The NS-SEC sequence is linear, whilst the sequence round the MDPREF unit circle is of course circular, returning to the same point, so we should not expect the two sequences to be linearly correlated (they are actually negatively correlated, linearly, $r = -0.207$).[17]

The sequencing OUG vector ends do not directly mirror the NS-SEC sequence, yet there is a reasonable degree of fit at the grosser level, at least in terms of the main groupings such as managers, clerks and craft workers. Thus, knowing the ERC profile of an OUG alone gives a fair estimate of where it fits in the NS-SEC classification, but the fit is not good enough to use the ERC profile as a predictor or allocation rule to assign to the NS-SEC scale on its own. As other criteria are also used in the NS-SEC assignment (including managerial, supervisory or employee status, and for some managers, the number of employees managed), this analysis lends support to the general credibility of the new measure.

CONCLUSIONS

This chapter set out to inspect the criterion validity of the NS-SEC by reference to the seven dichotomised employment relations questions asked in the LFS. The sheer variety of individual combinations of the seven ERC is staggering: 128 patterns occur in the data, but with differing frequencies.

To inspect the covariation of the dichotomies, two suitable presence/absence measures were chosen which differed simply in whether they took account of negative matches. The Jaccard measure, excluding negative mismatches, was found to be the more suitable, and the two measures correlated very highly, with the exception of some values involving control over tasks, which show a different pattern of interrelations with the other criteria when the respondents *do not* have influence in designing their employment tasks.

In the scaling representation of the measures, period of notice and timing of payment form the tight core of a larger cluster of employment relations, which also include promotion opportunities, control of tasks, and ability to plan work. By contrast, control over starting and leaving time is far distant from the other points, indicating that it is not articulated with the other ERC in terms of the covariation between them.

Aggregating the data into the ninety largest OUGs made it possible to examine the joint relationship of occupational group membership and the seven employment relations, using a two-mode multidimensional analysis of prefer-ence model. Although the gross characteristics of the relationship between the ERC remain the same, the relationship between the OUGs with respect to the ERC changes dramatically when the scores are standardised. New information relating 'opposite profile' OUGs suggests interesting modes of future analysis, but the most striking fact is that the sequences generated by the NS-SEC and ERC profiles are similar at the molar level, even though considerable and consistent differences emerge. Nevertheless, as other criteria are also included in the final assignment to NS-SEC categories, the degree of correlation between the two scales found here does lend support to the general validity of this scale.

It is always easy to finish a chapter by pointing to the need for further work. The question as to whether the employment relation variables are best considered to be constitutive criteria for, or independent predictors of, the NS-SEC remains unanswered. Given the clues indicated by the two-mode repre-sentation, a more intriguing issue is: are there significant, systematic and important differences in the sequences of the ERC profile as opposed to the NS-SEC sequence? Do the ERC profile data in effect generate a discernibly different classification? Cursory inspection would suggest that there are systematic differences. Indeed, differences in ordering in a wide range of OUGs are so discrepant that they would in any system be allocated to different categories of the classification, and whole sections of the sequence would need to be differently located to render them simply compatible. The scaling technology exists to make such comparison methodologically safe, so it is a feasible operation, but that would be a somewhat different enterprise to this one.

In any case, as previously observed, constructing a classification such as the NS-SEC can never be driven solely by statistical analysis, however sophisticated.

APPENDIX

Table 5.A1   *Response patterns for the seven criteria*

A B C D E F G	Frequency	%
0 0 0 0 0 0 0	3,967	6.56
0 0 0 0 0 0 1	1,457	2.41
0 0 0 0 0 1 0	112	0.19
0 0 0 0 0 1 1	710	1.17
0 0 0 0 1 0 0	903	1.49
0 0 0 0 1 0 1	1,234	2.04
0 0 0 0 1 1 0	104	0.17
0 0 0 0 1 1 1	3,392	5.61
0 0 0 1 0 0 0	2,537	4.19
0 0 0 1 0 0 1	1,292	2.14
0 0 0 1 0 1 0	108	0.18
0 0 0 1 0 1 1	561	0.93
0 0 0 1 1 0 0	292	0.48
0 0 0 1 1 0 1	354	0.59
0 0 0 1 1 1 0	33	0.05
0 0 0 1 1 1 1	680	1.12
0 0 1 0 0 0 0	288	0.48
0 0 1 0 0 0 1	193	0.32
0 0 1 0 0 1 0	16	0.03
0 0 1 0 0 1 1	133	0.22
0 0 1 0 1 0 0	64	0.11
0 0 1 0 1 0 1	124	0.20
0 0 1 0 1 1 0	12	0.02
0 0 1 0 1 1 1	450	0.74
0 0 1 1 0 0 0	286	0.47
0 0 1 1 0 0 1	211	0.35
0 0 1 1 0 1 0	16	0.03
0 0 1 1 0 1 1	151	0.25
0 0 1 1 1 0 0	42	0.07
0 0 1 1 1 0 1	82	0.14
0 0 1 1 1 1 0	11	0.02
0 0 1 1 1 1 1	194	0.32
0 1 0 0 0 0 0	839	1.39
0 1 0 0 0 0 1	344	0.57
0 1 0 0 0 1 0	34	0.06

Table 5.A1   *continued*

A B C D E F G	Frequency	%
0 1 0 0 0 1 1	131	0.22
0 1 0 0 1 0 0	85	0.14
0 1 0 0 1 0 1	87	0.14
0 1 0 0 1 1 0	10	0.02
0 1 0 0 1 1 1	129	0.21
0 1 0 1 0 0 0	1,558	2.58
0 1 0 1 0 0 1	734	1.21
0 1 0 1 0 1 0	62	0.10
0 1 0 1 0 1 1	360	0.60
0 1 0 1 1 0 0	120	0.20
0 1 0 1 1 0 1	115	0.19
0 1 0 1 1 1 0	13	0.02
0 1 0 1 1 1 1	171	0.28
0 1 1 0 0 0 0	146	0.24
0 1 1 0 0 0 1	76	0.13
0 1 1 0 0 1 0	8	0.01
0 1 1 0 0 1 1	48	0.08
0 1 1 0 1 0 0	19	0.03
0 1 1 0 1 0 1	24	0.04
0 1 1 0 1 1 0	3	0.00
0 1 1 0 1 1 1	51	0.08
0 1 1 1 0 0 0	277	0.46
0 1 1 1 0 0 1	188	0.31
0 1 1 1 0 1 0	11	0.02
0 1 1 1 0 1 1	179	0.30
0 1 1 1 1 0 0	21	0.03
0 1 1 1 1 0 1	56	0.09
0 1 1 1 1 1 0	8	0.01
0 1 1 1 1 1 1	97	0.16
1 0 0 0 0 0 0	818	1.35
1 0 0 0 0 0 1	344	0.57
1 0 0 0 0 1 0	30	0.05
1 0 0 0 0 1 1	215	0.36
1 0 0 0 1 0 0	138	0.23
1 0 0 0 1 0 1	238	0.39
1 0 0 0 1 1 0	26	0.04
1 0 0 0 1 1 1	840	1.39
1 0 0 1 0 0 0	874	1.44
1 0 0 1 0 0 1	569	0.94
1 0 0 1 0 1 0	50	0.08
1 0 0 1 0 1 1	417	0.69
1 0 0 1 1 0 0	114	0.19
1 0 0 1 1 0 1	139	0.23
1 0 0 1 1 1 0	19	0.03
1 0 0 1 1 1 1	438	0.72
1 0 1 0 0 0 0	707	1.17
1 0 1 0 0 0 1	502	0.83
1 0 1 0 0 1 0	57	0.09
1 0 1 0 0 1 1	415	0.69
1 0 1 0 1 0 0	104	0.17
1 0 1 0 1 0 1	189	0.31
1 0 1 0 1 1 0	14	0.02
1 0 1 0 1 1 1	821	1.36

Table 5.A1   *continued*

A B C D E F G	Frequency	%
1 0 1 1 0 0 0	1,112	1.84
1 0 1 1 0 0 1	1,021	1.69
1 0 1 1 0 1 0	110	0.18
1 0 1 1 0 1 1	1,346	2.22
1 0 1 1 1 0 0	176	0.29
1 0 1 1 1 0 1	341	0.56
1 0 1 1 1 1 0	70	0.12
1 0 1 1 1 1 1	1,818	3.01
1 1 0 0 0 0 0	287	0.47
1 1 0 0 0 0 1	173	0.29
1 1 0 0 0 1 0	19	0.03
1 1 0 0 0 1 1	111	0.18
1 1 0 0 1 0 0	36	0.06
1 1 0 0 1 0 1	44	0.07
1 1 0 0 1 1 0	7	0.01
1 1 0 0 1 1 1	125	0.21
1 1 0 1 0 0 0	874	1.44
1 1 0 1 0 0 1	591	0.98
1 1 0 1 0 1 0	65	0.11
1 1 0 1 0 1 1	563	0.93
1 1 0 1 1 0 0	133	0.22
1 1 0 1 1 0 1	190	0.31
1 1 0 1 1 1 0	31	0.05
1 1 0 1 1 1 1	473	0.78
1 1 1 0 0 0 0	560	0.93
1 1 1 0 0 0 1	444	0.73
1 1 1 0 0 1 0	46	0.08
1 1 1 0 0 1 1	391	0.65
1 1 1 0 1 0 0	134	0.22
1 1 1 0 1 0 1	185	0.31
1 1 1 0 1 1 0	37	0.06
1 1 1 0 1 1 1	564	0.93
1 1 1 1 0 0 0	2,011	3.32
1 1 1 1 0 0 1	2,136	3.53
1 1 1 1 0 1 0	281	0.46
1 1 1 1 0 1 1	3,559	5.88
1 1 1 1 1 0 0	659	1.09
1 1 1 1 1 0 1	1,080	1.79
1 1 1 1 1 1 0	198	0.33
1 1 1 1 1 1 1	4,406	7.28

Valid cases 60,498   Missing cases 2,854

Binary criteria:
A Timing of payment monthly or weekly/hourly/by the piece.
B The presence or absence of regular pay increments.
C Have/not have period of notice to quit of at least one month.
D The presence or absence of promotion opportunities.
E Have/not have some control over starting and leaving time.
F Have/not have influence over planning in the workplace.
G Have/not have influence in designing daily employment tasks.

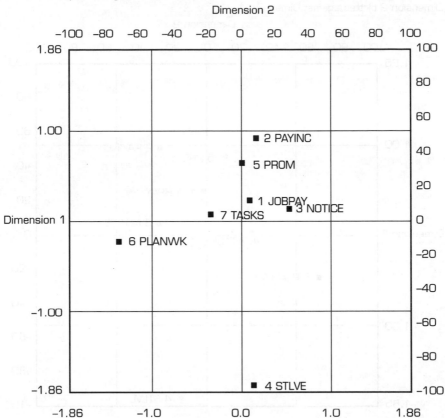

Figure 5.A1 *Ordinal scaling Russell and Rao similarity: seven criteria*

Task number 1
Final configuration (stress1 [DHAT] = .0003)
Dimension 2 plotted against Dimension 1

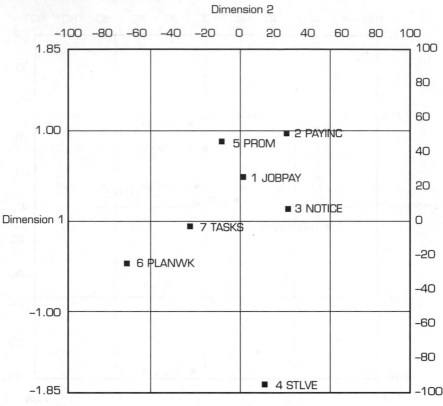

Figure 5.A2 *Ordinal scaling Jaccard similarity: seven criteria*

NOTES

This chapter updates an earlier paper produced to test the criterion validity of the NS-SEC and presented at the Social-Economic Classification (SEC) Validation Workshop, held at the University of Essex, December 1998.

1 In the technical, not the evaluative, sense. A partition P is finer than a partition Q if and only if each cell $c \varepsilon P$ is contained in some cell $d \varepsilon Q$ (equivalently, the fineness of a partition is the least upper bound of distances between c and d).

2 Partition: Given m sub-sets/categories/cells of a set P of objects: $c_1, c_2, \ldots, c_m$, this constitutes a partition of set P if and only if:

- The union of the sub-sets is the set P ($\cup_i c_i = P$).
- For every i and j, their intersection is the empty set ($c_i \cap c_j = \emptyset$).

That is, the sub-sets c_1 are a partition of P only if each element of P is in one and only one sub-set.

3 'Proximity' is used here as a general term in preference to '(dis)similarity' for referring to measures. It implies nothing about particular forms of metric, or representation.

4 The combination 0110110 is that of having regular pay increments, notice periods of at least one month, control over starting and leaving time, and influence over planning at work, but not having a period of payment shorter than one month, not having promotion opportunities, and not having influence over daily tasks.

5 The second-largest category, the category containing workers who have unfavourable status on all seven conditions, includes 3,967 people, 6.56 per cent of respondents. The third-largest category, the response pattern 1111011, includes 3,559 people, 5.88 per cent of the respondents. The third-largest response pattern category includes people who enjoy favourable status on all conditions except control over starting and leaving time. The fourth-largest category, the response pattern 0000111, includes 3,392 people, 5.61 per cent of the respondents. This category covers people who have control over starting and leaving time, planning and tasks, but unfavourable status on the other conditions. Other response patterns are significantly smaller.

6 Also known as the Sokal, Michener, or Russell and Rao measure.

7 Given that the ERC can be construed as functional alternatives (a suggestion of John Goldthorpe) the Jaccard coefficient in effect measures the extent to which the conjunction of two ERC outweighs the exclusive alternate possibility. Moreover, the scaling behaviour of the Jaccard coefficient is known to be good (Simmen, 1996).

8 In the normal way, MDS would not be used for these data as the compression ratio (of data to parameters) is only 1.5 and the solution is therefore not highly constrained. For ratios less than unity, the solution may be degenerate.

9 Ordinal 2-D multidimensional scaling. Badness of fit Stress1 (d hat) is virtually zero (0.000003; perfect fit) for Jaccard, and 0.0026 for Russell and Rao.

10 Linear 2-D multidimensional scaling. Badness of fit: alienation = 0.085 for Jaccard and 0.074 for Russell and Rao. The metric solutions differ chiefly in the (arbitrary) property of being a dimensional reflection of the ordinal pattern.

11 Data from the LFS were selected for respondents: (1) who were economically active; (2) whose employment status could be computed; (3) who were employees (not self-employed or on training schemes); (4) who answered all seven criteria questions; and (5) who reported working in one of ninety OUGs with the highest number of respondents.

12 Accounting for 74 per cent of variation.

13 This version of the CA algorithm allows distances to be compared across row/column sets – unlike conventional CA algorithms – but to do so would make the resulting diagram unreadable.

14 In the case of MDPREF, the row data are often pre-standardised (by the removal of the means of the columns, or by normalisation), and after singular value decomposition (SVD) the row points are represented in the column (ERC) space as vectors.

15 Vectors are here represented by small circles at the corresponding vector end in order to avoid obscuring the central part of the joint plot with the 'shafts' of the vectors.

16 The profile values are, however, of the original scores and *not* of the standardised scores.

17 The two orders do become comparable if the OUG vector ends are projected back onto a vector starting with 1112 (directors).

REFERENCES

Arabie, P. and Hubert, L.J. (1992) 'Combinatorial data analysis', *Annual Review of Psychology*, 43: 169–203.

Bland, R. (1979) 'Measuring social class: a critique of the Registrar General's classification', *Sociology*, 13: 283–91.

Breiger, R. (1981) 'The social class structure of occupational mobility', *American Journal of Sociology*, 87: 578–611.

Carmines, E.G. and Zeller, R.A. (1980) *Measurement in the Social Sciences*. London: Cambridge University Press.

Carroll, J.D., Green, P.E. and Schaffer, C.M. (1986) 'Interpoint distance comparisons in correspondence analysis', *Journal of Marketing Research*, 23: 271.

Chang, J.J. and Carroll, J.D. (1969) *How to Use MDPREF: A Computer Program for Multidimensional Analysis of Preference Data, Computer Manual*. Murray Hill, NJ: Bell Laboratories.

Coxon, A.P.M., Davies, P.M. and Jones, C.L. (1986) *Images of Social Stratification*. London: Sage.

Hubalek, Z. (1982) 'Coefficients of association and similarity, based on binary (presence-absence) data: an evaluation', *Biological Review*, 57: 669–89.

Johnson, S.C. (1967) 'Hierarchical clustering schemes', *Psychometrika*, 32: 241–54.

Lazarsfeld, P.F. and Henry, N.W. (1968) *Latent Structure Analysis*. Boston: Houghton Mifflin.

Lebart, L., Morineau, A. and Warwick, K.M. (1984) *Multivariate Descriptive Statistical Analysis: Correspondence Analysis and Related Techniques for Large Matrices*. London: John Wiley.

McCutcheon, A.L. (1987) *Latent Class Analysis*. Newbury Park, CA: Sage.

O'Reilly, K. and Rose, D. (1997) 'Criterion validation of the interim revised social classification', in D. Rose and K. O'Reilly (eds) *Constructing Classes: Towards a New Social Classification for the UK*. Swindon/London: ESRC/ONS. pp. 62–77.

Simmen, M.W. (1996) 'Multidimensional scaling of binary dissimilarities: direct and derived approaches', *Multivariate Behavioral Research*, 31: 47–67.

Snijders, T.A.B., Dormaar, M. and van Schuur, W.H. (1990) 'Distribution of some similarity coefficients for dyadic binary data in the case of associated attributes', *Journal of Classification*, 7: 5–31.

Weller, S. and Romney, A.K. (1990) *Metric Scaling: Correspondence Analysis*. Newbury Park, CA: Sage.

6

An Initial Exploration of the Employment Conditions of Full-time and Part-time Workers Using the NS-SEC

Kimberly Fisher

As we have seen, the NS-SEC was developed for the Office for National Statistics using data from the 1997 Labour Force Survey (LFS), which included questions about the employment relations and conditions of employees. In the construction phase of the NS-SEC, Goldthorpe noted that:

> For purposes of implementing the class schema, part-time employment has no implications in itself . . . it will be consequential to the extent that part-time employment does in fact entail different employment relations to full-time employment *and* that certain OUGs [Occupational Unit Groups] are ones in which part-time employment predominates. (1997: 47, emphasis in the original)

Following on from this are a number of issues concerning the classification of part-time employees in relation to the NS-SEC that uses OUGs as one of the main means by which to classify individuals. We would generally expect that part-time employees have less favourable employment conditions than full-time employees within the same OUG. At the same time, those OUGs with a majority or substantial minority of part-time employees would then be expected to show an overall lower mean service relationship score – one of the elements used in the construction of the NS-SEC – and thus be allocated to a 'lower' class. We would also expect that only a small number of OUGs, within particular sectors of industry, would show high proportions of part-time employees, especially the service sector (see also Chapter 12). The thirty-eight SOC2000 OUGs with 50 per cent or more of the employees working part-time are given in Table 6.1.

This chapter takes a slightly different approach to that above and investigates the differences between the workplace experiences of part-time and full-time employees within each of the NS-SEC classes after controlling for sex.

Through an initial examination of how the employment conditions asked in the 1997 LFS are distributed among full-time and part-time women and men in each of the NS-SEC classes, this chapter demonstrates that such differences do in fact emerge. To an extent, future variations between the conditions of full-time and part-time workers will diminish following the passage of legislation which requires employers to offer the same contractual conditions to both full-time and part-time employees working in comparable positions, 'unless such

Table 6.1 Percentage of full-time/part-time and NS-SEC allocations for all SOC2000 OUGs with 50%+ part-time employment (ten or more employees)

OUG no.	Name	% part-time employees	No. of employees	% female employees	NS-SEC (operational)	NS-SEC (7 class)
9243	School crossing patrol attendants	100.0	39	66.7	13.1	7
9244	School mid-day assistants	100.0	230	98.7	13.1	7
6123	Playgroup leaders/assistants	94.3	105	100.0	12.7	6
6213	Travel and tour guides	88.7	53	84.9	13.1	7
9233	Cleaners, domestics	85.6	1,467	85.5	13.4	7
9251	Shelf fillers	82.5	399	52.4	12.1	6
9225	Bar staff	82.4	410	65.6	13.1	7
4137	Market research interviewers	81.1	37	64.9	12.6	6
7112	Retail cashiers and check-out operators	81.1	631	82.9	12.1	6
7111	Sales and retail assistants	77.7	2,512	78.5	12.1	6
9226	Leisure and theme park attendants	77.3	22	54.6	13.1	7
9223	Kitchen and catering assistants	75.5	811	76.9	13.1	7
3442	Sports coaches, instructors and officials	72.7	33	69.7	7.2	3
6211	Sports and leisure assistants	72.5	69	53.6	12.2	6
9224	Waiters, waitresses	71.6	409	77.8	13.1	7
3229	Therapists n.e.c.	71.4	14	92.9	4.1	2
5496	Floral arrangers, florists	70.0	20	100.0	13.1	7
2319	Teaching professionals n.e.c.	69.2	78	78.2	7.3	3
3443	Fitness instructors	67.7	31	74.2	12.2	6

Table 6.1   *continued*

OUG no.	Name	% part-time employees	No. of employees	% female employees	NS-SEC (operational)	NS-SEC (7 class)
4135	Library assistants/clerks	67.5	77	80.5	7.1	3
7124	Market and street traders and assistants	66.7	12	66.7	13.1	7
6124	Educational assistants	64.7	343	97.1	12.7	6
3212	Midwives	62.5	24	100.0	4.1	2
4214	Company secretaries	62.5	24	100.0	7.1	3
7125	Merchandisers and window dressers	62.5	40	82.5	7.2	3
9259	Elementary sales occupations n.e.c.	62.1	29	55.2	12.1	6
3413	Actors, entertainers	61.5	13	38.5	4.1	2
6231	Housekeepers and related occupations	60.3	58	89.7	12.2	6
6115	Care assistants and home carers	57.0	1,213	90.9	12.2	6
4213	School secretaries	55.4	83	98.8	7.1	3
9249	Elementary security and safety occupations n.e.c.	55.3	38	26.3	12.2	6
9245	Car park attendants	54.6	22	9.1	13.4	7
6111	Nursing auxiliaries and assistants	54.3	420	88.6	7.3	3
4216	Receptionists	53.1	556	97.7	12.6	6
2312	Further education teaching professionals	52.6	209	55.5	4.1	2
9229	Elementary personal services occupations n.e.c.	52.6	19	68.4	13.1	7
2215	Dental practitioners	50.0	10	60.0	3.1	1
3222	Occupational therapists	50.0	20	90.0	4.1	2

treatment can be objectively justified' (Lourie, 2000: i). Nevertheless, the new legislation will not necessarily change differences in the informal conditions of full-time and part-time work, and past patterns are more likely to recede with time rather than to vanish completely as data from the year 2000 become available. The scale of variation between the sexes as well as between full-time and part-time workers in the 1997 LFS underlies the need to include sex and full-time or part-time status as variables in any assessment of workplace conditions at the individual level for the immediate future.

THE IMPORTANCE OF ACCOUNTING FOR FULL-TIME OR PART-TIME STATUS AND SEX

The disadvantages faced by women and part-time workers in the labour markets of industrialised countries have been extensively documented for some time. More women work in part-time employment, and, to a large extent, gender and full-time/part-time status issues in the workplace overlap (Kelly, 1991).

The British Household Panel Survey data indicate that labour market conditions for men and women, as well as for part-time and full-time workers in the UK, have been changing through the 1990s. Halpin (1997) observed that occupation and social class structures have become increasingly flexible in the UK, with men and women across the age cohorts moving in and out of the labour market and moving between occupation-based categories. Flexibility of movement between occupations, however, has not tended to change patterns of full-time and part-time work. Most British employees of both sexes who work full time in one year work full time in later years, and most people who work part time or who are inactive remain in the same state across the years (Booth et al., 1996: 7).

Men make more transitions between part-time and full-time employment than women, and Booth et al. (1996: 20) conclude that 'it is clear that there is not yet convergence in patterns of labour market transition between men and women'. Booth et al. found that women with young children and women with health problems were more likely to work part time or not be in the labour force, while women with higher levels of education, women who were them-selves owner–occupiers of their accommodation, and women whose pre-adult teenage years were spent with a mother working in a managerial or professional job were more likely to work full time than part time, suggesting a role-model effect (1996: 11–13). Men whose fathers were skilled manual workers, who suffered limiting health problems, and who had previous experiences of unemployment were more likely to work part time than full time, while men whose highest level of education was A-levels, whose partners worked, and who own their own homes were more likely to work full time (1996: 13).

The British government, along with other governments from the European Union, has expressed interest in the gaps in the conditions of full-time and part-time workers. EU Directive 97/81/EC, extended to the UK by EU Directive 98/23/EC in April 1998 and implemented in British law from July 2000, prohibits employers from offering fewer contractual privileges to part-time workers than are offered to full-time workers performing equivalent jobs (Lourie, 2000). The legislation particularly emphasises that part-time workers should receive pro rata equity with full-time workers for such conditions as rates of pay, overtime rates, selection for redundancy, access to training, maternity and parental leave rights, and entry to pensions schemes (Lourie, 2000). Some of the conditions examined in the LFS data from 1997 include some less formal contractual conditions which are not explicitly covered by the new legislation. Historically, the full-time/part-time and sex divides reflected social relations which extended beyond the workplace, and the recent legislation will not eliminate the variance overnight. Reviewing the conditions of full-time and part-time women and men across the NS-SEC classes in the 1997 LFS will reveal employment condition variations for these groups.

THE DATA

The data used in the subsequent analysis are drawn from the first quarter of the LFS for 1997. As we saw in the introduction to Part II, the LFS included eight questions on employment conditions. A question asking whether employees held secure (or permanent) contracts as opposed to temporary contracts has regularly appeared in the LFS. Seven other questions were included specifically for the development of the NS-SEC.

The range of response options for each employment condition question were recoded into favourable (coded as 1) and unfavourable (coded as 0) categories for the initial testing of the NS-SEC on the LFS data. In this recoding (similar to what we have seen in previous chapters), respondents receive a favourable coding if they are paid on a monthly basis, have a recognised pay increment scale, have to give at least one month's notice to quit, have opportunities of promotion, have a say in when they start and leave work, have a say in planning their work, and have an influence over which tasks they perform. Though the permanent contract question was not included in the initial analysis of the NS-SEC, it has been included here as the data are available and their inclusion adds some minimal extra insight. The overall picture produced by the data, however, is the same if this variable is excluded. For purposes of this chapter, having a permanent contract is also defined as a favourable employment condition.

The employment condition questions were asked of all respondents, and for those people who were out of the labour market or who were unemployed, the questions were asked in relation to the last job or in relation to a present training scheme for employment. The first quarter of the 1997 LFS included another experimental element, the recoding of occupations into new OUGs classified to SOC2000. The SOC2000 codes were recoded from the original occupation descriptions supplied by the respondents who described themselves as presently employed (either employees or self-employed). To reduce the possibility of recall bias regarding conditions from a previous job and to incorporate the NS-SEC codes based on SOC2000, this chapter excludes apprentices, unpaid family workers, as well as all people not presently employed. The employment questions are not fully relevant to self-employed people. Thus, to ensure that the answers to the employment questions are equally relevant to all respondents, this chapter examines only the data-related employees.

Most employees in the LFS sample answered all eight questions. Only 4.3 per cent of employed people did not answer all eight of the employment condition questions. The majority of the 2,788 people who failed to answer at least one question failed to answer six or more questions. As these people account for a small percentage of the sample and gave little information, they are excluded from most of the subsequent analysis and no effort was made to impute for missing values.

This chapter first uses the Jaccard nearest neighbour, single linkage, hierarchical clustering technique to examine relationships between the answers to the eight condition questions (the appropriateness of this statistical method for this analysis was discussed in the previous chapter). The presence or absence of favourable status across the conditions was summed to create a scale with a score of 0 representing the worst conditions, and a score of 8 representing the best conditions. The additive scaling of these eight items effectively produces an extended service relationship score (SRS; see Chapter 3). Dendrograms from the clustering, the means and medians of the scale and the percentage of workers coded as having a favourable answer to each condition question serve as the basis for analysis.

CLUSTERING

The initial dendrograms for all employees, for male workers, and then for female employees are shown in Figures 6.1 to 6.3 respectively. People having favourable status on the method of payment question also tended to have a favourable period of notice to quit, particularly women. Likewise, having a permanent job is closely associated with having prospects of promotion. For

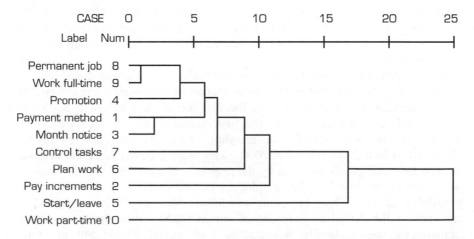

Figure 6.1 *All employees answering all eight employment condition questions*

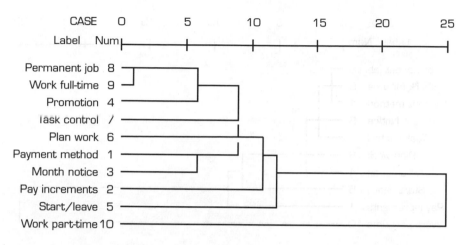

Figure 6.2 *Male employees who answered all eight condition questions*

men and all employees, having prospects of promotion and a permanent job are also associated with working full time. Working full time is not closely associated with other positive working conditions for women. The significance of full-time status for men reflects the fact that most men work full time, while the absence of similar significance for women reflects the fact that women are nearly equally likely to work full time or part time. For all workers, regardless of sex, having control over starting and leaving time and working part time has no clear association with favourable or unfavourable status on the other employment conditions.

Some clear distinctions separate the NS-SEC classes (Figures 6.4 to 6.9, but note that Class 4 is excluded as this class only includes people who are self-employed). For Classes 1 (higher managerial and professional occupations) and

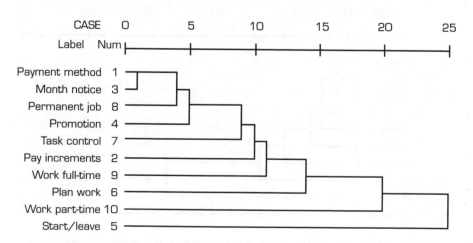

Figure 6.3 *Female employees who answered all eight condition questions*

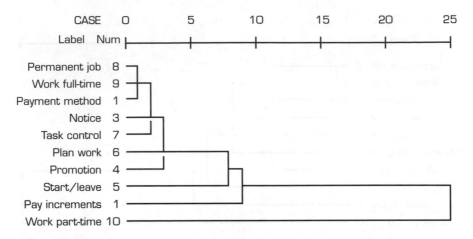

Figure 6.4 *NS-SEC Class 1 – higher managerial and professional occupations answering all eight condition questions*

2 (lower managerial and professional occupations), six and seven employment conditions (respectively) are closely associated. People in both Classes 1 and 2 share the strongest tendencies to work full time, to have a favourable method of payment and to have a permanent contract. Having influence over tasks, a long period of notice to quit, and promotion prospects are less closely linked to these favourable conditions for Classes 1 and 2. The looser clusters for lower managerial and professional occupations also include the ability to plan work. Employees in lower managerial and professional occupations also are less likely to have control over starting and leaving time than those in higher managerial and professional occupations.

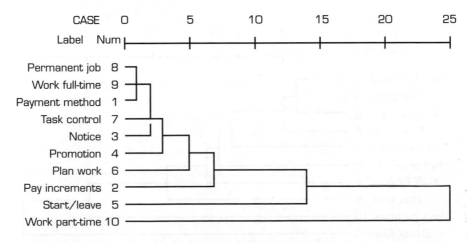

Figure 6.5 *NS-SEC Class 2 – lower managerial and professional occupations answering all eight condition questions*

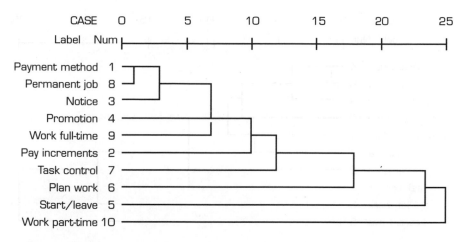

Figure 6.6 *NS-SEC Class 3 – intermediate occupations answering all eight condition questions*

Employees in Classes 3 (intermediate occupations), 5 (lower supervisory and technical occupations) and 6 (semi-routine occupations) enjoy clusters of three favourable employment conditions. The cluster of favourable conditions for Class 3 includes a monthly period of payment, permanent contracts, and longer periods of notice to quit. Employees in Classes 5 and 6, in contrast, are likely to work full time and have opportunities for promotion. Employees in these two classes only share a likelihood of having a permanent contract with inter-mediate workers. Employees in all three of these classes were not likely to have influence over starting and leaving time. People in Class 6 have less control over planning of work and less influence over tasks, but are more likely than

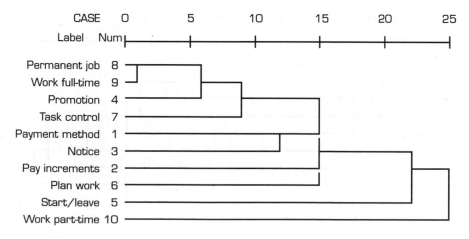

Figure 6.7 *NS-SEC Class 5 – lower supervisory and technical occupations answering all eight condition questions*

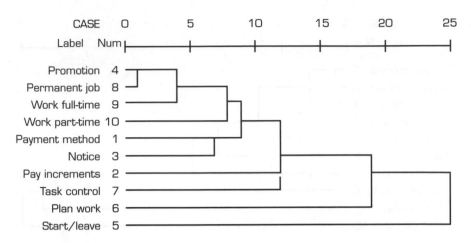

Figure 6.8 *NS-SEC Class 6 – semi-routine occupations answering all eight condition questions*

intermediate or craft and related workers to work part time. People in Class 5 were less likely to work part time, to have regular pay increments, or to have the possibility of planning their work.

For Class 7 (routine occupations), only two employment conditions are closely related, having a permanent contract and working full time. That is, having a favourable status on any other condition is not likely to be associated with favourable status on another. Accordingly, employees in Class 7 are least likely to have a longer payment period, longer period of notice to quit, or influence over either planning at work or starting and leaving time.

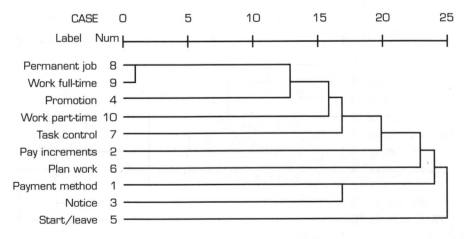

Figure 6.9 *NS-SEC Class 7 – routine occupations answering all eight condition questions*

THE DISTRIBUTION OF SCORES ON THE EXTENDED SRS

Both male and female employees who responded to the first quarter of the 1997 LFS were more likely to work full time than part time, but the difference in levels of part-time work is striking: 45.1 per cent of female employees who answered all eight employment condition questions in the 1997 LFS worked part time, compared with only 8.4 per cent of the male employees. Male employees accounted for only 15.8 per cent of all part-time employees in this sample. The low percentage of men in part-time employment must be kept in mind when reviewing the subsequent tables.[1]

As one would expect, Table 6.2 reveals that both male and full-time employees had higher scores on the scale of eight conditions than female and part-time employees respectively. The advantage of working full time appears pronounced among all employees, as well as when male employees working full time and part time, and female employees working full time and part time, are compared. The mean sex differential is slight, though still sufficiently large to be statistically significant. Male employees also have a higher median score than female employees. When both sex and full-time or part-time status are combined, however, the sex advantage reverses. Full-time female employees gained a higher mean (though not median) score than full-time male employees, and part-time female employees gained a higher mean (though not median) score than part-time male employees. Again, the differentials in the means are slight, but nonetheless they are sufficiently large to be statistically significant.[2]

Table 6.3 indicates that the full-time/part-time gap persists across the NS-SEC classes. Within the NS-SEC classes, the overall sex differences are slight (and indeed the mean scores are identical for women and men in Class 5). For

Table 6.2 *Mean and median scores by sex and full-time/part-time status across all eight conditions for people who answered all eight questions*

	Mean	Median	Standard deviation	Levene's test for equality of variance	t-test for equality of means & two-tailed significance
Men	4.63	5	2.16	$F = 28.031$	t-value 9.680
Women	4.45	4	2.06	$p < 0.00$	$p < 0.000$
Full time	4.93	5	2.06	$F = 326.230$	t-value 73.052
Part time	3.48	3	1.85	$p < 0.000$	$p < 0.000$
Full-time men	4.80	5	2.11	$F = 292.258$	t-value 42.875
Part-time men	2.82	3	1.74	$p < 0.000$	$p < 0.000$
Full-time women	5.15	5	1.96	$F = 40.112$	t-value 65.115
Part-time women	3.61	3	1.85	$p < 0.000$	$p < 0.000$
Full-time men	4.80	5	2.11	$F = 268.778$	t-value −16.245
Full-time women	5.15	5	1.96	$p < 0.000$	$p < 0.000$
Part-time men	2.82	3	1.74	$F = 35.227$	t-value −18.751
Part-time women	3.61	3	1.85	$p < 0.000$	$p < 0.000$

Table 6.3 *Mean scores and standard deviations (sd) on the extended SRS across the NS-SEC classes for employees who answered all eight questions*

NS-SEC class	FT	PT	Women	Men	FT women	FT men	PT women	PT men
1 Higher managerial and professional occupations	6.57 sd 1.32	5.42 sd 1.87	6.47 sd 1.42	6.53 sd 1.36	6.59 sd 1.32	6.57 sd 1.32	5.80 sd 1.78	4.60 sd 1.80
2 Lower managerial and professional occupations	6.12 sd 1.46	5.19 sd 1.73	5.97 sd 1.54	6.00 sd 1.55	6.19 sd 1.41	6.06 sd 1.50	5.29 sd 1.69	4.52 sd 1.81
3 Intermediate occupations	5.14 sd 1.66	4.34 sd 1.69	4.81 sd 1.70	5.13 sd 1.71	5.08 sd 1.66	5.24 sd 1.64	4.39 sd 1.67	3.32 sd 1.74
5 Lower supervisory and technical occupations	4.00 sd 1.68	3.61 sd 1.59	3.95 sd 1.67	3.95 sd 1.67	4.12 sd 1.71	3.97 sd 1.67	3.66 sd 1.57	3.36 sd 1.69
6 Semi-routine occupations	3.42 sd 1.68	2.97 sd 1.51	3.26 sd 1.60	3.10 sd 1.62	3.67 sd 1.71	3.26 sd 1.64	3.06 sd 1.51	2.53 sd 1.41
7 Routine occupations	2.63 sd 1.43	2.32 sd 1.32	2.45 sd 1.32	2.57 sd 1.45	2.52 sd 1.35	2.66 sd 1.45	2.41 sd 1.31	1.98 sd 1.34

FT, full time; PT, part time.

Table 6.4   Percentage of full-time and part-time women and men who enjoy favourable status for each employment condition*

NS-SEC class	Payment method	Pay increments	Notice to quit	Start/leave time	Promotion prospects	Influence over tasks	Able to plan work	Permanent contract
1 Higher manager/professional								
Full-time women	92.2	66.6	83.4	59.4	83.9	83.5	73.7	91.4
Full-time men	90.7	58.2	82.4	63.4	82.2	86.6	80.2	94.6
Part-time women	82.5	61.3	68.9	67.5	72.2	74.5	68.1	80.7
Part-time men	65.3	33.7	47.5	58.4	43.6	82.2	62.4	52.5
2 Lower manager/professional								
Full-time women	88.2	70.1	80.0	37.9	81.9	82.2	62.4	95.2
Full-time men	82.2	54.9	72.4	51.3	75.9	83.6	68.3	95.8
Part-time women	76.3	65.6	64.3	31.1	68.8	77.3	51.7	80.7
Part-time men	63.4	41.8	47.7	44.3	49.5	73.5	61.0	60.6
3 Intermediate occupations								
Full-time women	82.9	58.9	70.3	31.4	69.3	55.5	28.5	92.8
Full-time men	80.1	61.8	66.3	29.6	79.6	56.9	38.3	93.2
Part-time women	69.6	50.0	56.0	39.1	54.9	50.2	21.0	90.1
Part-time men	44.8	26.9	32.4	37.2	40.7	45.5	28.2	68.3
5 Lower supervisory/technical								
Full-time women	45.1	39.8	38.3	15.9	64.7	63.4	30.9	95.7
Full-time men	39.5	41.0	36.4	15.8	68.4	56.3	28.7	96.7
Part-time women	39.5	35.2	29.1	17.0	56.5	61.2	22.5	93.6
Part-time men	32.1	28.6	17.1	21.4	50.0	55.7	28.6	85.0
6 Semi-routine occupations								
Full-time women	52.7	37.7	38.4	10.9	57.5	46.7	16.6	91.7
Full-time men	32.6	37.0	28.3	10.8	61.5	36.2	12.5	94.3
Part-time women	43.9	32.8	25.5	11.6	50.1	35.4	10.0	88.9
Part-time men	31.4	30.3	14.1	13.8	48.6	22.4	8.2	79.2
7 Routine occupations								
Full-time women	17.1	26.3	15.7	9.5	42.2	28.6	10.4	92.3
Full-time men	19.9	29.2	18.4	11.8	43.8	30.0	11.4	92.4
Part-time women	20.7	19.6	11.9	19.1	27.8	37.2	6.9	88.4
Part-time men	17.7	14.8	6.8	14.3	28.3	24.0	7.2	76.5

* Including people who did not answer all eight questions.

Table 6.5   Number of part-time women and men who enjoy favourable status for each employment condition*

NS-SEC class	Payment method	Pay increments	Notice to quit	Start/leave time	Promotion prospects	Influence over tasks	Able to plan work	Permanent contract
1 Higher manager/professional								
Part-time women	175	130	146	143	153	158	138	171
Part-time men	66	34	48	59	44	83	65	53
2 Lower manager/professional								
Part-time women	1,377	1,183	1,160	561	1,242	1,395	932	1,456
Part-time men	182	120	137	127	142	211	175	174
3 Intermediate occupations								
Part-time women	1,732	1,244	1,393	973	1,367	1,248	523	2,242
Part-time men	65	39	47	54	59	66	38	99
5 Lower supervisory/technical								
Part-time women	228	203	168	98	326	353	130	540
Part-time men	45	40	24	30	70	78	40	119
6 Semi-routine occupations								
part-time women	2,093	1,565	1,213	552	2,385	1,689	477	4,234
Part-time men	317	306	142	139	491	226	63	800
7 Routine occupations								
Part-time women	511	484	294	472	687	917	220	2,180
Part-time men	114	95	44	92	182	154	46	492

* Including people who did not answer all eight questions.

full-time employees the sex differences are too small to be significant. Among part-time employees, significant differences that favour women only emerge in Classes 1 and 3. Only the difference in Class 3 is likely to be meaningful, however, as women greatly outnumber men among part-time workers in that class (see Table 6.5).

Table 6.4 displays the percentage of full-time and part-time female and male employees who reported a favourable status for each employment condition across the NS-SEC classes. This table again reflects the overwhelming advantage of working full time, especially for male employees. The percentage of male employees working part time who have favourable status is lower than the percentages for female employees working both full and part time and for male employees working full time in thirty-seven of the forty-eight cells. Part-time male employees are worst off in twenty-five of the forty-eight cells. Part-time male employees are also more likely than other groups in Class 5 to have control over starting and leaving time.

This apparent disadvantage for male part-time employees nonetheless should be viewed in the context that few men actually work part time. Table 6.5 displays the number of women and men working part time who have a favourable score for each employment condition. In all cells, women predominate by large ratios. These ratios are smallest, ranging from 2:1 women to men to 4:1, in NS-SEC Class 1. Part-time female employees appear in the largest numbers in the intermediate occupations (Class 3), where the number of women having a favourable condition to the number of men enjoying the same status ranges to as high as 32:1 (having pay increments).

CONCLUDING REMARKS

The examination of the distribution of favourable employment conditions across the NS-SEC, full-time/part-time status and sex variables lends general support to the distinctions between the classes in the NS-SEC. This chapter also demonstrates that full-time workers enjoyed clear advantages over part-time workers in 1997. While most part-time workers then (as now) were women, even before the passage of the new legislation, the distribution of favourable employment conditions between the sexes was complex. Women did not experience the same level of disadvantage in the employment conditions which they faced in other aspects of the labour market, such as pay. One need not accept the eight employment condition questions asked in the 1997 LFS as the only conditions of consequence. Provision of employee pension schemes or provision of day care facilities at or near the workplace[3] are among many other potential employment conditions which could prove relevant to future analysis.

While the new legislation will require employers to give greater concern to the contractual status of full-time and part-time workers, it will not eliminate differences in the labour market experiences either between women and men or between people working thirty-five hours or more per week and people working fewer hours. The *Part-Time Workers (Prevention of Less Favourable Treatment) Regulations 2000* neither create a right to part-time work nor require change for all part-time workers (Lourie, 2000). The legislation only prevents the use of 'part-time' status as a sole determinant for different contractual conditions, but where part-time and full-time workers perform different or incomparable jobs in a company, no such adjustments are required (Lourie, 2000).

Moreover, there is evidence that some groups of employers are circumventing the legislation.[4] While this evidence thus far is confined to media reports, the general climate in the UK might suggest that such circumvention could occur. The UK has been ranked at the low end of scales of the equity of the treatment of both female employees as well as of part-time employees (Bolton, 2001b). In spite of the British government's acceptance of European directives on part-time work, and in spite of a House of Lords ruling in February 2001 that part-time workers can take up further pension rights, few part-time employees have taken advantage of their pension rights (Bolton, 2001a). A Confederation of British Industry survey conducted in the spring of 2001 found that some employees at 71 per cent of British employers of between 500 and 4,999 workers had opted out of the Working Time Directive limitation on maximum hours of work (Buckley, 2001: 25).

Even if the legislation did achieve the effect of levelling the conditions of employees doing similar work, regardless of the number of hours worked per week, the changing status of part-time work will not necessarily mean that the gap between the proportion of women and men working part time will change. The part-time and full-time employment condition gaps and gender-based employment condition gaps are interrelated. Researchers using the NS-SEC for individual-level analysis would be wise to control for both sex and full-time or part-time status in order to prevent effects related to these employment condition gaps from colouring the subsequent analysis.

NOTES

1 Indeed, Table 6.1 reveals that women account for two-thirds or more of employees in twenty-nine of the thirty-eight OUGs where 50 per cent or more of the employees in the OUG work part time. Men only constitute a larger percentage of employees in three of the OUGs: actors/entertainers; elementary security and safety occupations; and car park attendants. Also, the relative proportion of people working in the largely part-time OUGs where men predominate is small compared with the number of people working in other OUGs where many employees work part time.

2 Nevertheless, employment conditions on their own do not present the full picture with regard to the level of social and economic power held by women and men. Women in the UK and other European countries face a greater risk of living in poverty than men, and poor women are more likely to endure more spells and longer spells of poverty than men (Ruspini, 1997). Women continue to face a glass ceiling blocking, or at least slowing, their promotion to the highest levels of business management and ownership (Yang, 1998), and men continue both to earn more than women and to enjoy employment opportunities in a greater range of occupations (Anker, 1997). Moreover, employed women continue to perform the lion's share of housework, with the participation of employed men in domestic labour increasing, but at a slow rate

(Gershuny, 2000). In spite of this, the LFS 1997 data do reveal that men do not enjoy the entirety of the advantages in the workplace.

3 The provision of convenient day care would allow some people who might otherwise not work to become economically active, and also facilitate the option for some part-time employees to switch to full-time employment.

4 The BBC Radio 4 programme *You and Yours*, for example, has taken up the cases of further education lecturers who previously worked on part-time contracts, but, since the passage of this legislation, have been made redundant, then rehired on a casual contracts basis through private contracting firms specialising in providing temporary further education teaching. The further education colleges which made their part-time lecturing staff redundant now no longer hire part-time lecturing staff, but put teaching requirements not covered by full-time staff out to private contract. In some cases, the private contractors have offered the redundant part-time lecturers less pay and fewer benefits than they previously enjoyed, though these employees are doing the same work which they performed under their old contracts (White and Barclay, 2001).

REFERENCES

Anker, R. (1997) 'Theories of occupational segregation by sex: an overview', *International Labour Review*, 136: 315–39.

Bolton, J. (2001a) 'Part-timers slow to take up pensions', *The Times*, 8 August.

Bolton, J. (2001b) 'Sexist Britain', *The Times*, 28 February.

Booth, A.L., Garcia-Serrano, C. and Jenkins, S.P. (1996) 'New men and new women: is there convergence in patterns of labour market transition?', *Working Papers of the ESRC Research Centre on Micro-Social Change*, Paper 96-9. Colchester: University of Essex.

Buckley, C. (2001) 'Many workers give up their right to limit on hours', *The Times*, 15 June.

Gershuny, J. (2000) *Changing Times: Work and Leisure in Post-Industrial Society*. Oxford: Oxford University Press.

Goldthorpe, J.H. (1997) 'The "Goldthorpe" class schema: some observations on conceptual and operational issues in relation to the ESRC Review of Government Social Classifications', in D. Rose and K. O'Reilly (eds) *Constructing Classes: Towards a New Social Classification for the UK*. Swindon/London: ESRC/ONS.

Halpin, B. (1997) 'Is class changing? Evidence from BHPS retrospective work-life histories', *Working Papers of the ESRC Research Centre on Micro-Social Change*, Paper 97-13. Colchester: University of Essex.

Kelly, R.M. (ed.) (1991) *The gendered economy: work, careers, and success*. Document originally produced for the Arizona's Fifth Women's Townhall, September 1990. London: Sage.

Lourie, J. (2000) *Part-time work*, Research Paper 00/05, 15 May. London: Business and Transport Section, House of Commons Library.

Ruspini, E. (1997) 'Gender and dynamics of poverty: the cases of (West) Germany and Great Britain', *Working Papers of the ESRC Research Centre on Micro-Social Change*, Paper 97-24. Colchester: University of Essex.

White, P. and Barclay, L. (2001) *You and Yours*, BBC Radio 4 programme, 24 April.

Yang, N. (1998) 'An international perspective on socio-economic changes and their effects on life stress and career success of working women', *SAM Advanced Management Journal*, 63: 15–21.

Part III
Construct validation

The main issue that the chapters in Part III address is whether the NS-SEC adds value to the explanation of life chances. Is it a better measure to use than, say, SOC2000 major groups? Does it compare well with or improve upon the current instantiation of the Goldthorpe schema? How does it compare with the previous government classifications – SC and SEG? How useful is it for the investigation of relevant problems? These are issues of construct validation. That is, judging a concept and its measurement in terms of empirical consequences and analytic transparency.

However, and as we have seen for criterion validation, such comparisons cannot be settled by statistical measures alone. What we should be concerned about, as we noted previously, is whether using the NS-SEC improves our understanding of social processes, not just with whether it produces higher (or lower) correlations with dependent variables. Construct validation must be a theoretically driven process. As O'Reilly has noted:

> If the variable is intended to reflect a particular *construct*, to which attach certain *meanings*, then hypotheses can be constructed and tested based on what we understand about the construct. In other words, 'construct validity focuses on the assessment of whether a particular measure relates to other measures consistent with theoretically derived hypotheses concerning the concepts (or constructs) that are being measured'. (Rose and O'Reilly, 1998: Appendix 10, para 17, emphasis in original)

Hence, in all construct validation exercises, the points we rehearsed in Chapter 2 concerning a proper understanding of the conceptual basis of the NS-SEC and all that flows from this, must be noted and understood.

THE VALIDATION STUDIES

Most of the chapters in Part III focus on how the NS-SEC relates to various dimensions of health inequalities. However, there is one exception. Elias and McKnight in Chapter 7 use data from both the Labour Force Survey and the British Household Panel Survey (BHPS) to assess how the NS-SEC classes relate to earnings and prospective experiences of unemployment. Large-scale registration data are used in Chapters 8 and 9. In Chapter 8, Fitzpatrick uses death registration data to examine differences in mortality rates and, in Chapter 9, Pevalin uses birth registration data to investigate differentials in low-weight births. Cooper and Arber, in Chapter 10, analyse data from the General Household Survey to examine gender and age differences in self-reported health and limiting long-term illness in relation to the NS-SEC, with a special focus on allocation to Class 8. Although Heath, Martin and Beerten in Chapter 11 use three distinct outcomes – smoking, housing tenure and voting intention – in their analysis of BHPS data, its basic concern is to offer a guide to researchers on continuity issues between SC and the NS-SEC.

We should also note that the final version of the NS-SEC, as based on SOC2000, had to be validated in these studies using an SOC90-based approximation to it.[1] The fact is that, at the time the studies were undertaken, of all the data sets available to us only our 1996/97 LFS data had been coded to SOC2000.

In the course of all the subsequent chapters, some of the general issues we discussed in Part I are further elaborated, such as the analysis of the allocation of 'never worked' and 'long-term unemployed' status by Cooper and Arber in Chapter 10.

NOTES

1 This approximation is referred to as SEC90 by ONS.

REFERENCES

Rose, D. and O'Reilly, K. (1998) *The ESRC Review of Government Social Classifications*. London/Swindon: ONS/ESRC.

7
Earnings, Unemployment and the NS-SEC

Peter Elias and Abigail McKnight

INTRODUCTION

As explained in Chapter 2, the NS-SEC derives its structure from concepts based upon the nature of the employment relationship, defined via the contract of employment that exists between the employer and the employee or, in the case of self-employed workers, with reference to the nature of the goods and services provided. In this chapter we examine the link between the NS-SEC and other dimensions of the employment relationship, specifically the derived economic rewards and the degree of risk or insecurity associated with it. In terms of economic reward, we study the relationship between the earnings of employees and the NS-SEC. As a measure of risk in the employment relationship, we examine the subsequent exposure to unemployment of persons who occupy a particular socio-economic position at a point in time.

We have undertaken these investigations for two reasons. First, and as part of the NS-SEC construct validation programme, we wished to examine the nature of the relationship between earnings, unemployment and the NS-SEC and also to contrast the NS-SEC with other socio-economic classifications. Our intention is to portray the general nature of these associations and to gain some further insight into the ability of the NS-SEC to discriminate between groups in terms of their earnings or experience of unemployment. Second, we want to explore further the nature of these relationships – do they arise indirectly through 'intervening' factors such as age, gender or job tenure, or does there appear to be some more fundamental link between risk, reward and the nature of the employment relationship?

This chapter is in two parts. The first part explores the link between earnings and socio-economic classifications. Here we examine the additional 'explanatory' power that knowledge of an individual's social position provides about his/her earnings, over and above factors such as age, gender and job tenure. In this part we compare and contrast three earlier socio-economic classifications with the NS-SEC. The second part presents a similar investigation of the links between socio-economic positions and the subsequent experience of unemployment. We should stress at the outset, however, that these two investigations differ markedly in one important analytical sense. The study of earnings is *contemporaneous* in that it examines the nature of the link between the job held by a respondent and through which the respondent's social position is defined and his/her earnings are derived from that job. In contrast, the study of unemployment is *prospective*. It measures social position at a point in time, and then investigates the future experience of unemployment, relating this experience to the earlier social class position.

SOCIAL AND OCCUPATIONAL CLASSIFICATIONS

Systems of socio-economic classification differ from occupational classifications in that the former are designed to provide the means whereby a large and varied amount of information about the social and economic situation of an individual or household can be reduced to a smaller set of categories or 'classes' for analytical purposes. For operational reasons, most systems of socio-economic classification utilise occupational information in their construction. They should not, however, be confused with occupational classifications, designed to summarise information about the type of work undertaken by an individual or groups of individuals (i.e. the nature of the tasks and duties involved in the competent performance of a job).

The two main occupational classifications in use in UK official statistics over the past fifteen years have been the *Classification of Occupations 1980* (CO80) and the *Standard Occupational Classification 1990* (SOC90). CO80 and SOC90 are used in the construction of both the former UK social classifications (Social Class based on Occupation and Socio-economic Groups) and the Goldthorpe schema (Goldthorpe and Heath, 1992) when combined with information on status in employment and, in certain circumstances, establishment size.[1]

The recent introduction of the successor to SOC90, the 2000 version of the Standard Occupational Classification (SOC2000) required that the NS-SEC should be defined in terms of SOC2000. For our analysis of earnings we needed information on the earnings of individuals classified to both SOC90 and SOC2000. The winter quarter of the 1996/97 Labour Force Survey (LFS) provided such information. For the study of unemployment and socio-economic classifications, however, no relevant cross-classified data exist. To achieve comparability between classifications we make use of the NS-SEC approximation that uses SOC90, namely SEC90 (see the introduction to Part III).

DIFFERENTIATING EARNINGS BY SOCIAL CLASS

Information on gross weekly earnings from employment is extracted from the LFS. This source facilitates statistical control for variations associated with a number of factors that are not directly related to the effect of the class variables under investigation. These are referred to in the following analysis as 'control' variables and include age and job tenure effects, gender and full-time/part-time working.

The natural logarithm of employee earnings is selected as the dependent variable in an ordinary least squares regression framework consisting of a set of categorical variables for the constituent groups of the classification under

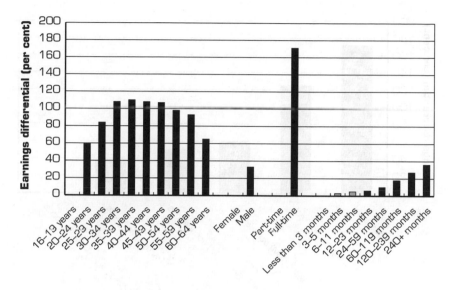

Figure 7.1 *Earnings differentials – control variables (LFS)*

investigation. The coefficients on these variables, translated into percentage differences in earnings from the various reference categories we have chosen, are shown in the following figures.

Figure 7.1 shows the variation in earnings associated with the control variables.[2] It can be seen that the effects of age, job tenure, location, gender and working time are strong and well defined. Age has the well-known curvilinear relationship with earnings while job tenure effects have a smaller but clearly defined positive relationship with earnings. The gender difference remains at about 30 per cent in the presence of all other control variables.[3] Grey bars in the series indicate that an earnings differential is not significantly different from the reference category at the 5 per cent level.

Figure 7.2 portrays the earnings differentials for the Social Class based on Occupation categories in the presence of the control variables. Here a clear gradient is evident and each category is distinctly different from any other category. 'Higher' social classes are associated with higher average gross weekly earnings relative to 'lower' social classes.

Figure 7.3 shows the same information by Socio-economic Groups. No significant difference in earnings from the reference category (unskilled manual) is associated with membership of the categories 'farmers' or 'agricultural workers'. Employers and managers (large establishments) do not exhibit a significant differential from professional workers (employees) in terms of their earnings. The exclusion of the self-employed results in employers being excluded from the group and their exclusion could alter the position of this group in terms of relative gross weekly earnings. Similarly, intermediate non-manual workers and managers (small establishments) have similar earnings differentials from the reference category.

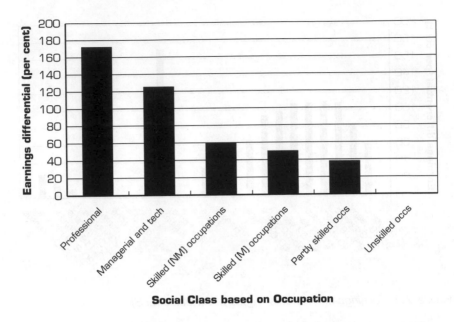

Social Class based on Occupation

Figure 7.2 *Earnings differentials – Social Class based on Occupation (LFS)*

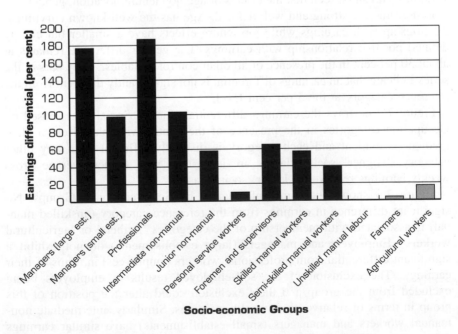

Socio-economic Groups

Figure 7.3 *Earnings differentials – Socio-economic Groups (LFS)*

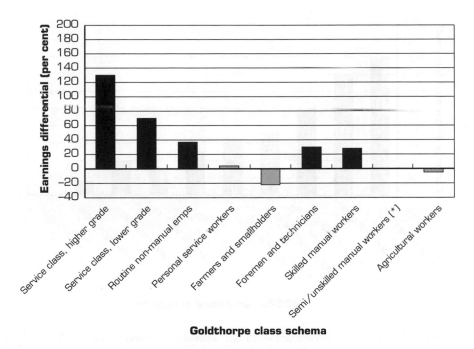

Goldthorpe class schema

Figure 7.4 *Earnings differentials – Goldthorpe classes (LFS)*

Figure 7.4 portrays results for the Goldthorpe class schema. As with the Socio-economic Groups, information on those categories defined as self-employed is unavailable, given that the LFS does not include relevant earnings information for this group. This means not only that some classes are missing but that the composition of other classes will be altered. For example, farmers and smallholders would normally include self-employed workers and their exclusion could change the relative position of this class in terms of average weekly earnings. While the two service class categories appear reasonably distinct, two sets of categories are not well differentiated in terms of their associated earnings. These are routine non-manual employees, foremen and technicians, and skilled manual workers on the one hand and semi- and unskilled manual workers, personal service workers and agricultural workers on the other. However, the latter categories collapse together to form the working class in Goldthorpe's seven-class model and so this result is as would be expected. Similarly, foremen and technicians form a single class (Class V) in the seven-class schema.

The earnings differentials associated with the NS-SEC are shown in Figures 7.5 and 7.6. The operational version of the NS-SEC provides the most detailed view of earnings differentials. As explained in Chapter 1, this version of the NS-SEC has been developed to maximise continuity with Socio-economic Groups and Social Class based on Occupation. It is unlikely that this level of detail will be used for the type of analytic purposes that concern us here. Higher tiers of the classification are obtained by collapsing the operational

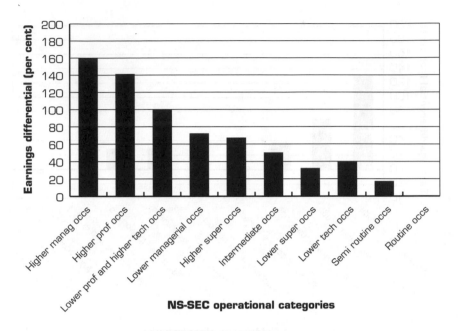

Figure 7.5 *Earnings differentials – NS-SEC operational categories (LFS)*

categories. However, in the analysis of earnings differentials we have chosen to focus on both the operational version and the seven-class version. Looking first at the operational version (Figure 7.5) it can be seen that the various categories are well differentiated in terms of the average earnings associated with each category. Lower technical occupations show a higher average earnings differential than lower supervisory occupations. This is unsurprising given that the latter category includes the supervisors of semi-routine and routine occupations.

Figure 7.6 shows the earnings differentials of employees in the seven-class version of the NS-SEC. This tier of the classification shows a clear gradient in earnings, with each group differentiated from the others.

In summary, we note that earnings and socio-economic classifications correlate quite well. After adjusting earnings for the effects of age, gender, job tenure and for full-time/part-time working, and at the broad level, we find that the categories of both Social Class based on Occupation and the NS-SEC exhibit a marked gradient with earnings. This gradient most likely reflects the correlation between pay and the terms and conditions of employment, the conceptual basis of the NS-SEC. It is worth pointing out, however, that the similarity between these two classifications and earnings does not imply that either is equally good at differentiating earnings. The highest and the lowest categories of Social Class based on Occupation are much smaller classes than the corresponding two classes in the NS-SEC. In the former the two classes account for just over 11 per cent of employees, whereas the top and bottom categories of the NS-SEC cover more than 25 per cent of employees.

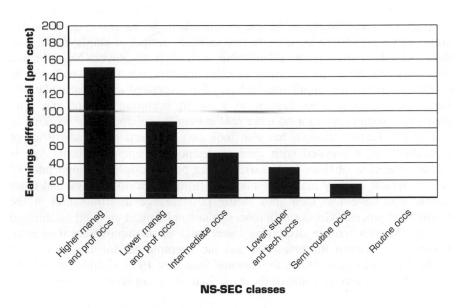

Figure 7.6 *Earnings differentials – NS-SEC classes (LFS)*

SOCIO-ECONOMIC CLASSIFICATIONS AND THE EXPERIENCE OF UNEMPLOYMENT

In this section we examine the relationship between socio-economic classifications and the experience of unemployment. As mentioned in the introduction to this chapter, this analysis differs from the earnings analysis in that we use it to reveal the extent to which those who occupy a particular position within a socio-economic classification at a point in time are likely to experience future spells of unemployment with varying degrees of risk. In analysing earnings our intention was to show the links between the economic rewards from a particular job and the associated contractual relationship. While the categories and classes of the NS-SEC are not intended to be an ordinal set, it is clear from the preceding analysis that they rank, as one would anticipate, in terms of earnings. Here we attempt a similar analysis with unemployment, using unemployment as an indication of the labour market 'risk' associated with different forms of employment relationship. To achieve this we require information about the *subsequent* experience of unemployment for persons occupying a particular social class position. For this purpose we make use of nine years of panel data from the British Household Panel Survey (BHPS), examining the relationship between their socio-economic position in 1991 and later experiences of unemployment between September 1991 and August 1999.

The NS-SEC is defined in terms of the nature of the employment relationship. As we saw in Chapter 2, these cover a spectrum that varies between the service relationship on the one hand and the labour contract on the other. It is reasonable to hypothesise that different employment relations are linked to the subsequent experience of unemployment, in that those who hold a labour contract are more likely to be made redundant, or to leave an employer voluntarily without moving directly into another contract of employment, than those who hold a 'service' relationship with their employer. Nevertheless, unemployment arises for a variety of other reasons, not all of which can be considered part of the employment relationship associated with a particular job. For example, those who happen to work in declining sectors may find themselves unemployed for no other reason than the misfortune of working in that sector. Earlier research has also indicated that certain characteristics of individuals are associated with their experiences of unemployment. Age is perhaps the most obvious factor, with young people displaying high rates of unemployment as they make the transition from education to work and older people who have lost their jobs facing possible age discrimination in the recruitment process. Gender differences in unemployment are well established in the UK, with women displaying lower rates of unemployment than men. Differences between the employed and the unemployed are also evident in terms of marital status (Office for National Statistics, 1998; Gallie et al., 1994), though the causality of some of these associations is difficult to determine.

DIFFERENTIATING UNEMPLOYMENT BY SOCIAL CLASS

To test the hypothesis that socio-economic positions carry a 'risk' of unemployment, we make use of information from Waves 1 to 9 of the BHPS. Each wave carries information on the experience of unemployment recorded in the preceding year.[4] This information, collected in October/November, is used to construct a summary indicator of the annual experiences of unemployment, the number of weeks in each year (1 September to 31 August) for which the respondent recorded him/herself as unemployed. The information utilised in this study is restricted to those persons for whom information is available in each and every wave of the BHPS, from Wave 1 to Wave 9. This restriction yields a sample of 6,080 persons.[5]

We use two different but related measures of the experience of unemployment. The first, and possibly most interesting of these for our purpose, records whether or not the respondent had experienced *any* unemployment over the period 1 September 1991 to 31 August 1999. This is a measure of the incidence of unemployment and distinguishes between those who never experience any unemployment and those who do. The second measure is derived from the cumulative experience of unemployment over this same period, classifying respondents as having a *long-term* experience of unemployment if the cumulative amount of time spent unemployed during this eight-year period exceeds one year. This will reflect not only the risk of becoming unemployed in the period under consideration, but also the risk of remaining unemployed and the experience of repeat spells of unemployment.

Table 7.1 shows, by age group (age in 1991), the cumulative experience of unemployment for this sample as recorded in Waves 2 to 9 of the BHPS. Overall, approximately three-quarters of these respondents record no experience of unemployment at all throughout this eight-year period. Young people record significantly more, mainly due to the fairly short spells of unemployment they experience on entry to the labour market. However, the experience of very long-duration unemployment (two years or more out of the eight years for which information is available) is much higher among the youngest members of the sample, with one in twelve of those aged 18 and under in 1991 recording a cumulative total of two years or more spent unemployed between September 1991 and August 1999.

MODELLING THE EXPERIENCE OF UNEMPLOYMENT BY SOCIAL CLASS

From Table 7.1 it can be seen that the group most likely to experience unemployment consists of those aged 23 years and under in 1991. From a separate analysis of the incidence and duration of these spells we determined that most are of relatively short duration and are associated with the transition from education to work. These experiences of unemployment do not relate closely to our investigation. Additionally, classification of these individuals in 1991 either is not possible (because they have no experience of work) or may be inappropriately based upon part-time, vacation or student employment (see Chapter 12). To overcome this problem we focus the following analysis upon those aged 23 to 51 years in 1991. This has the effect of limiting the sample studied to 3,624 persons

Figure 7.7 shows the profile of unemployment experienced by this age group as recorded in the nine waves of the panel study. It is interesting to observe that the significant national decline in unemployment noted over this period manifests itself via the decline in the extent to which a group of men aged 23–51 years in 1991 have experienced unemployment. For a similar group of

Table 7.1   *Cumulative experience of unemployment, September 1991 to August 1999, by age in 1991 (column per cent)*

Cumulative experience of unemployment	Age in 1991 (years)							
	18 and under	19–23	24–33	34–43	44–53	54–63	64+	Total
Missing or proxy	13.2	9.5	7.2	6.5	7.1	5.6	4.7	6.9
None	41.0	49.7	72.8	72.4	71.7	82.8	94.5	73.9
>0 and <1 month	4.1	3.5	1.8	1.9	0.9	0.9	0.1	1.5
1 month but <3 months	9.4	7.7	3.7	3.9	4.2	1.6		3.6
3 months but <6 months	10.5	7.5	2.7	3.5	3.4	0.9	0.1	3.1
6 months but <1 year	7.5	9.5	5.1	5.3	5.9	3.4	0.6	4.9
1 year but <2 years	6.0	7.3	3.4	3.1	3.7	2.5		3.2
2 years but <4 years	3.8	4.4	2.2	1.9	2.0	1.7		1.9
4 years or more	4.5	1.1	1.1	1.5	1.1	0.7		1.1
Total sample (=100%)	266	455	1,342	1,240	1,112	767	898	6,080

Source: BHPS

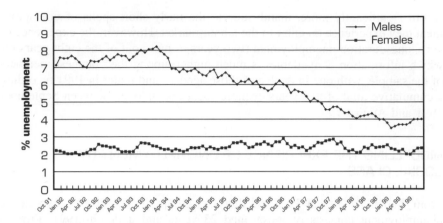

Figure 7.7 *The experience of unemployment between October 1991 and September 1999 for BHPS respondents ages 23–51 years in 1991 (BHPS)*

women, their reported experience of unemployment remains much lower than that of men but stays virtually constant over the period.

Figure 7.8 shows the relationship between Social Class based on Occupation and the subsequent experience of unemployment. There is a reasonably clear gradient linking these social class categories and the experience of *any* unemployment, with the exception of skilled manual workers. In line with earlier research based on this same data source (Elias, 1997) we note that

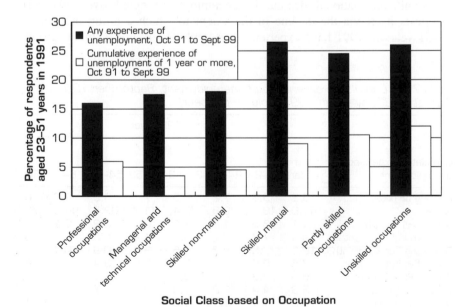

Figure 7.8 *Percentage of respondents with experience of unemployment 1991–9, by social class based on occupation (BHPS)*

persons who occupied skilled manual positions in 1991 were most vulnerable to redundancies arising from the labour market restructuring which took place in the early 1990s. In terms of the cumulative experience of unemployment the relationship is not so clear. Persons occupying professional occupations in 1991 have a cumulative experience of unemployment in the subsequent eight-year period that exceeds those in managerial, technical and skilled non-manual positions. This may be due to the fact that this measure of unemployment will reflect subsequent difficulties experienced in *regaining* employment, as well as the risk of becoming unemployed. This may, in turn, be associated with age effects. However, it should be pointed out that persons who occupied a professional position in 1991 were only half as likely as those who are in unskilled occupations to have a cumulative record of one year or more unemployment from 1991 to 1999.

Figure 7.9 shows this same information using the eleven-class version of the Goldthorpe schema. This classification yields more insight into the structure of unemployment than is gained from Social Class based on Occupation. In particular, the lower experience of unemployment among small proprietors with employees, farmers and smallholders is evident, as is the concentration of unemployment among those who occupied skilled, semi-skilled and unskilled manual positions in 1991.

Figure 7.10 utilises the seven-class version of the NS-SEC to explore these dimensions of unemployment. This classification shows the higher than average experience of unemployment among those who were classified to 'routine

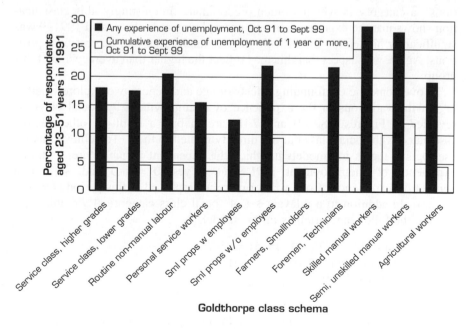

Figure 7.9 *Percentage of respondents with experience of unemployment 1991–9, by Goldthorpe classes (BHPS)*

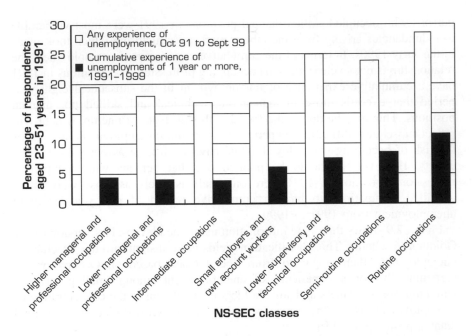

Figure 7.10 *Percentage of respondents with experience of unemployment 1991–9, by NS-SEC classes (BHPS)*

occupations' in 1991 and the lowest experience among 'intermediate occupations', a category in which women predominate. Interestingly, this classification shows that the experience of any unemployment in the period 1991–9 was significantly higher for those in the higher managerial and professional positions. Again, we suspect that this may reflect the higher than average age of this group.

To overcome the confounding effects of age and gender, we explore whether or not the variations in the experience of unemployment by social class, as revealed in Figures 7.8, 7.9 and 7.10, are in part a result of other factors associated with social class but not directly related to them. To achieve this we use logistic regression models in which the dependent variables are, first, *any* experience of unemployment 1991–9 (1 = yes, 0 = no) and, second, a *cumulative* experience of one year or more unemployed in this period (1 = yes, 0 = no). In addition to a relevant set of social class categorical variables, we include the following variables in this model:

* age groups (23–34, 35–44, 45–51 years)
* youngest child under 2 years in 1991
* marital status in 1991
* gender

Figures 7.11 and 7.12 reveal how the odds of experiencing any unemployment and the odds of experiencing one year or more of unemployment vary by the classes of the NS-SEC, with and without the control variables listed above.

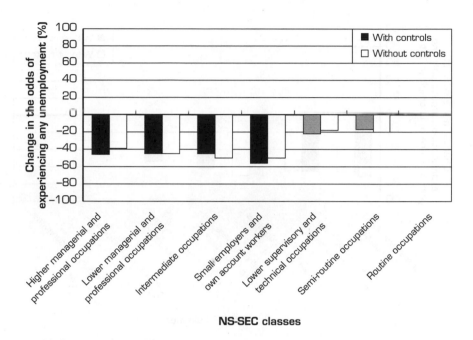

NS-SEC classes

Figure 7.11 *NS-SEC classes and the experience of any unemployment 1991–9 (BHPS)*

Examining first the experience of any unemployment, the white bars show how these odds change relative to the reference category (routine occupations) without the additional variables. Four categories show significantly lower odds. When the additional variables are added (the solid bars) they remain significantly different from the reference category. We note that the introduction of this correction for age and gender effects reduces the odds associated with the higher managerial and professional category. For the cumulative experience of unemployment (Figure 7.12) some similar results are obtained, with significantly lower odds of experiencing a cumulative duration of one year or more for those who occupy 'service class' positions and for small employers and own account workers.

SUMMARY

In this chapter we have investigated the links between socio-economic classifications and the economic rewards and risks associated with the categories of these classifications. We have compared the earnings differentials of constituent categories in three existing socio-economic classifications (Social Class based on Occupation, Socio-economic Groups and Goldthorpe class schema). For the NS-SEC we have considered two tiers of the classification (the operational version and the seven-class version) and assessed the ability of the NS-SEC to differentiate between groups of employees in terms of earnings. In

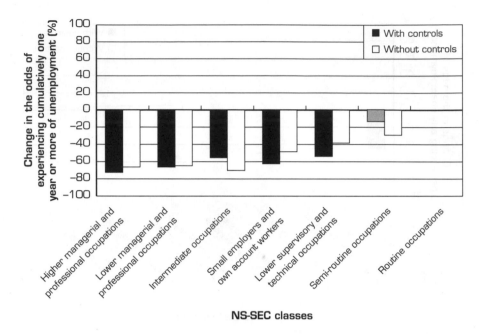

Figure 7.12 *NS-SEC classes and the cumulative experience of one year or more of unemployment 1991–9 (BHPS)*

terms of risk, we analysed the links between social class and subsequent exposure to unemployment, utilising two different measures of the experience of unemployment.

The categories of Social Class based on Occupation exhibit a clear gradient in earnings. There is no such gradient apparent in the relationship between Socio-economic Groups and earnings.[6] The Goldthorpe schema identifies a strong differential between service class (higher) and service class (lower) but in other parts of the classification there is very little difference between its constituent groups in terms of earnings.

The seven-class version of the NS-SEC has a clearly defined ordinal gradient in earnings which persists *after* controlling for the separate effects of age, gender, hours worked and job tenure on earnings.

The links between the three socio-economic classifications investigated here and the experience of unemployment reveal a more complex pattern. The experience of unemployment does correlate with the NS-SEC classes, but the distinction appears greatest between the 'service relationship' classes on the one hand and the 'labour contract' classes on the other. This is an unsurprising finding, given that the labour contract is usually defined in terms of the labour services required and is terminated when such services are no longer in demand.

In summary, we conclude that the NS-SEC in its seven-class version has, like Social Class based on Occupation, a significant and distinctive relationship with earnings. This is a useful and important property, in that it facilitates the use of the new classification as a proxy measure of earnings in situations where such information is unavailable (the 2001 Census of Population, for example). The more balanced structure of the NS-SEC compared with Social Class based on Occupation will make the former a more useful tool in this respect. The relationship between the NS-SEC and unemployment is consistent with its conceptual basis – those who hold a service type of employment relationship are at a significantly lower risk of subsequent unemployment than those who hold a labour contract.

APPENDIX

Table 7.A1   *Earnings and Social Class based on Occupation – regression results*

		Coeff.	SE	Sig.
	Constant	3.014	0.041	0.00
Age	16–19 years*			
	20–24 years	0.510	0.030	0.00
	25–29 years	0.660	0.029	0.00
	30–34 years	0.782	0.029	0.00
	35–39 years	0.793	0.029	0.00
	40–44 years	0.787	0.030	0.00
	45–49 years	0.772	0.030	0.00
	50–54 years	0.727	0.031	0.00
	55–59 years	0.682	0.034	0.00
	60–64 years	0.541	0.041	0.00
Sex	Female*			
	Male	0.282	0.013	0.00
Working time	Part-time*			
	Full-time	1.029	0.015	0.00
Job tenure	Less than 3 months*			
	3–5 months	0.014	0.033	0.67
	6–11 months	0.039	0.032	0.22
	12–23 months	0.060	0.030	0.05
	24–59 months	0.091	0.029	0.00
	60–119 months	0.172	0.029	0.00
	120–239 months	0.257	0.030	0.00
	240+ months	0.321	0.033	0.00
Social class	Professional	1.005	0.035	0.00
	Managerial & technical	0.814	0.028	0.00
	Skilled (NM) occupations	0.468	0.028	0.00
	Skilled (M) occupations	0.391	0.030	0.00
	Partly skilled occupations	0.229	0.029	0.00
	Unskilled occupations*			
	Armed forces	0.766	0.089	0.00
	N	9,122		
	R^2	0.665		

* Reference category.
Source: LFS

Table 7.A2   *Earnings and Socio-economic Groups – regression results*

		Coeff.	SE	Sig.
	Constant	3.061	0.041	0.00
Age	16–19 years*			
	20–24 years	0.511	0.030	0.00
	25–29 years	0.649	0.029	0.00
	30–34 years	0.768	0.029	0.00
	35–39 years	0.778	0.029	0.00
	40–44 years	0.769	0.029	0.00
	45–49 years	0.753	0.030	0.00
	50–54 years	0.712	0.031	0.00
	55–59 years	0.667	0.034	0.00
	60–64 years	0.539	0.041	0.00
Sex	Female*			
	Male	0.248	0.013	0.00
Working time	Part-time*			
	Full-time	0.987	0.015	0.00
Job tenure	Less than 3 months*			
	3–5 months	0.019	0.033	0.56
	6–11 months	0.037	0.032	0.25
	12–23 months	0.052	0.030	0.08
	24–59 months	0.084	0.028	0.00
	60–119 months	0.158	0.029	0.00
	120–239 months	0.237	0.029	0.00
	240+ months	0.292	0.032	0.00
SEG	Managers (large est.)	1.014	0.031	0.00
	Managers (small est.)	0.685	0.035	0.00
	Professionals	1.050	0.035	0.00
	Intermediate non-manual	0.712	0.029	0.00
	Junior non-manual	0.456	0.028	0.00
	Personal service workers	0.082	0.034	0.01
	Foremen & supervisors	0.510	0.036	0.00
	Skilled manual workers	0.446	0.032	0.00
	Semi-skilled manual	0.325	0.031	0.00
	Unskilled manual*			
	Farmers	0.044	0.216	0.84
	Agricultural workers	0.150	0.080	0.06
	Armed forces	0.826	0.088	0.00
	N	9,122		
	R^2	0.676		

* Reference category.
Source: LFS

Table 7.A3   *Earnings and Goldthorpe class – regression results*

		Coeff.	SE	Sig.
	Constant	3.296	0.034	0.00
Age	16–19 years*			
	20–24 years	0.478	0.030	0.00
	25–29 years	0.616	0.029	0.00
	30–34 years	0.731	0.029	0.00
	35–39 years	0.740	0.029	0.00
	40–44 years	0.729	0.029	0.00
	45–49 years	0.715	0.030	0.00
	50–54 years	0.680	0.031	0.00
	55–59 years	0.636	0.034	0.00
	60–64 years	0.481	0.041	0.00
Sex	Female*			
	Male	0.270	0.013	0.00
Working time	Part-time*			
	Full-time	0.985	0.015	0.00
Job tenure	Less than 3 months*			
	3–5 months	0.024	0.033	0.47
	6–11 months	0.041	0.032	0.19
	12–23 months	0.058	0.030	0.05
	24–59 months	0.087	0.028	0.00
	60–119 months	0.162	0.029	0.00
	120–239 months	0.244	0.029	0.00
	240+ months	0.295	0.032	0.00
Goldthorpe	Service class, higher grade	0.827	0.019	0.00
	Service class, lower grade	0.523	0.018	0.00
	Routine non-manual employees	0.309	0.019	0.00
	Personal service workers	0.038	0.022	0.08
	Farmers & smallholders	–0.257	0.186	0.17
	Foremen & technicians	0.253	0.024	0.00
	Skilled manual workers	0.239	0.024	0.00
	Semi/unskilled manual workers*			
	Agricultural workers	–0.073	0.077	0.34
	N	9,122		
	R^2	0.676		

* Reference category.
Source: LFS

Table 7.A4 *Earnings and the NS-SEC (operational categories) – regression results*

		Coeff.	SE	Sig.
	Constant	3.209	0.035	0.00
Age	16–19 years*			
	20–24 years	0.466	0.030	0.00
	25–29 years	0.610	0.029	0.00
	30–34 years	0.727	0.029	0.00
	35–39 years	0.738	0.029	0.00
	40–44 years	0.732	0.029	0.00
	45–49 years	0.720	0.029	0.00
	50–54 years	0.683	0.031	0.00
	55–59 years	0.651	0.033	0.00
	60–64 years	0.501	0.040	0.00
Sex	Female*			
	Male	0.277	0.013	0.00
Working time	Part-time*			
	Full-time	0.996	0.015	0.00
Job tenure	Less than 3 months*			
	3–5 months	0.016	0.033	0.63
	6–11 months	0.051	0.031	0.10
	12–23 months	0.059	0.029	0.04
	24–59 months	0.091	0.028	0.00
	60–119 months	0.157	0.028	0.00
	120–239 months	0.240	0.029	0.00
	240+ months	0.305	0.032	0.00
NS-SEC	Higher managerial	1.031	0.029	0.00
	Higher professional	0.889	0.026	0.00
	Lower professional & higher technical	0.707	0.021	0.00
	Lower managerial	0.604	0.026	0.00
	Higher supervisory	0.520	0.035	0.00
	Intermediate	0.430	0.021	0.00
	Lower supervisory	0.291	0.025	0.00
	Lower technical	0.367	0.032	0.00
	Semi-routine	0.161	0.019	0.00
	Routine*			
	N	9,122		
	R^2	0.682		

* Reference category.
Source: LFS

Table 7.A5   *Earnings and the NS-SEC (classes) – regression results*

		Coeff.	SE	Sig.
	Constant	3.211	0.035	0.00
Age	16–19 years*			
	20–24 years	0.462	0.030	0.00
	25–29 years	0.605	0.029	0.00
	30–34 years	0.726	0.029	0.00
	35–39 years	0.737	0.029	0.00
	40–44 years	0.734	0.029	0.00
	45–49 years	0.721	0.029	0.00
	50–54 years	0.682	0.031	0.00
	55–59 years	0.652	0.033	0.00
	60–64 years	0.502	0.041	0.00
Sex	Female*			
	Male	0.279	0.013	0.00
Working time	Part-time*			
	Full-time	0.995	0.015	0.00
Job tenure	Less than 3 months*			
	3–5 months	0.016	0.033	0.62
	6–11 months	0.051	0.031	0.10
	12–23 months	0.059	0.029	0.04
	24–59 months	0.090	0.028	0.00
	60–119 months	0.154	0.028	0.00
	120–239 months	0.239	0.029	0.00
	240+ months	0.304	0.032	0.00
NS-SEC	Higher managerial & professional occupations	0.950	0.022	0.00
	Lower managerial & professional occupations	0.657	0.019	0.00
	Intermediate occupations	0.431	0.021	0.00
	Lower supervisory & technical occupations	0.318	0.022	0.00
	Semi-routine occupations	0.161	0.019	0.00
	Routine occupations*			
	N	9,122		
	R^2	0.679		

* Reference category.
Source: LFS

Table 7.A6 *Experience of any unemployment and the NS-SEC classes – regression results*

		Coeff.	SE	Sig.
	Constant	−1.279	0.133	0.00
Partnership status	Married*			
in 1991	Living as a couple	0.647	0.143	0.00
	Widowed	−0.025	0.457	0.95
	Divorced	0.689	0.183	0.00
	Separated	1.155	0.227	0.00
	Never married	0.501	0.131	0.00
Sex	Female*			
	Male	0.466	0.090	0.00
Children in	Children in household aged	0.166	0.134	0.21
household	0–2 years			
Age	24–33 years	−0.257	0.119	0.03
	34–43 years	−0.032	0.110	0.77
	44–51 years*			
NS-SEC	Higher managerial & professional occupations	−0.622	0.169	0.00
	Lower managerial & professional occupations	−0.610	0.135	0.00
	Intermediate occupations	−0.591	0.154	0.00
	Small employers & own account workers	−0.787	0.183	0.00
	Lower supervisory & technical occupations	−0.277	0.158	0.08
	Semi-routine occupations	−0.151	0.147	0.30
	Routine occupations*			
	Missing	0.707	1.423	0.61
	Inapplicable	0.107	0.484	0.82
	Never had a job	0.027	0.364	0.94
	-2LL (constant only)	3,730.34		
	-2LL (model)	3,586.16		
	Goodness of fit	3,641.51		
	Cox & Snell R^2	0.039		
	Nagelkerke R^2	0.061		

* Reference category.
Source: BHPS

Table 7.A7   *Cumulative experience of one year or more of unemployment and the NS-SEC classes – regression results*

		Coeff.	SE	Sig.
	Constant	–3.109	0.223	0.00
Partnership status in 1991	Married*			
	Living as a couple	0.074	0.221	0.00
	Widowed	0.526	0.750	0.48
	Divorced	1.422	0.265	0.00
	Separated	1.641	0.324	0.00
	Never married	1.034	0.201	0.00
Sex	Female*			
	Male	1.350	0.161	0.00
Children in household	Children in household aged 0–2 years	0.655	0.208	0.00
Age	24–33 years	–0.438	0.200	0.03
	34–43 years	–0.164	0.186	0.38
	44–51 years*			
NS-SEC	Higher managerial & professional occupations	–1.352	0.294	0.00
	Lower managerial & professional occupations	–1.064	0.223	0.00
	Intermediate occupations	–0.812	0.264	0.00
	Small employers & own account workers	–0.941	0.277	0.00
	Lower supervisory & technical occupations	–0.772	0.248	0.00
	Semi-routine occupations	–0.159	0.222	0.47
	Routine occupations*			
	Missing	1.543	1.450	0.29
	Inapplicable	–0.188	0.799	0.81
	Never worked	0.951	0.430	0.03
	-2LL (constant only)	1,777.36		
	-2LL (model)	1,579.95		
	Goodness of fit	3,889.16		
	Cox & Snell R^2	0.053		
	Nagelkerke R^2	0.137		

* Reference category.
Source: BHPS

NOTES

1 Status in employment classifications reflect the type of explicit or implicit contract of employment of a worker with other persons (employers, clients, other family members) which regulates the working relationship. The basic criteria used to define groups in the International Classification of Status in Employment (ICSE–93) are 'the type of economic risk, an element of which is the strength of the attachment between the person and the job, and the type of authority over establishments and other workers which the job incumbents have or will have' (ILO, 1993). Typically, status in employment classifications distinguish between employees, employers and own account workers.

2 Figure 7.1 shows the transformed coefficients on the control variables in the regression containing the operational version of the NS-SEC. The results are similar in all the regressions (see the Appendix).

3 This is equivalent to a female to male earnings ratio of 77 per cent.

4 Information on spells of unemployment is obtained via the following sequence of questions:

I'd like to ask you a few questions now about what you might have been doing since September 1ˢᵗ last year in the way of paid work, unemployment, or things like time spent retired or looking after the family. . . . As we need to get as complete a picture as possible I'd like you to tell me about any spells you may have had in or out of paid employment, even it they were just a few days when you were waiting to take up another job.

5 In the analysis presented here no correction has been made for differential rates of attrition in the BHPS. While reweighting of the sample provides a method for the partial elimination of bias due to attrition in descriptive statistical analysis, it does not assist in eliminating selection bias in the multivariate analysis of individual-level data presented in this chapter.

6 It is interesting to note that, if SEGs are collapsed to an approximation of the Goldthorpe schema, the groups which are merged are those which show similar earnings differentials from the reference category.

REFERENCES

Elias, P. (1997) 'Restructuring, reskilling and redundancy: a study of the dynamics of the UK labour market, 1990–95', *Working papers of the ESRC Research Centre on Micro-social Change*, Paper 97-20. Colchester: University of Essex.

Gallie, D., Marsh, C. and Vogler, C. (1994) *Social Change and the Experience of Unemployment*. Oxford: Oxford University Press.

Goldthorpe, J.H. and Heath, A. (1992) 'Revised class schema', *Joint Unit for the Study of Social Trends*, Working Paper No. 13.

ILO (1993) *Report of the Conference*. 15th International Conference of Labour Statisticians, 18–28 January 1993. Geneva: International Labour Office.

Office for National Statistics (1998) *Social Focus on the Unemployed*. London: The Stationery Office.

8
Examining Mortality Rates by the NS-SEC Using Death Registration Data and the 1991 Census

Justine Fitzpatrick

BACKGROUND TO HEALTH INEQUALITIES

Measuring and monitoring socio-economic differentials in mortality has been a key part of the work of the office responsible for the registration of deaths since the establishment of the General Register Office (GRO) in 1837. The GRO has since been subsumed within the Office for National Statistics (ONS) and it is ONS that now carries on the tradition of reporting on these differentials today. This role continues to be of major importance as health inequalities are as much a public health issue in the 1990s as they were over 150 years ago, when the GRO was set up.

The work of William Farr and the findings from the early reports produced by the first Registrars General have been well documented elsewhere (Drever and Whitehead, 1997). These early analyses, coinciding with the beginning of national registration of births, marriages and deaths, pre-dated the development of official social classifications. The development of Social Class based on Occupation gave a clear framework for identifying and understanding health differentials within the population in a more systematic way, and demonstrated that there was a gradient in health – in particular mortality rates – across the social scale.

The setting up of the National Health Service in 1948 was seen as a major step towards redressing inequalities in health through the provision of health care services for all. However, although class differences in access to health care narrowed, inequalities in health have persisted (Wilkinson, 1986).

There is much evidence that substantial socio-economic inequalities in health persisted in the 1990s (Acheson, 1997; Drever and Whitehead, 1997). Overall, those in partly skilled and unskilled occupations tended to have higher mortality rates and lower life expectancy than those in professional and managerial occupations. Infant mortality rates are higher for babies born to fathers in unskilled and partly skilled jobs compared with those whose fathers are in professional occupations. The average birthweight for babies born to fathers in unskilled occupations is lower than those born to fathers in professional occupations.

These inequalities are of continuing concern. The recent White Paper *Saving Lives: Our Healthier Nation* (Department of Health, 1999a) acknowledges that health inequalities are widening and has a commitment to 'improve the health of everyone and the worst-off in particular'. More recently the *NHS Plan* (Department of Health, 1999b) for England aims to bring improvements in health across the board and to reduce health inequalities.

Quantifying the absolute and relative differences in people's health within a population is a prerequisite for developing appropriate strategies to address them, be it at a local, regional or national level. Identifying and measuring health inequalities is essential for monitoring public health, for planning and targeting health care services and the distribution of resources, for identifying new and emerging health problems, for assisting in the discovery of causal factors, and for formulating and developing effective health service policies.

BACKGROUND TO THE STUDY

As noted above, the ONS (and formerly the Office of Population Censuses and Surveys) has traditionally used occupationally based classifications – principally Social Class based on Occupation – to measure and report health differences between sub-groups within the population. The recommendation arising from the recent review of government social classifications to replace Social Class based on Occupation (SC) and Socio-economic Groups (SEG) with a single new National Statistics Socio-economic Classification (NS-SEC) is therefore of crucial importance to how we continue to measure and monitor social inequalities in health.

This chapter describes work carried out in the latter stages of the review to validate the new NS-SEC as a construct using, primarily, death registration data and the 1991 Census. The starting point for this research was an analysis of male mortality by SC in the early 1990s, presented in *Health Inequalities* (Drever and Bunting, 1997). The objectives of our study were, first, to see whether we could classify the data used in this earlier analysis by the NS-SEC and, second, if successful, to recreate the analysis using the NS-SEC instead of SC and compare our results with the published analysis using the latter. We later extended our analysis to include a comparison of all measures of infant mortality and stillbirth rates by SC and NS-SEC. These results are also presented here.

DATA SOURCES

The main analysis of adult mortality that we set out to recreate using the NS-SEC was:

1   All-cause and cause-specific standardised mortality ratios in men aged 20–64, 1991–3.
2   Age-specific and age-cause-specific mortality rates.

We therefore needed data from two sources – death registration data (to provide the numerator for the calculation of rates) and the 1991 Census (to provide the denominator). The ten-yearly Censuses provide the only national breakdown of the whole population by occupation, and therefore SC. This means that we had to focus our analysis around 1991. Like the earlier analysis, we combined three years of death registration data to ensure that we had sufficient numbers of deaths by age group and by cause to allow rigorous analysis.

We later extended our analysis to include:

3   Perinatal, neonatal, postneonatal and infant mortality rates in 1996.
4   Stillbirth rates in 1996.

Variations in infant mortality rates by socio-economic status have traditionally been analysed using the ONS-linked infant mortality database. In this database, details of all deaths in infancy (under 1 year of age) are linked to details of the infant's birth in order to pick up additional information supplied at the time of birth, for example birthweight. We did not have to restrict these data to years around the 1991 Census as the denominator for infant mortality rates is births and not population.

ALLOCATING THE NS-SEC TO DEATH REGISTRATION DATA

The last gainful occupation of the deceased is recorded at the registration of death for everybody over the age of 16 and under the age of 75. In the case of married women or widows the occupation of their husband is also recorded. The occupation stated for the deceased is coded using the prevailing occupational classification system; for the data years used in this study, the 1990 Standard Occupational Classification (SOC90). For those who have an occupation, their employment status is also recorded, although the informant supplies this on a voluntary basis.[1] However, information on the size of organisation in which the individual worked is *not* collected at death registration. We have therefore had to use the reduced method of deriving the NS-SEC based on SOC90 (see Chapter 1) to classify death registration data.

In classifying death registration data by NS-SEC, we concentrated on assigning the seven-class version of the NS-SEC as that is the version that approximates most closely to SC and is therefore the one we are most likely to use in describing health inequalities. The operational version of the NS-SEC has too many categories, with too few numbers in each group, to enable a meaningful analysis and in any case is not intended for such purposes.

We allocated the NS-SEC to all deaths between 1991 and 1993 for those aged 20–64. There were 175,838 deaths in men over this time period, of which 93 per cent were classified to one of the categories of the NS-SEC. The remaining 12,300 (7 per cent) could not be classified to any particular NS-SEC as their occupation was either not stated or inadequately described. A small number of cases were classified using the simplified method of deriving the NS-SEC as the combination of SOC90 and employment status stated at death registration were not allowed in the matrix for the reduced derivation of the NS-SEC and were not edited to accord with it.

Between 1991 and 1993, there were 107,086 deaths in women aged 20–64. Of these 57,455 (54 per cent) could not be classified as their occupation was either not stated or inadequately described. The large percentage of female deaths that were unclassified was mainly due to the fact that until very recently (September 1997) it was only possible to record regular gainful employment on a death certificate. For women who were not in employment at the time of their death, an occupation was only recorded if they had been in employment for most of their life. This is in contrast to the situation for men where their last gainful occupation would be recorded, irrespective of whether or not they were in employment at the time of their death. The high proportion of women for whom an NS-SEC group could not be allocated makes the analysis of female mortality rates very difficult.

COMPARING THE DISTRIBUTION OF DEATHS BY NS-SEC WITH THAT FOR SC

Tables 8.1 and 8.2 show the distribution of deaths by SC and NS-SEC for men and women aged 20–64 in 1991–3. These tables also show the percentage of deaths falling into each SC and each category of NS-SEC.

For deaths among both men and women it is apparent that there is not a one-to-one relationship between SC and NS-SEC. Deaths to those at the two ends of the SC scale, Classes I and V, are fairly concentrated in particular NS-SEC classes. Deaths to those in Class I are concentrated in NS-SEC Class 1.2 (higher professional occupations), and those in Class V are concentrated in NS-SEC Class 7 (routine occupations). Deaths to people within other social classes are spread across many different NS-SEC classes. This also applies to deaths among those in the armed forces. These had previously been assigned to a separate armed forces class, but they are now allocated to two different NS-SEC classes on the basis of rank. Officers are assigned to NS-SEC Class 1.1 while non-commissioned officers and other ranks are assigned to NS-SEC Class 3 (intermediate occupations). A particular point to note is that deaths to those in managerial occupations (part of Class II) have been separated into higher and lower managerial occupations (NS-SEC Classes 1.1 and 2 respectively) and those who are self-employed have been allocated to NS-SEC Class 4.

The same deaths are in the residual classes of both classifications. This is because SC, like NS-SEC, is also derived from occupation and employment status. The NS-SEC therefore does not enable us to classify any more people than would have previously been classified using SC.

For men, one-third of all deaths were to those in SC Class IIIm, and just under one-fifth to those in Classes II and IV. NS-SEC Class 7 contained the largest percentage of all deaths, but this group was made up of deaths largely previously assigned to SC Classes IIInm, IIIm and IV.

For women, over half of deaths could not be classified to either SC or NS-SEC. The largest number of deaths were in SC Classes IIInm and II, accounting

Table 8.1   NS-SEC by SC, male deaths aged 20–64, England and Wales, 1991–3

NS-SEC	I	II	IIInm	IIIm	IV	V	Armed forces	Unclassified	Total	Row %
1.1	56	5,627					298		5,981	3
1.2	6,550	1,206							7,756	4
2	456	18,126	3,202	396					22,180	13
3		940	8,032	1,525	266		815		11,578	7
4		5,879	1,672	8,036	1,491	515			17,593	10
5		338	611	21,063	3,338	428			25,778	15
6		662	1,651	7,873	15,334	961			23,481	15
7		95	52	21,550	9,689	14,802			45,188	26
Unclassified								12,300	12,300	7
Total	7,062	32,873	15,220	60,443	30,118	16,706	1,113	12,300	175,835	100
Col. %	4	19	9	34	17	10	1	7	100	

Three deaths have no social class information.

Table 8.2   *NS-SEC by SC, female deaths aged 20–64, England and Wales, 1991–3*

NS-SEC	SC						Armed forces	Unclassified	Total	Row %
	I	II	IIInm	IIIm	IV	V				
1.1	4	645					7		656	1
1.2	710	178							888	1
2	22	9,762	1,133	56					10,973	10
3		1,398	10,249	285	133		19		12,084	11
4		1,557	533	166	185	27			2,468	2
5		183	307	1,756	279	11			2,536	2
6		227	3,834	1,382	4,812	405			10,660	10
7		7	69	1,298	3,485	4,503			9,362	9
Unclassified								57,455	57,455	54
Total	736	13,957	16,125	4,943	8,894	4,946	26	57,455	107,082	100
Col. %	1	13	15	5	8	5	0	54	100	

Four deaths have no social class information.

Table 8.3 The allocation of NS-SEC with and without using establishment size information, men aged 20–64, England and Wales, 1991

NS-SEC by reduced method	NS-SEC by full method									
	1.1	1.2	2	3	4	5	6	7	Unclassified	Total
1.1	46,820		43,557							90,377
1.2	2	103,205	724							103,931
2	1,654		236,926							238,580
3				120,753						120,753
4	451				178,491					178,942
5			247			175,970				176,217
6			1,961				172,150			174,111
7								233,813		233,813
Unclassified									105,080	105,080
Total	48,927	103,205	283,415	120,753	178,491	175,970	172,150	233,813	105,080	1,421,804

for 15 per cent and 13 per cent respectively. The largest NS-SEC category was Class 3, which was made up of deaths largely previously in Class IIInm. Thus men and women have very different profiles, reflecting the differences in occupation and employment status between the sexes.

ALLOCATING THE NS-SEC TO 1991 CENSUS DATA

As stated earlier, the 1991 Census is used as the denominator for calculating mortality rates. The 1991 Census in England and Wales collected information on the occupation and employment status of all residents over the age of 16. In addition, respondents were asked about the size of the organisation that they worked in. Therefore, the population of England and Wales can be classified using the full method of deriving the NS-SEC, not just the reduced method. However, we classified the Census data using both methods of the NS-SEC to try and identify differences in the class distributions obtained with and without using the establishment size information. If the use of the reduced method alters the size of the NS-SEC categories in some way, the Census data should also be classified using the reduced method to avoid a mismatch between the numerator and the denominator when calculating mortality rates.

Table 8.3 shows the relationship between the population of men aged 20–64, classified using the full derivation method (including the establishment size information) and the reduced derivation method of the NS-SEC.

Table 8.3 shows that, overall, there is 97 per cent continuity between the two methods of deriving the NS-SEC. That is, 97 per cent of the population will be in the same NS-SEC class using both the full and the reduced method of deriving the NS-SEC. However, Table 8.3 also shows that, using the reduced method, the size of NS-SEC Class 1.1 (large employers and higher managerial occupations) increased by 85 per cent.[2] These cases have been transferred from NS-SEC Class 2 (lower managerial and professional occupations) to NS-SEC Class 1.1. The size of NS-SEC Class 2 has decreased by 16 per cent. However, not all those transferred out of NS-SEC Class 2 by using the reduced method move to NS-SEC Class 1.1. Others are transferred to NS-SEC Classes 1.2, 5 and 6. In addition, a small number of cases have transferred from NS-SEC Class 1.1 into NS-SEC Classes 1.2, 2 and 4. All these changes appear to have affected all age groups in a similar way. The age distribution of NS-SEC classes is similar using both versions of the classification.

Therefore, the use of the reduced method of deriving the NS-SEC *does* alter the size of the NS-SEC groups quite considerably. For this reason, the reduced version of NS-SEC was used for the denominator in this analysis.

COMPARISON OF OVERALL MORTALITY RATES FOR MEN BY SC AND BY NS-SEC

This section compares the previous analysis of mortality in men by SC to that obtained with NS-SEC. Figure 8.1 shows standardised mortality ratios[3] for men aged 20–64 in England and Wales by SC, 1991–3. Class IIInm has a mortality

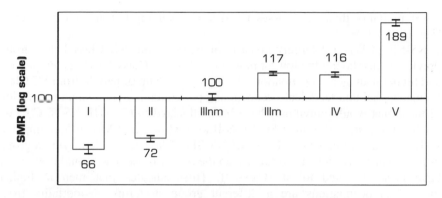

Figure 8.1 *SMRs by SC, men aged 20–64, England and Wales, 1991–3*

rate very similar to England and Wales as a whole. Classes I and II have lower mortality than England and Wales as a whole, and all other social classes have higher mortality. There is a general gradient across the social scale, with the lowest mortality in Class I (professional occupations) and the highest in Class V (unskilled occupations). The ratio of the mortality rate in Class V to Class I is 2.9, indicating that men aged 20–64 in Class V have nearly three times the mortality rate of those aged 20–64 in Class I. The SMRs for those in the armed forces are not shown here as they tend to have unusually high mortality.

Figure 8.2 shows SMRs for men aged 20–64 in England and Wales between 1991 and 1993 by NS-SEC. It shows that the highest SMR is found in NS-SEC Class 7. Class 1.1 has the lowest SMR. Although the NS-SEC is not designed to be an ordinal scale, we can see a general trend for an increase in SMRs, the higher the NS-SEC class. This is not surprising given what we know about mortality by SC and which social classes make up which NS-SEC classes. The ratio of the highest to the lowest SMR based on NS-SEC groupings is 2.8, very similar to that obtained for SC. However, NS-SEC Classes 1.1 and 7 have

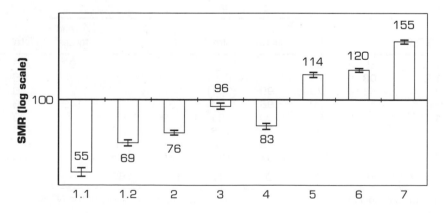

Figure 8.2 *SMRs by NS-SEC, men aged 20–64, England and Wales, 1991–3*

lower mortality than SC Classes I and V respectively but are much larger in size, too.

NS-SEC Class 1.2 largely consists of people from SC Class I, the group previously displaying the lowest mortality. NS-SEC Class 1.1 (large employers and higher managerial occupations) is largely made up of people from SC Class II (managerial and technical occupations), but contains only a small proportion of those that would previously have been allocated to Class II. NS-SEC Class 1.1 has lower mortality than SC Class II as a whole (an SMR of 55 compared with 72). Therefore, we can infer that NS-SEC Class 1.1 is identifying a group of people that have lower mortality than the rest of those who would previously have been allocated to SC Class II. This indicates that men in higher managerial occupations are a different group in terms of mortality from managers as a whole. However, we have already seen that by using the reduced method of deriving the NS-SEC we are allocating people to NS-SEC Class 1.1 that would be allocated to Class 2, if establishment size information was available. Therefore, although we are seeing a big difference in mortality between NS-SEC Classes 1.1 and 2, use of the reduced NS-SEC may be making these groups more similar than they would be if establishment size information were available.

NS-SEC Class 4 (small employers and own account workers) is also an interesting group. This group contains people from many different social classes, who are found also to have low mortality rates.

To aid understanding of the reasons behind the pattern of mortality by NS-SEC, we calculated SMRs for all possible combinations of SC and NS-SEC. The results are presented in Table 8.4. Generally, within each SC class there is increasing mortality as we move down the NS-SEC scale. For example, people in NS-SEC Class 6 from SC Class IIIm have higher mortality than those in NS-SEC Class 5 from SC Class IIIm.

Table 8.4   *SMRs for different combinations of SC and NS-SEC, men aged 20–64, England and Wales, 1991–3*

NS-SEC	I	II	IIInm	IIIm	IV	V	Armed forces	Total
				SC				
1.1	(65)	**53**					97	55
1.2	**68**	74						69
2	46	**73**	99	(251)				76
3		79	**96**	94	98		143	96
4		84	100	**81**	79	67		83
5		(250)	125	**116**	96	120		114
6		99	122	132	**116**	112		120
7		(137)	(487)	**136**	138	216		155
Total	66	72	100	117	116	189		

Numbers in **bold** indicate the social class that makes up the majority of the NS-SEC class.
Numbers in brackets are based on a small number of events.

Table 8.4 confirms some of the points made above about the pattern of mortality by NS-SEC. Those from SC Class II allocated to NS-SEC Class 1.1 do have lower mortality than those allocated to other NS-SEC categories. The table also shows the low mortality of all those allocated to NS-SEC Class 4. This group identifies and isolates people, previously from many different social classes that have low mortality. The two social classes that contribute the greatest number of people to this group are SC Classes IIIm and II. Those from Class IIIm that are allocated to NS-SEC Class 4 have by far the lowest mortality (SMR 81) than those from Class IIIm that are allocated elsewhere.

Table 8.4 also shows the mortality rates of people in the armed forces. The armed forces are distributed across two different NS-SEC groups, whereas they had their own SC group. The armed forces have higher mortality rates than the NS-SEC classes that they are allocated to, as we might expect.

AGE-SPECIFIC MORTALITY PATTERNS BY SC AND NS-SEC

Figure 8.3 shows age-specific mortality rates by SC for men aged 20–64 in England and Wales between 1991 and 1993. The rank order of the classes is fairly constant across age bands, with SC Classes I and II being the lowest at every age group and Class V the highest. The patterns illustrated by overall SMRs shown in Figure 8.2 by NS-SEC classes hold when individual age groups are examined in Figure 8.4. Like SC, this graph shows very little crossover between the groups, that is the rank order of NS-SEC classes by age is fairly constant. However, one striking point to note is that displayed in NS-SEC Class 4 at the older ages. At ages up to 20–34 this class has the lowest mortality. Up to ages 55–59, SMRs in the class are not the lowest, but one of

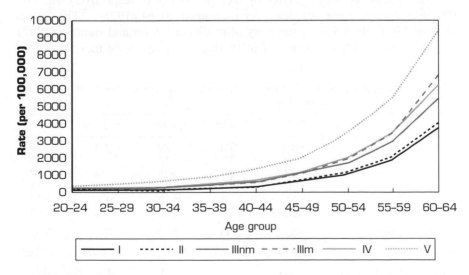

Figure 8.3 *Age-specific mortality rates by SC, men aged 20–64, England and Wales, 1991–3*

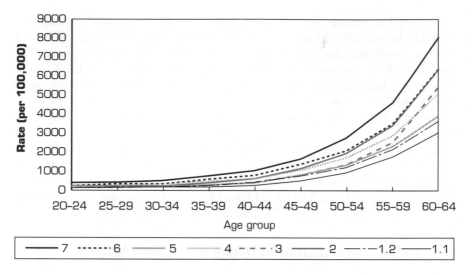

Figure 8.4 *Age-specific mortality rates by NS-SEC, men aged 20–64, England and Wales, 1991–3*

the lowest, but at age group 60–64, the mortality rate increases dramatically. Thus, the mortality advantage of the NS-SEC Class 4 is not so marked in older age groups. This is an issue that would repay further analysis.

COMPARISON OF *OUR HEALTHIER NATION* CAUSES OF DEATH FOR MEN BY SC AND NS-SEC

Tables 8.5 and 8.6 show SMRs by SC and NS-SEC respectively for *Our Healthier Nation* causes of death for men aged 20–64, 1991–3. The figures presented in Table 8.5 are a summary of results in Drever and Bunting (1997). For SC there is a clear gradient of increasing mortality as we move down the

Table 8.5   *SMRs by SC for* Our Healthier Nation *causes of death, men aged 20–64, England and Wales, 1991–3*

SC	CHD	Stroke	Cancer	Accidents	Suicide
I	63	70	78	54	55
II	73	67	79	57	63
IIInm	107	96	101	74	87
IIIm	125	118	126	107	96
IV	121	125	116	106	107
V	182	219	165	226	215
England and Wales	100	100	100	100	100
Number	52,219	8,350	55,205	10,275	9,725
Ratio of highest to lowest	2.9	3.1	2.1	4.2	3.9

Source: Drever and Bunting (1997)

Table 8.6   *SMRs by NS-SEC for* Our Healthier Nation *causes of death, men aged 20–64, England and Wales, 1991–3*

NS-SEC	CHD	Stroke	Cancer	Accidents	Suicide
1.1	59	46	66	40	31
1.2	66	69	81	59	60
2	77	73	84	62	66
3	100	90	94	82	91
4	91	89	97	38	49
5	123	112	122	98	90
6	123	125	120	119	116
7	156	166	147	176	166
England and Wales	100	100	100	100	100
Number	52,215	8,350	55,205	10,275	9,725
Ratio of highest to lowest	2.6	3.6	2.2	4.6	5.3

social scale for every cause of death, which is very similar to the all-cause pattern of mortality. For NS-SEC the pattern is not so clear cut. The rank order of NS-SEC categories for some causes of death is not the same as that shown for all causes combined. Generally NS-SEC Class 1.1 has the lowest mortality, except in the case of accidents where NS-SEC Class 4 (the non-professional self-employed) has the lowest mortality. For most causes of death the unusually low mortality for Class 4 is maintained, except for cancers where the advantage is much reduced.

The ratio of the highest to lowest SMR is very similar to that seen using SC for most causes of death, except for suicide. For suicide the ratio of the highest to the lowest with NS-SEC is 5.3, compared with 3.9 for SC, largely because the mortality of those in NS-SEC Class 1.1 is very low.

Figures 8.5 to 8.9 plot the age pattern of mortality by NS-SEC for these *Our Healthier Nation* causes of death. For ischaemic heart disease and stroke the age pattern of mortality is very similar to that for overall mortality. The rank order of NS-SEC classes holds at every age group, except for the increase in mortality in NS-SEC Class 4 at older age groups, especially for stroke, which is also seen for all-cause mortality. For cancer, the advantage of NS-SEC Class 4 group is smaller, but there is still this pattern of an increase at older age groups.

For accidents and suicide the age pattern of mortality by NS-SEC is not so straightforward. For both causes there is no clear increase in mortality rates with age. For both causes NS-SEC Classes 6 and 7 show the highest mortality rates with much crossover between other categories. For accidents NS-SEC Class 4 shows the lowest mortality at younger age groups, but not older ages over 40. For suicide NS-SEC Classes 1.1 and 4 have the lowest mortality across the age bands. An interesting point to note is the different age patterns for the different NS-SEC classes for deaths from suicide. For NS-SEC Classes 6 and 7, mortality rates are at the lowest at the younger and older age bands. There is a peak in suicide mortality rates for these NS-SEC classes between

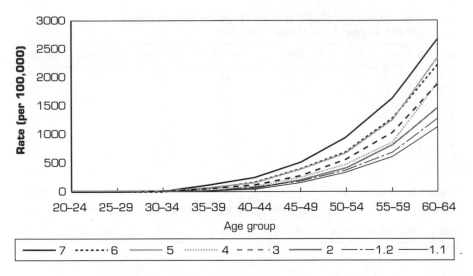

Figure 8.5 *Age-specific mortality rates for ischaemic heart disease by NS-SEC, men aged 20–64, England and Wales, 1991–3*

ages 30 and 44. This is similar to what is seen for suicide deaths in SC Class V (Drever and Bunting, 1997). However, for NS-SEC Classes 1.1 and 4, like all other social classes, there is an increase in mortality rates with age. For other causes of death the different NS-SEC classes have the same age pattern of mortality.

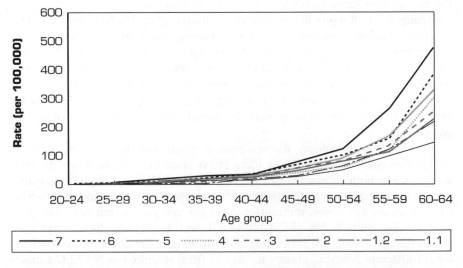

Figure 8.6 *Age-specific mortality rates for stroke by NS-SEC, men aged 20–64, England and Wales, 1991–3*

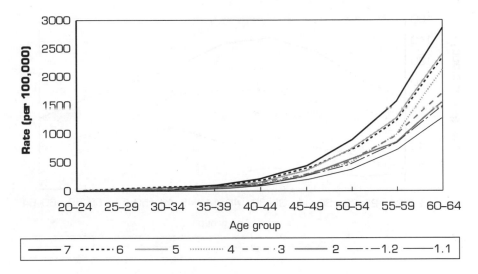

Figure 8.7 *Age-specific mortality rates for cancer by NS-SEC, men aged 20–64, England and Wales, 1991–3*

ALLOCATING THE NS-SEC TO INFANT MORTALITY AND BIRTHS DATA

As stated earlier, the data source used for this analysis is the linked infant mortality file. We allocated the NS-SEC to all deaths during 1996 to infants under 1 year of age, regardless of the year of birth, and to all live and stillbirths in 1996 using the father's occupation *at birth* and the reduced method of

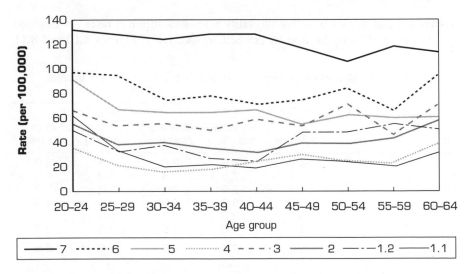

Figure 8.8 *Age-specific mortality rates for accidents by NS-SEC, men aged 20–64, England and Wales, 1991–3*

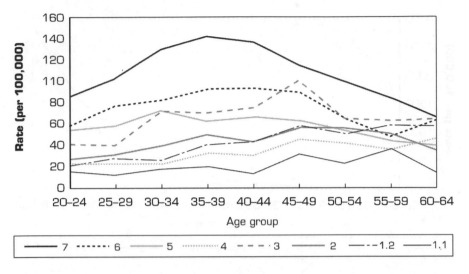

Figure 8.9 *Age-specific mortality rates for suicide and undetermined injury by NS-SEC, men aged 20–64, England and Wales, 1991–3*

deriving the NS-SEC based on SOC90. Mother's occupation has been requested at birth registration in recent years, but is not well recorded. Again, we have concentrated on assigning the seven-class version of the NS-SEC. As we have used father's occupation at birth to determine both SC and NS-SEC, births that are registered by the mother alone are excluded from this analysis.

COMPARISON OF INFANT MORTALITY AND STILLBIRTH RATES BY SC AND NS-SEC

Tables 8.7 and 8.8 show infant mortality rates and stillbirth rates[4] in England and Wales in 1996 by SC and by NS-SEC respectively. Figures 8.10 and 8.11

Table 8.7   *Stillbirth and infant mortality rates by SC, England and Wales, 1996*

SC	Stillbirth	Perinatal mortality	Neonatal mortality	Post-neonatal mortality	Infant mortality
I	4.4	6.6	2.8	1.1	3.9
II	4.7	7.5	3.4	1.3	4.6
IIInm	4.7	7.9	4.1	1.7	5.7
IIIm	5.2	8.3	4.0	1.9	5.9
IV	5.9	9.2	4.3	2.1	6.4
V	6.4	10.8	5.8	2.8	8.7
England and Wales	5.3	8.4	4.0	1.8	5.8
Number	3,180	5,059	2,400	1,113	3,513
Ratio of highest to lowest	1.5	1.6	2.1	2.6	2.3

Table 8.8   *Stillbirth and infant mortality rates by NS-SEC, England and Wales, 1996*

NS-SEC	Stillbirth	Perinatal mortality	Neonatal mortality	Post-neonatal mortality	Infant mortality
1.1	4.1	6.5	2.9	1.1	4.0
1.2	4.3	6.7	2.9	1.0	3.9
2	4.8	7.5	3.4	1.4	4.8
3	4.7	7.8	3.8	1.9	5.6
4	4.3	6.6	2.9	1.0	3.8
5	5.2	8.5	4.3	1.7	6.0
6	5.8	9.1	4.4	2.3	6.7
7	6.4	10.5	5.3	2.7	8.0
England and Wales	5.3	8.4	4.0	1.8	5.8
Number	3,180	5,059	2,400	1,113	3,513
Ratio of highest to lowest	1.6	1.6	1.8	2.7	2.1

show stillbirth and infant mortality rates by SC and NS-SEC respectively as a ratio of the rate for England and Wales as a whole. A rate ratio of 1 means that a social class has the same rate as England and Wales as a whole. Ratios of more than 1 indicate a higher than average rate and a ratio of less than 1 indicates a lower rate. Again, there is a smooth gradient in infant deaths and stillbirths by SC – with Classes IV and V having by far the highest rates and Classes I and II the lowest. The largest class differential is seen in postneonatal mortality rates and the smallest in stillbirths.

NS-SEC Classes 1.1, 1.2 and 4 have the lowest stillbirth and infant mortality rates relative to the whole of England and Wales. The low rates in Class 4 are even more pronounced than that shown for adult mortality. As with adult

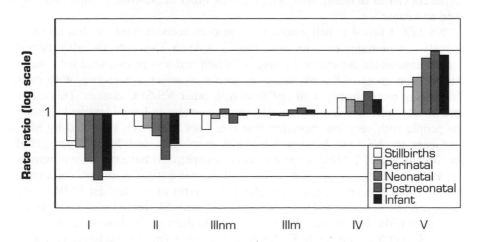

Figure 8.10 *Rate ratios by SC for stillbirths and infant mortality, England and Wales, 1996*

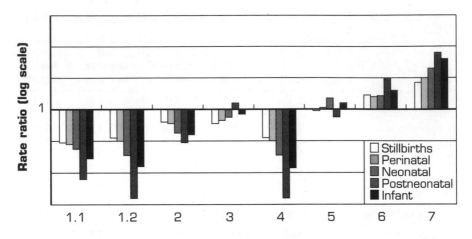

Figure 8.11 *Rate ratios by NS-SEC for stillbirths and infant mortality, England and Wales, 1996*

mortality, infants born to fathers in NS-SEC Classes 6 and 7 have by far the highest mortality rates. The largest class differential in rates is seen in the postneonatal mortality rate.

CONCLUSIONS FROM THE ANALYSIS

There are substantial differences in standardised mortality ratios in men by NS-SEC classes. However, there is a less clear gradient of increasing mortality across the social scale than shown with SC. The rank order of the social class groups for male mortality is very similar for different age groups and for different causes of death. However, the rank order of NS-SEC groups varies by age and cause.

NS-SEC Class 4 (small employers and own account workers) has comparatively low mortality rates for most causes of death. However, the advantage is more pronounced for external causes of death and less pronounced for cancer. In addition, most of the advantage is seen at younger age groups, with rates increasing more sharply with age than with other NS-SEC classes. This class, previously split across many social classes, appears to have identified a group of people with very low mortality that could not have been identified by SC.

Generally NS-SEC Classes 1.1 (large employers and higher managerial occupations) and 1.2 (higher professional occupations) have the lowest mortality rates for all age groups and causes, and Classes 6 (semi-routine occupations) and 7 (routine occupations) the highest. The ratio of the highest SMR to the lowest SMR is very similar to that obtained with SC for all causes of death, except suicide. For suicide the ratio of the highest to the lowest SMR is 3.9 with SC and 5.3 with NS-SEC. NS-SEC Classes 1 and 7 have lower mortality than SC Classes I and V respectively for all causes of death, but the ratio of the highest to lowest mortality rate remains the same for the two classifications.

The armed forces have been shown to have much higher mortality rates than the NS-SEC classes that they have been allocated to. However, these may not be true rates, as there are often problems with a mismatch between the numerator and denominator. The number classified as the armed forces at death may not correspond to the number classified as the armed forces at Census.

The reduced method of deriving the NS-SEC results in a very different distribution of the number of people by NS-SEC class than the full derivation method using establishment size. NS-SEC Class 1.1 increased by 85 per cent if the reduced method was used and Class 2 decreased by 16 per cent. However, overall there was 97 per cent continuity between the two methods.

There are substantial differences in infant mortality rates by NS-SEC class. For all measures of infant mortality NS-SEC Classes 6 and 7 have by far the highest rates and Classes 1.1, 1.2 and 4 have the lowest rates. The largest class differential in infant mortality is seen in postneonatal mortality rates, and the smallest in stillbirth rates.

DISCUSSION

The analysis presented in this chapter has focused on using SC and NS-SEC to identify and describe socio-economic differentials in adult and infant mortality, and in stillbirths. Such work is key to understanding inequalities in health. The results provide a first comparison with previous analyses of mortality using SC. However, they also raise some important questions about the application and use of NS-SEC, both in the analysis of health data and in the wider context of social reporting, and point to further investigations needed.

One area for further research is the different treatment of the armed forces in the two classifications, and its influence on mortality rates. In SC the armed forces were assigned to a separate category and have traditionally been excluded from mortality analyses as they have unusually high mortality rates (Table 8.4). In the NS-SEC the armed forces were allocated to Classes 1.1 (large employers and higher managerial occupations) and 3 (intermediate occupations). We highlighted earlier the probable effect on mortality rates of including the armed forces within these two classes. It will be important to examine this effect more closely, by excluding the armed forces from the analysis, as this will give a better understanding of how to interpret these and future results using the NS-SEC.

This chapter also highlights a number of other areas where differences between SC and NS-SEC give rise to new or different findings in the mortality data: for example, the identification of comparatively low mortality among the class for small employers and own account workers (NS-SEC Class 4), and differences in mortality between those in the higher and lower managerial occupations (NS-SEC Classes 1.1 and 2). All of these issues raise questions about how we interpret trends in health inequalities over time when moving to a new classification. While the NS-SEC provides a conceptually more robust basis for examining occupationally based analyses, it also presents a challenge in how to monitor time trends, separating real change from the inevitable discontinuity of using a new classification system.

Equally, if not more, important is a thorough understanding of the effects on analyses of using two methods of deriving the NS-SEC – the full and the reduced methods. This chapter has demonstrated the difference in the relative size of the NS-SEC classes, depending on which method of derivation is used. However, this raises immediate questions about the difficulties of comparing and interpreting results from data sets that use the different methods of deriving the NS-SEC. Any comparison of socio-economic variations between morbidity and mortality experience would first need to take account of which method of deriving the NS-SEC had been used for analysis.

NOTES

1 Employment status categories for birth and death registration data:

1   Employee
2   Manager
3   Foreman/Supervisor
4   Self-employed – with employees
5   Self-employed – without employees

2 The 1996/97 LFS data show a 28 per cent increase in NS-SEC Class 1.1 using the reduced method of derivation. In both the Census and LFS data, SOC90 OUGs 110 and 121 appear to be the largest contributors to these increases. SOC90 OUG 110 appears to be over-represented in the 1991 Census. It may, in part, be due to the use of the index entry – 110 Manager (manufacturing) – as the Census coders may have used this more often than the LFS interviewers who would probably have made greater use of the information in description of tasks or between 1991 and 1996/97 there may have been a genuine drop in the numbers in OUG 110 (ONS, personal communication).

3 Standardised mortality ratios (SMRs). An SMR allows the comparison of death rates in two or more groups of the population by eliminating the effect of differences in the age structure of those groups. In this case, the observed deaths in a social group are expressed as a ratio of the expected deaths in that social group if it had the same age-specific death rates as the population of England and Wales, and are multiplied by 100. Values greater than 100 indicate higher than average mortality, values lower than 100 indicate lower than average mortality. The SMRs in this chapter are presented on log scales with the axis crossing at 100.

4 Infant mortality rate definitions:

Stillbirth rate: the number of stillbirths per 1,000 total births (stillbirths and live births).
Perinatal mortality rate: the number of stillbirths plus the number of deaths to babies aged under 7 days per 1,000 total births.
Neonatal mortality rate: the number of deaths to babies aged under 28 days per 1,000 live births.
Postneonatal mortality rate: the number of deaths to babies aged 28 days and over, but under 1 year, per 1,000 live births.
Infant mortality rate: the number of deaths to children under 1 year, per 1,000 live births.

REFERENCES

Acheson, D. (1997) *Independent Inquiry into Inequalities in Health Report.* London: The Stationery Office.

Department of Health (1999a) White Paper. *Saving Lives: Our Healthier Nation.* London: The Stationery Office.

Department of Health (1999b) White Paper. *The NHS Plan.* London: The Stationery Office.

Drever, F. and Bunting, J. (1997) 'Patterns and trends in male mortality', in F. Drever and M. Whitehead (eds) *Health Inequalities.* London: The Stationery Office. pp. 95–107.

Drever, F. and Whitehead, M. (eds) (1997) *Health Inequalities.* London: The Stationery Office.

Wilkinson, R.G. (1986) *Class and Health: Research and Longitudinal Data.* London: Tavistock Publications.

9
Social Class and the Incidence of Low-weight Births

David J. Pevalin

INTRODUCTION

The association between the incidence of low-weight births and social class, usually measured by Social Class based on Occupation (SC) – previously known as Registrar General's Social Class – has previously been demonstrated (e.g. Rutter and Quine, 1990; ONS, 1999). With the introduction of the National Statistics Socio-economic Classification (NS-SEC) to replace both SC and Socio-economic Groups (SEG) as the official classification schema, it is appropriate to assess the construct validity of the NS-SEC against the incidence of low-weight births.

As noted in the introduction to Part III, construct validation requires that the NS-SEC demonstrates empirical associations with the outcomes of interest as predicted by theory (see also Rose and O'Reilly, 1998). This chapter presents the results of a construct validation study using data from the register of all births in England and Wales from 1996 to 1998. The remainder of this section briefly reviews the potential consequences of low birthweight in childhood and beyond and draws some plausible hypotheses of how the NS-SEC could be associated with the incidence of low-weight births. Further sections of this chapter describe the data and analytic sample, the results of the analyses, and a discussion of the results.

BACKGROUND

There is a wealth of evidence from the medical literature that low-birthweight infants require higher levels of medical intervention at birth and are at increased risk for developmental deficits and poor health outcomes (Barker, 1998; Breslau, 1995; Cohen, 1995; Cohen et al., 1996; Speechley and Avison, 1995). Children born with low birthweights also have higher neonatal, post-neonatal and infant mortality rates. For example, in 1998 the overall neonatal mortality (death before 28 days) rate was 3.8 deaths per 1,000 live births but this varied from a rate of 185.9 per 1,000 for birthweights less than 1,500 g to 5.3 per 1,000 for those weighing 2,000–2,499 g to 0.7 per 1,000 for those weighing 3,500 g and over (ONS, 1999). In addition, Barker and colleagues (1989; 1998) have shown that smaller size at birth is associated with increased risks of hypertension and death from ischaemic heart disease in adulthood (see also Leon et al., 1998) indicating that the consequences for health may not be confined to childhood.

Of particular interest is the 'Barker hypothesis' on the fetal origins of adult disease, especially heart disease. Barker and colleagues (1989; 1998) found that the highest risks of heart disease were in overweight adults who were small at birth. This finding led to the hypothesis that in order to adapt to insufficient nutrition, endocrine and metabolic changes occur in the fetus. These adaptations become maladaptive if, later, nutrition is plentiful and then predisposes the person to obesity.

Bartley et al. (1994) in their analysis of the British 1958 birth cohort study (the NCDS) have also shown that low birthweight (under 6 lb, 2,721 g in this instance) is associated with socio-economic disadvantage, as indicated by household overcrowding and amenities, housing adequacy and financial difficulties, in both childhood and adulthood. It is clear that birthweight is a marker for a number of potential adverse consequences in childhood and adulthood and may be, as Bartley et al. (1994: 1475) note, an indicator of the 'life chances conferred by the family of origin'. However, the complex mechanisms by which birth outcomes interact with social circumstances throughout life and their consequences for later health are still being uncovered.

For instance, accepting that low-weight births are more likely to occur in families with higher levels of socio-economic disadvantage, then another biological maladaptation hypothesis[1] is relevant to the adult health of these children. Brunner and colleagues (1996; 1997; 1999) posit a number of plausible mechanisms involving the unintended consequences of the physiological reactions to the fight-or-flight response under chronic low-level stress. Socio-economic disadvantage is thought to provoke low-level stress and one biological response to this stress is the increased output of fibrogen in the blood in response to the hormones generated by the fight-or-flight response. Fibrogen increases the blood's ability to clot and may lead to the formation of arterial plaques that lead to increased risk of ischaemic heart disease and stroke. Therefore, childhood experience of socio-economic disadvantage may, by itself, have adverse consequences for adult health.

The psychosocial and emotional adjustment of small at birth infants appears to depend largely on the interaction between medical conditions and family functioning, especially effective parent–child dyads (Plunkett and Meisels, 1989; Spiker et al., 1993). Other research has shown that, in addition to generalised social disadvantage, low-weight births are also more likely in families with higher levels of dysfunction and lower levels of maternal education (Kramer et al., 2000; Pevalin et al., 2001). This further suggests that low-birthweight infants will more likely have a family environment ill-equipped to supply the effective parent–child interaction required to compensate for the medical and developmental risks associated with such a birth.

The co-occurrence of low-weight births, social disadvantage and family dysfunction reinforces the complexity of the interactions of fetal, infant, child and family circumstances as they relate to future health outcomes. In other words, it still remains uncertain to what extent adult health is determined by biological changes in the fetus, by the socio-economic circumstances of the family in and around the time of birth, and by the social reproduction of advantage and disadvantage over the lifecourse.

Where does a socio-economic classification fit into all this? As we explained in Chapter 2, at the most general level, it is hoped that the clearer conceptual basis of the NS-SEC, compared with SC and SEG, will remove some of the barriers to a fuller explanation of the complex mechanisms involved in the studies of health outcomes and their aetiology. However, in many cases, what the NS-SEC actually measures, employment relations, may not have a direct bearing on the outcome of interest. However, as Rose and Pevalin have previously noted, the theory behind the NS-SEC proposes that employment relations are

> central to delineating the structure of socio-economic positions in modern societies. . . . The positions defined by the NS-SEC categories exist independently of the individuals who occupy them at any particular time, but they condition and shape the lives of their occupants. That is, the life chances of individuals and families depend mainly on their position in the division of labour and on the material and symbolic advantages that derive from it. (2000: 1123)

This approach, discussed in more detail in Chapter 2, links health, in all its forms, with social organisation and the differential access to resources, both physical and intellectual. It also places individual behaviours in a social context that emphasises processes and mechanisms while moving away from the highly individualistic focus on 'proximal risk factors' (cf. Link and Phelan, 1995).

We would argue that a family's socio-economic position at the time of the birth of its children is related to the parents' behaviour and their access to resources during the pregnancy as well as being related to the risk of future socio-economic disadvantage. For example, as Elias and McKnight have shown in Chapter 7, the future risks of unemployment vary by class.

An association between socio-economic position and behaviour and re-sources during pregnancy returns us to the Barker hypothesis. Socio-economic position, by way of NS-SEC classes, may be linked to differing rates of low-weight births via differential levels of nutrition during pregnancy. It is not unreasonable to hypothesise that families with less favourable socio-economic positions are more likely to suffer from poorer nutrition either through inadequate financial resources or through lack of knowledge, the latter being based in the knowledge levels of the parents and/or through restricted access to adequate prenatal care and education.[2]

Another possible link between socio-economic position and low-weight births may be through differential rates of maternal smoking during pregnancy. The adverse effects of smoking during pregnancy have been demonstrated in numerous studies. Heath, Martin and Beerten demonstrate in Chapter 11 that the prevalence of smoking varies by NS-SEC class with those in routine occupations being more than twice as likely to smoke than those in higher professional and managerial occupations.[3]

While this construct validity study cannot explore these hypothesised mechanisms, they do raise the anticipation that the NS-SEC classes should be associated with differential incidence rates of low-weight births.

METHOD

Data

Data for these analyses come from the birth registration records for 1996–8 from England and Wales – approximately 1.9 million births. A random 10 per cent of all joint registered live birth records and all joint registrations of stillbirths have the father's occupation coded to the Standard Occupational Classification 1990 (SOC90) and have supplementary questions on whether the father was self-employed or an employee, or of managerial or supervisor status, and if self-employed whether he has employees or not.

Sample

Excluding stillbirths, 170,922 records had a three-digit SOC90 code. Multiple births were also excluded as multiple birth status was highly associated with low birthweight – 55.5 per cent of multiple births were low birthweight (odds ratio (OR) 18.5, 95 per cent CI 18.2–18.8). This left a sample of 165,985 live, singleton births.

These live, singleton births were divided into three types of registration: within marriage; outside marriage but living at the same address; and outside marriage and living at different addresses. The method of registration was associated with differential rates of low-birthweight infants as shown in Table 9.1.

Therefore, the validation analyses were conducted on the sample of 114,382 live, singleton births that were registered within marriage.

Measures

The 'reduced' form of derivation was used to create the NS-SEC variable. As we have seen, the reduced form was specifically designed for use with registration data where size of establishment information is not collected. The

Table 9.1   *Percentages and odds ratios of low birthweight (LBW) by registration type for live, singleton births, 1996–8, England and Wales*

Type of registration	n	% LBW	OR	95% CI
Within marriage	114,382	5.25	ref.	
Outside marriage, same address	39,616	6.60	1.27	1.21–1.33
Outside marriage, different address	11,987	7.87	1.54	1.43–1.65
Total	165,985	5.77		

Table 9.2   *Distributions of all births, LBW and VLBW by classes of the SC for live, singleton births within marriage, 1996–8, England and Wales*

SC	All births		Low birthweight		Very low birthweight	
	n	Col. %	*n*	Row %	*n*	Row %
I	11,145	9.74	465	4.17	85	0.76
II	35,764	31.27	1,567	4.38	248	0.69
IIInm	13,003	11.37	656	5.04	109	0.84
IIIm	32,586	28.49	1,878	5.76	290	0.89
IV	15,488	13.54	1,044	6.74	164	1.06
V	4,254	3.72	298	7.01	39	0.92
VI	2,142	1.87	100	4.67	19	0.89
Totals	114,382	100	6,008	5.25	954	0.83

derivation matrix was based on the SOC90 approximation to the final version. SC was coded onto the records by ONS. Although the NS-SEC was based solely on the father's occupation, in this chapter we shall treat that as a crude indicator of household class (see Chapter 1 for fuller descriptions of the forms of derivation, approximations of the NS-SEC, and methods of deriving a household-level measure).

Low birthweight (LBW) was defined as infants weighing less than 2,500 g at birth. Defining LBW as less than 2,500 g is generally not considered to be extreme by today's standards but this cut-off is retained in official statistics and World Health Organisation definitions. Very low birthweight (VLBW) was defined as infants weighing less than 1,500 g at birth. The raw distributions of all births, LBW, and VLBW by SC and NS-SEC classes are presented in Tables 9.2 and 9.3.

As the mother's age at the time of birth is usually associated with LBW and VLBW outcomes it was included in the analyses. From the available registration data it was only possible to have a dichotomous variable indicating if the mother was 21 years of age or younger at the time of birth. This cut-off identified 3.97 per cent of the live, singleton births registered within marriage.

Table 9.3   *Distributions of all births, LBW and VLBW by classes of the NS-SEC for live, singleton births within marriage, 1996–8, England and Wales*

NS-SEC	All births		Low birthweight		Very low birthweight	
	n	Col. %	*n*	Row %	*n*	Row %
1	22,426	19.61	897	4.00	153	0.68
2	20,881	18.26	958	4.59	164	0.79
3	12,882	11.26	600	4.66	103	0.80
4	14,416	12.60	750	5.20	116	0.80
5	12,103	10.58	656	5.42	91	0.75
6	15,555	13.60	1,036	6.66	149	0.96
7	16,119	14.09	1,111	6.89	178	1.10
Totals	114,382	100	6,008	5.25	954	0.83

The broad range of this categorisation would tend to hide the increased risks that teenage mothers have for low-weight births. However, even this variable was strongly associated with both birthweight outcomes (LBW: OR 1.71, 95 per cent CI 1.61–1.99; VLBW: OR 1.51, 95 per cent CI 1.15–1.98).

RESULTS

The raw distributions of all births, low-weight and very low-weight births presented in Tables 9.2 and 9.3 show a much more even distribution across the classes of the NS-SEC compared with those of SC. This reflects the distributions found in surveys of working-age males and is not surprising. SC usually has a disproportionately low number of cases in Classes I and V. For example, SC Class V contains only 3.72 per cent of all births and of those 7.01 per cent are LBW. In contrast NS-SEC Class 7 has 14.09 per cent (nearly four times as many) of all births, of which 6.89 per cent are LBW. A similar situation is found when comparing SC Class I, which has 9.74 per cent of all births and 4.17 per cent LBW, with NS-SEC Class 1, which has 19.61 per cent of all births with 4.0 per cent LBW. Neither the NS-SEC nor the SC classes produce a regular pattern with VLBW.

Tables 9.4 and 9.5 present the odds ratios of LBW and VLBW for SC and NS-SEC classes, adjusted for the mother's age at the time of birth. The differences observed in Tables 9.2 and 9.3 are confirmed in the logistic regression analysis. Table 9.4 shows that the odds of a low-weight birth are 64 per cent higher in SC Class V compared with Class I. A similar difference in odds, 71 per cent, is observed in Table 9.5 between NS-SEC Classes 1 and 7. It is worth noting that this difference is generated between two NS-SEC classes with 33.7 per cent of all births, as opposed to 13.5 per cent in the relevant two classes of SC. The NS-SEC classes provide slightly more distinction in very low-weight births with Classes 6 and 7 being significantly higher than Class 1, whereas SC Class IV is the only one significantly higher than Class I.

Table 9.4 *Odds ratios and 95% confidence intervals of LBW and VLBW for classes of SC for live, singleton births within marriage, 1996–8, England and Wales (n = 114,382)*

SC	Low birthweight		Very low birthweight	
	OR*	95% CI	OR*	95% CI
I	ref.	–	ref.	–
II	1.04	0.94–1.16	0.90	0.70–1.15
IIInm	1.19	1.05–1.34	1.08	0.81–1.44
IIIm	1.37	1.23–1.52	1.14	0.90–1.46
IV	1.59	1.42–1.78	1.35	1.04–1.76
V	1.64	1.41–1.91	1.16	0.79–1.70
VI	1.07	0.86–1.34	1.13	0.68–1.86
χ^2 (df)	266.2 (7)		25.7 (7)	

* Adjusted for the age of the mother.

Table 9.5   *Odds ratios and 95% confidence intervals of LBW and VLBW for classes of the NS-SEC for live, singleton births within marriage, 1996–8, England and Wales (n = 114,382)*

NS-SEC	Low birthweight		Very low birthweight	
	OR*	95% CI	OR*	95% CI
1	ref.	–	ref.	–
2	1.14	1.04–1.25	1.14	0.91–1.43
3	1.15	1.03–1.28	1.16	0.90–1.49
4	1.29	1.17–1.43	1.16	0.91–1.48
5	1.34	1.21–1.49	1.08	0.83–1.41
6	1.64	1.50–1.80	1.37	1.09–1.72
7	1.71	1.56–1.87	1.58	1.27–1.97
χ^2 (df)	308.2 (7)		29.3 (7)	

* Adjusted for the age of the mother.

The lower tails of the birthweight distributions by SC and NS-SEC classes are shown in Figures 9.1 and 9.2. These reinforce the suggestion from the regression analyses that the differences in the probability of low-weight births across SC classes only become apparent for those birthweights from 1,500 to 2,499 g. Again, a similar pattern is observed for NS-SEC classes but in Figure 9.2 the seven classes tend to form four different distributions with Class 1 on its own, Classes 2 and 3 together, 4 and 5 together, and 6 and 7 together.

In order to add some depth to the pattern of low-weight births observed in both the SC and the NS-SEC classes, Table 9.6 presents the percentage of low-weight births for each cell of a cross-tabulation of SC by NS-SEC classes. Inspecting the rows of the table reveals the percentage of low-weight births in each category of NS-SEC broken down by the SC class they would have been in under the previous classification, and vice versa for the columns and classes of SC.

Overall, the figures show more consistency along the rows rather than down the columns, indicating that the NS-SEC categories select groups with a similar incidence of low-weight births regardless of their SC class. For example, NS-SEC Class 4 – self-employed non-professionals – has a similar incidence of about 5.2 per cent whether they were allocated to SC Classes II, IIInm, IIIm or IV. The row for NS-SEC Class 6 – semi-routine occupations – shows a similar result with all cells having an incidence of about 6.7 per cent regardless of SC allocation to Classes IIInm, IIIm or IV. Similar findings were reported in the previous chapter. However, the same is not observed in the columns of the SC classes. The classes of the NS-SEC appear to distinguish differential incidence rates of low-weight births within the SC class. For example, within SC Class IV the NS-SEC classes distinguish groups with different rates from 5 to 8 per cent. Some inconsistencies do also appear along the rows for NS-SEC Classes 2 and 7. Those in NS-SEC Class 2 that are also allocated to SC Class IIInm have a higher incidence than the category overall. In NS-SEC Class 7 those in SC Class IV have the highest incidence of all the cells, 8.13 per cent, but those from SC Class IIIm are considerably lower at 6.1 per cent.

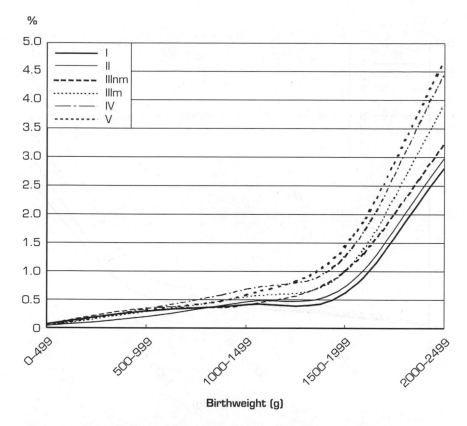

Figure 9.1 *Distribution of birthweights less than 2,500 g by classes of the SC for live, singleton births within marriage, 1996–8 England and Wales (n = 6,008)*

The armed forces who were allocated to a separate class in SC (VI) are now allocated to NS-SEC Classes 1 (officers) and 3 (other ranks). The incidence of low-weight births for these divisions of SC Class VI appears to match the other cases in the appropriate NS-SEC classes. This result is therefore rather different from that revealed by mortality analyses in the last chapter. It therefore reminds us of the need to think about how the armed forces are treated in different types of health analysis.

DISCUSSION

The results reported above confirm that the classes of the NS-SEC produce differential incidence rates of low-weight births. As expected, children born to fathers in semi-routine and routine occupations are at a significantly higher risk of being low-weight births than those born to fathers in both higher and lower professional and managerial occupations. Moreover, the NS-SEC produces monotonic differences in the prevalence of low-weight births across all classes.

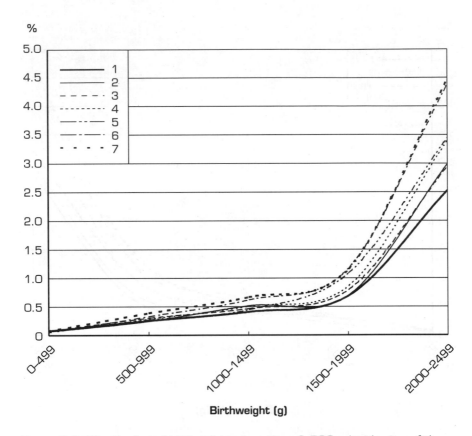

Figure 9.2 *Distribution of birthweights less than 2,500 g by classes of the NS-SEC for live, singleton births within marriage, 1996–8 England and Wales (n = 6,008)*

Table 9.6 *Percentages of low-weight births for combinations of SC and NS-SEC for live, singleton births within marriage, 1996–8, England and Wales (n = 114,382)*

NS-SEC	SC							Row %
	I	II	IIInm	IIIm	IV	V	VI	
1	4.20	3.82	–	–	–	–	[3.74]	4.00
2	[3.46]	4.56	5.26	*	–	–	–	4.59
3	–	[3.83]	4.51	5.34	[6.00]	–	4.83	4.66
4	–	5.12	5.56	5.21	5.21	[5.00]	–	5.21
5	–	*	*	5.52	5.02	*	–	5.42
6	–	[6.34]	6.74	6.72	6.62	[6.89]	–	6.66
7	–	*	*	6.11	8.13	7.40	–	6.89
Col. %	4.17	4.38	5.04	5.76	6.75	7.01	4.67	5.25

[] Less than 1,000 births.
* Less than 200 births.

These results thus add to the empirical evidence of the construct validity of the NS-SEC.

However, as the NS-SEC is a nominal classification that cannot be wholly ordered, the monotonic differences observed in this case cannot be expected for other outcomes. For example, the incidence of low-weight births for NS-SEC Class 4 – self-employed non-professionals – happened to be between the values for Classes 3 and 5. Compare the pattern of these results with those for adult mortality rates produced by Fitzpatrick in the previous chapter where the value for NS-SEC Class 4 is similar to that of Class 2 and lower than Class 3, thus producing a non-monotonic pattern across the classes.

Using registration data for these analyses had two important limitations. First, only the father's occupation was used to derive the NS-SEC and SC measures. As we saw in Chapter 1, this is a crude, and somewhat outdated, method of inferring a household level of social class. Second, no further information was available to investigate any of the hypothesised mechanisms linking social class with low-weight births. On the other hand, the use of registration data allowed the analyses to be based on a large random sample of all births thus improving the generalisability of and confidence in the results.

However, notwithstanding these limitations, the results presented in this chapter indicate that the classes of the NS-SEC do have differential rates of low-weight births, as did the former classification schema – the SC. What remains to be seen is how, with more detailed data, the more explicit conceptual basis of the NS-SEC can be used in furthering the explanations of how social class is linked to adverse birth outcomes as discussed in Chapter 2.

NOTES

1 These hypotheses are controversial. As Brunner and Marmot note:

> First, is it plausible that the organization of work, degree of social isolation, and sense of control over life, could affect the likelihood of developing and dying from chronic diseases . . .? The answer is an empathic 'yes'. The second issue is more complicated: do any of the plausible biological pathways actually operate . . .? The evidence on this is incomplete and is an important topic for current and future research, but it is sufficiently suggestive to point to hypotheses for testing. (1999: 17–18)

2 Research using the NS-SEC needs to be conducted to investigate its prospective relationship with similar outcomes.

3 The association between smoking during pregnancy and the NS-SEC needs to be demonstrated on appropriate data to test this hypothesised link.

REFERENCES

Barker, D.J.P. (1998) *Mothers, babies and health in later life*. Edinburgh: Churchill Livingstone.

Barker, D.J.P., Osmond, C., Winter, P.D., Margetts, B. and Simmonds, S.J. (1989) 'Weight in infancy and death from ischaemic heart disease', *Lancet*, 2: 577–80.

Bartley, M., Power, C., Blane, D., Davey Smith, G. and Shipley, M. (1994) 'Birth weight and later socioeconomic disadvantage: evidence from the 1958 British cohort study', *British Medical Journal*, 309: 1475–8.

Breslau, N. (1995) 'Psychiatric sequelae of low birthweight', *Epidemiologic Reviews*, 17: 96–106.

Brunner, E.J. (1997) 'Stress and the biology of inequality', *British Medical Journal*, 314: 1472–6.

Brunner, E.J., Davey Smith, G., Marmot, M.G., Canner, R., Beksinska, M. and O'Brien, J. (1996) 'Childhood social circumstances and psycholosocial and behavioural factors as determinants of plasma fibrinogen', *Lancet*, 347: 1008–13.

Brunner, E. and Marmot, M. (1999) 'Social organization, stress, and health', in M. Marmot and R.G. Wilkinson (eds) *Social Determinants of Health*. Oxford: Oxford University Press. pp. 17–43.

Cohen, S.E. (1995) 'Biosocial factors in early infancy as predictors of competence in adolescents who were born prematurely', *Journal of Developmental and Behavioral Pediatrics*, 16: 36–41.

Cohen, S.E., Beckwith, L., Parmalee, A.H., Sigman, M., Asarnow, R. and Espinosa, M.P. (1996) 'Prediction of low and normal school achievement in early adolescents born preterm', *Journal of Early Adolescence*, 16: 46–70.

Kramer, M.S., Seguin, L., Lydon, J. and Goulet, L. (2000) 'Socio-economic disparities in pregnancy outcome: why do the poor fare so poorly?', *Paediatric and Perinatal Epidemiology*, 14: 194–210.

Leon, D.A., Lithell, H.O., Vågerö, D., Koupilová, I., Mohsen, R., Berglund, L., Lithell, U.-B. and McKeigue, P.M. (1998) 'Reduced fetal growth and increased risk of death from ischaemic heart disease: cohort study of 15000 Swedish men and women born 1915–29', *British Medical Journal*, 317: 241–5.

Link, B. and Phelan, J. (1995) 'Social conditions as fundamental causes of disease', *Journal of Health and Social Behavior*, Extra Issue: 95–114.

Office of National Statistics (ONS) (1999) 'Report: infant and perinatal mortality by social and biological factors, 1998', *Health Statistics Quarterly*, 4 (Winter): 71–5.

Pevalin, D.J., Wade, T.J., Brannigan, A. and Sauve, R. (2001) 'Beyond biology: the social context of prenatal behaviour and birth outcomes', *Social and Preventive Medicine*, 46: 233–9.

Plunkett, J.W. and Meisels, S.J. (1989) 'Socioemotional adaptation of preterm infants at three years', *Infant Mental Health Journal*, 10: 117–31.

Rose, D. and O'Reilly, K. (1998) *The ESRC Review of Government Social Classifications*. London/Swindon: ONS/ESRC.

Rose, D. and Pevalin, D.J. (2000) 'Social class differences in mortality using the National Statistics Socio-economic Classification – too little, too soon: a reply to Chandola', *Social Science and Medicine*, 15: 1121–7.

Rutter, D.R. and Quine, L. (1990) 'Inequalities in pregnancy outcome – a review of psychosocial and behavioral mediators', *Social Science and Medicine*, 30: 553–68.

Speechley, K.N. and Avison, W.R. (1995) 'Admission to a neonatal intensive care unit as a predictor of long-term health', *Journal of Developmental and Behavioral Pediatrics*, 16: 397–405.

Spiker, D., Ferguson, J. and Brooks-Gunn, J. (1993) 'Enhancing maternal interactive behaviour and child social competence in low birth weight, premature infants', *Child Development*, 64: 754–68.

10
Gender, Health and Occupational Classifications in Working and Later Life

Helen Cooper and Sara Arber

INTRODUCTION

This chapter investigates how the NS-SEC discriminates the reported health of men and women at two stages of the lifecourse: working age (18–59 years) and older age (60 and above). First, a conceptual discussion relating to the measurement of occupational class for these two age groups is provided, highlighting gender differences in employment status and occupational position. A key issue, as we saw in Chapter 1, centres on the most appropriate way to classify working-age adults who have been actively seeking work for twelve months or more – the 'long-term unemployed'. The analysis examines how the method used to classify the long-term unemployed impacts on the nature of class inequalities in health found for working-age men and women. The analysis uses logistic regression models to provide a comparison of the NS-SEC with the two previous measures of occupational class, Socio-economic Groups (SEG) and the Social Class based on Occupation (SC), to model the relationship with health among working-age and, finally, among older men and women.

The analysis is based on the British General Household Survey (GHS), a large and nationally representative interview survey of all adults aged 16 and above. The analysis reported here uses combined data from the 1994/5 and the 1995/6 GHS: about 25,000 men and women aged 18–59 inclusive, and 9,500 men and women aged 60 and over. The GHS provides an annual sample of about 10,000 private households and had an overall response rate of approximately 80 per cent in 1994/5 and 1995/6 (Bennett et al., 1996; Rowlands et al., 1997).

Occupational class and the lifecourse

The lifecourse approach is increasingly adopted as a framework to assess social inequality in health, with longitudinal studies showing how the chances of good health in mid-life and later life are influenced by prior life experiences extending from early childhood (Wadsworth, 1991). Adult labour market position has been shown to be a key determinant of health, with social class gradients in self-assessed health and chronic illness (Arber, 1996; 1997; Drever and Whitehead, 1997). Occupation and patterns of employment during working life can determine not only an individual's exposure to health-related stressors, but also the individual's financial and material circumstances in later life, such as entitlement to an occupational pension (Ginn and Arber, 1999). Thus, occupational position during working life continues to be associated with health among older men and women, many years after individuals have left the labour market (Arber and Cooper, 1999).

Class inequalities in health may vary at different stages of the lifecourse because of cohort and generational differences in patterns of employment that reflect both historical and structural changes in society. Recent decades have witnessed the decline of traditional industries such as manufacturing and the expansion of service sector employment. Greater competition within the labour market and global economic forces have contributed to greater job insecurity, contractual or part-time employment, together with an expansion of further and higher education (ONS, 1999).

These age-related differences in the nature of employment cannot, however, be divorced from gender. Within an historical or social context, gender has a fundamental role in determining what is appropriate behaviour (Arber and Cooper, 2000). Profound changes in gender roles since the mid-1970s mean that the labour market profiles of men and women differ markedly both within and between age cohorts.

The rising employment participation of women (especially of married women) over the last two decades means that, by the mid-1990s, more working-age women than ever before were in paid work (ONS, 1998). This compares with the current generation of older women, the majority of whom either did not work or left employment upon marriage or the birth of their first child (Dex, 1984). Employment patterns among men differ markedly from women of the same age. Most older men were economically active throughout their working lives during a prolonged period of full employment following the Second World War. Today, a higher proportion of men in working-age groups are not in paid employment. In part, this reflects greater unemployment, particularly in industries such as manufacturing which were once the mainstay of male employment. It relates also to the longer time spent in education and the earlier labour market exit of men who increasingly retire in their fifties and early sixties. As we saw in Chapter 1, any social classification based on occupation needs to consider how to classify men and women not currently in paid employment. This is a more central issue when measuring class for women and among older age groups.

The employment status of working-age and older adults in the 1994–6 GHS[1] is shown in Table 10.1 for men and women. At both lifecourse stages, the percentage employed was greater for men than for women. At age 18–59, 83 per cent of men were in paid employment compared with 69 per cent of women. There are differences between the sexes in the hours worked: around one-third of working-age women were employed part time compared with only 5 per cent of men. Working-age women who were non-employed were most likely to be looking after the home or family (21 per cent), with only 1 per cent

Table 10.1 *Employment status of men and women aged 18–59 and 60+* *(rounded percentage values)*

	Age 18–59		Age 60+	
Current employment status	Men	Women	Men	Women
Employed	83	69	18	8
Part time (30 h/wk or less)	5	31	6	6
Full time (31 h/wk or more)	77	38	12	2
Not employed	17	31	82	92
Short-term unemployed (<12 mths)	5	2	<1	0
Long-term unemployed (12+ mths)	4	2	1	<1
Retired	1	2	74	64
Looking after home or family	1	21	1	26
Other inactive (includes disabled, temp. sick and students)	7	5	6	1
Col. %	100	100	100	100
N =	11,932	12,583	4,109	5,378

of working-age men in this employment category. The percentage of working-age men who were unemployed was approximately double that of women. This finding applied to short-term unemployment, defined as less than twelve months' duration, and long-term unemployment of twelve months or more. At age 18–59, there was less gender difference in the percentages who were economically inactive for other reasons, a group that represents adults who reported temporary sickness, disability or being in full-time education.

The gender difference in statutory retirement age is likely to contribute to the greater proportion of men than women over 60 who were in paid employment: 18 per cent and 8 per cent respectively. Among older workers, men continued to predominate in full-time work (12 per cent), with women more likely to be employed part time. As expected, the proportion of older adults who were classified as unemployed was negligible.

These age differences in employment status for men and women raise three issues about the assumed influence of social class on health at working and older ages:

1 Class-based influences on health are likely to be more marked for adults with a profile of consistent employment than for those with a more intermittent employment history. Since men typically have a more consistent employment profile than women, this may partly account for the finding of stronger class gradients in men's than women's health (Macintyre and Hunt, 1997; Stronks et al., 1995). However, despite a high level of employment during working life among the current generation of older men, class inequalities may be less pronounced at this stage of the lifecourse than for working-age groups because of time spent since leaving the labour market. For older women, there is the added difficulty of

representing those who never had a paid job or who may have left the labour market on marriage or first child-birth many years earlier.

2   To interpret the relationships between class and health, it is important to consider the conceptual basis of the class schema used, since this may also influence the magnitude of class differences found for men and women at different stages of the lifecourse. Established socio-economic measures such as SEG, and particularly SC, have been heavily criticised for their reliance on a 'male' occupational structure that cannot adequately capture gender segregation in the labour market. NS-SEC differs from both SEG and SC in considering women's occupations in much more detail and in being explicitly founded on the concept of employment relations (see Chapter 2 and Rose and O'Reilly, 1997) which can be used to generate hypotheses about the links between class and health. The NS-SEC, which encompasses aspects of the work and labour contract, is argued to be a better indicator of the labour market today than the skill or social status associated with occupations which formed the basis of SC, but may be a poorer representation of the labour market experienced by the current generation of older people.

3   Because the labour market is dynamic, changes in employment and working conditions that differentially affect men and women may give rise to new patterns of class inequality in health (Annandale and Hunt, 2000). Gender segregation in the labour market remains pervasive; women are concentrated in part-time work often in the 'secondary' sector and are more likely than men to experience low pay, job insecurity and poor working conditions (Equal Opportunities Commission, 2001). Women's employment is likely to differ from that of men in those dimensions of work closely related to the concept of employment relations underlying the NS-SEC, namely economic security, income and the work situation. However, women in the labour market cannot be characterised as uniformly disadvantaged; increasing numbers of women employed full time occupy 'advantaged' positions and a recent study shows that educational level, marital status and number of children are associated with marked socio-economic differences among women across the lifecourse (Rake, 2000).

The gendered distribution of working-age and older adults in the NS-SEC, based on their current occupation, and for those not in employment, based on their last main occupation, is shown in Table 10.2. It is important to note that all women are classified on the basis of their *own* occupational class, not that of their husbands or head of household. The extent to which the NS-SEC would yield different results using the 'conventional' approach of allocating women's class position discussed in Chapter 1 is a separate issue and one which is not considered in this analysis.

For both sexes, the NS-SEC has been collapsed into nine analytic classes where Class 1 is divided into Classes 1.1 and 1.2 and the long-term unemployed are combined with the never worked in Class 8 (the operational definitions of 'long-term unemployment' and 'never worked' are discussed in the next section).

Table 10.2 shows that, in the working-age group (18–59), women in the GHS were under-represented in NS-SEC Classes 1.1 and 1.2 relative to men. Only 4.4 per cent of all working-age women were classified in these higher professional or managerial occupations compared with 14.6 per cent of working-age men. Rather, women in this age group were concentrated in intermediate occupations or NS-SEC Class 3 (21.9 per cent) – a class that includes most clerical and some service sector employment – and which accounted for just 6.9 per cent of men. Men aged 18–59 were over twice as likely as women to be self-employed (NS-SEC Class 4) whilst a higher percentage of working-age women than men were currently or previously employed in semi-routine or routine occupations (NS-SEC Classes 6 and 7).

As expected, gender differences in the socio-economic profile of older adults were more marked than for the working-age group (Table 10.2). Only approximately 1 per cent of women aged 60+ were in NS-SEC Classes 1.1 and 1.2 compared with 12.4 per cent of older men. Older women were more likely than older men to be classified as in the semi-routine (NS-SEC Class 6) or routine (NS-SEC Class 7) classes and women in this age group also predominated in intermediate occupations (NS-SEC Class 3). Comparing the class profiles of older women with those currently of working-age suggests some degree of movement into professional and managerial occupations by working-age women, but the observed differences between men and women are consistent

Table 10.2 *NS-SEC classes by age and gender*

NS-SEC		Age 18–59		Age 60+	
		Men	Women	Men	Women
1.1	Large employers and higher managerial occupations	5.8	1.9	5.1	0.5
1.2	Higher professional occupations	8.8	2.5	7.3	0.7
2	Lower managerial/professional occupations	19.6	20.9	18.4	15.0
3	Intermediate occupations	6.9	21.9	5.6	20.1
4	Small employers and own account workers	13.4	5.3	10.7	5.7
5	Lower supervisory and technical occupations	14.2	5.2	19.9	6.9
6	Semi-routine occupations	11.8	22.0	14.1	23.7
7	Routine occupations	14.3	15.7	17.7	22.5
8	Never worked and long-term unemployed	5.4	4.6	1.2	5.0
	8.1 Long-term unemployed (12+ months)	4.8	2.1	1.1	0.1
	8.2 Never worked*	0.6	2.5	0.1	4.9
%		100	100	100	100
N =		11,914	12,568	4,106	5,369
N Full-time students		468	538	2	5
N Unclassified		722	698	21	26

* Defined as all adults who report never having had a paid job. Excludes full-time students.

with substantial gender segregation in the labour market at both lifecourse stages.

THE NEVER EMPLOYED AND LONG-TERM UNEMPLOYED

A relevant issue when investigating class inequalities in health concerns adults who have never worked, as well as the growing number of adults who are not in the labour market and so are excluded from current employment relations (Arber, 1997). Whilst a common approach is to categorise the 'non-employed' according to their last main job (as in Table 10.2), this is clearly not possible for those who have never been in paid employment.

As we saw in Chapter 1, 'never employed' is a complex category when considering health outcomes because of the likelihood that ill-health or disability is the cause, rather than the outcome, of never employment. To limit this possibility of 'reverse causation' between 'never employed' and poor health, it is recommended that health analysts define the never employed as all those who 'have never been in paid employment, but are available for paid work' (ONS, 2001). This definition increases the likelihood that the never employed category excludes the long-term sick or 'unable to work' but incorporates adults who, like the long-term unemployed, are excluded from current employment relations.

For the purposes of this analysis, however, 'never employed' includes all adults (excluding students) in the GHS who reported that they had never had a paid job. The wider definition of 'never employed' used in Table 10.2 shows that the likelihood of never having had a paid job is related to both age and gender. Using this wider definition, the never employed constitute only a small proportion of all working-age adults, but more women (2.5 per cent) than men (0.6 per cent). The same gender difference is evident for older adults but is of greater magnitude: only 0.1 per cent of men aged 60 and over report never having had a paid job, whereas the percentage of older women in this category is approximately double that of working-age women at 5 per cent. It would not be meaningful to use the narrower definition of 'never employed' for these older age groups.

The way in which 'never employed' is defined therefore has a significant bearing on the composition and meaning of this category for men's and women's health across the lifecourse. Adopting the narrower NS-SEC definition of 'never employed', which omits all those not available for paid work, would leave only a small number of working-age adults defined as such and this would not be a meaningful categorisation for older adults, particularly women. We therefore adopt a more inclusive definition: 'adults who report never having had a paid job and who are not in full-time education'. It is therefore important to remember how this differs from the NS-SEC definition of 'never employed', particularly when interpreting the relationship between a never employed status and health (see the 'health warning' in Chapter 1).

There are two alternative approaches to classifying the long-term unemployed using the NS-SEC. The first is to use the individual's last main occupation as an indicator of class position, and the second approach recommended to NS-SEC users is to combine the long-term unemployed with the never worked (but available for work). Although the latter is justified on the grounds that the NS-SEC will lack discriminatory power for long-term unemployed adults excluded from employment relations (Goldthorpe, 1997), user definitions of 'long-term unemployment' can vary from six months (the period for which Jobseekers Allowance is paid) to a year or more. The twelve-month rule has been used in Table 10.2, which reports the percentage of men and women in each age group who are long-term unemployed. As expected, long-term unemployment is largely confined to adults of working age and was more common for men (4.8 per cent) than for women (2.1 per cent).

Age and gender differences in the likelihood of being never employed or long-term unemployed are important because it is recommended that users of the NS-SEC combine these two groups into a single 'never worked and long-term unemployed' category for analysis (represented as NS-SEC Class 8 in Table 10.2). Using our definition of never worked (all who have never had a paid job), and long-term unemployment (twelve months or more), it can be clearly seen from Table 10.2 that the composition of this class is gendered for adults of working age: among men it is primarily composed of long-term unemployed while for women the majority are never employed. The next section focuses on this issue and discusses how the method used to classify the long-term unemployed has implications for studies of health inequality.

LONG-TERM UNEMPLOYMENT AND CLASS INEQUALITY IN HEALTH USING THE NS-SEC

The analysis presented in this section focuses on working-age adults who constitute the majority of the long-term unemployed. It considers how the method used to classify the long-term unemployed influences the magnitude of class inequalities in reported health using the NS-SEC.

The gendered composition of the 'long-term unemployed and never worked' in NS-SEC Class 8 (see Table 10.2) suggests that the health of men in this group will be associated in large part with morbidity reported by those long-term unemployed for twelve months or more. By contrast, the health of women in this group will primarily reflect the health of the never employed who predominate in this category. The reasons for never having had a paid job are gendered in ways that are likely to impact upon the reported health of men and women; research suggests that ill-health-related selection can largely account for the small number of working-age men who report never having had a paid job (Arber, 1997) whilst never employment among women of working age primarily relates to early child-bearing and childcare commitments. Owing to the way in which we have defined never employment in our analysis, there is a need to be cautious about inferring any causal relationship with health for men and women.

Separating the long-term unemployed in class analyses of health also poses the potential problem of reverse causation: that is, it is impossible to ascertain using cross-sectional data such as the GHS whether poor health outcomes precede or are preceded by the experience of long-term unemployment. In the GHS, the employment status variable codes adults as 'permanently unable to work' (a group that is likely to encompass largely those with disability) separately from those seeking paid employment or waiting to take up paid work. Adults classified as 'permanently unable to work', but who have previously been employed, are therefore classified in the NS-SEC according to their last main job.

The chances of being long-term unemployed are not evenly distributed across the NS-SEC classes. Figure 10.1 shows a clear relationship between long-term unemployment of twelve months or more and NS-SEC class position based on last main occupation. For men, 9.3 per cent who were classified in routine occupations (NS-SEC Class 7) were long-term unemployed compared with 7.4 per cent classified in semi-routine occupations (NS-SEC Class 6), 4 per cent in NS-SEC Class 5 or NS-SEC Class 4 and only 2.5 per cent of men in NS-SEC Classes 1.1 and 1.2 reported actively looking for work for twelve months or more. The relationship between class and long-term unemployment was also evident but weaker for women by comparison, which partly reflects the smaller proportion of working-age women who were categorised as long-term unemployed.

The finding that long-term unemployment is most common among the lower socio-economic classes, particularly for men, may have implications for the magnitude of social class gradients found in health. In the GHS, the proportion of long-term unemployed who reported having a limiting longstanding illness (LLI) was relatively low at 31 per cent of men and 28 per cent of women aged 18–59 and this may reflect the way in which employment status is coded in this survey. However, to the extent that there is high morbidity among long-term unemployed included in the NS-SEC, this may serve to amplify the health disadvantage of lower socio-economic classes because the likelihood of being

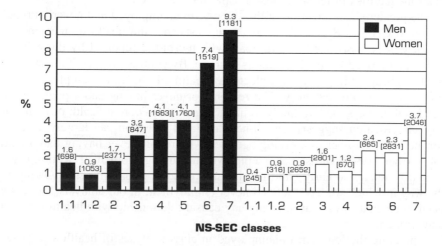

Figure 10.1 *Percentage of long-term unemployed within each NS-SEC class: men and women aged 18–59 (base numbers in square brackets)*

long-term unemployed is linked to class of previous occupation. Based on the proportion of the long-term unemployed in each NS-SEC class (see Figure 10.1), one might expect that combining the long-term unemployed with the never worked would result in weaker class gradients in health, particularly for men, than when the long-term unemployed are classified into classes according to their last occupation. However, using the GHS, class differences in LLI among long-term unemployed men and women differed little from the percentage distribution of long-term unemployment within each NS-SEC class (analyses not shown).

To consider this issue in more detail, the analysis now compares the nature of class inequalities in self-reported health for working-age men and women. Two measures of morbidity in the GHS are contrasted:

1   *Chronic illness* is based on whether individuals report any LLI. Respondents are asked 'Have you any longstanding illness, disability or infirmity? (By longstanding I mean anything that has troubled you over a period of time or is likely to affect you over a period of time.)' If the answer is 'yes', the respondent is asked 'Does this illness limit your activities in any way?' Those who reply 'yes' are categorised as having an LLI.
2   *Self-assessed health* is based on the question 'Over the last twelve months, would you say your health has on the whole been good, fairly good or not good?' For these analyses, morbidity is based on reports of 'less than good' (responses of 'fairly good' and 'not good' combined). This general health measure has been associated with mortality (Idler and Benyamini, 1997; Mossey and Shapiro, 1982).

Using these two health outcomes, logistic regression models are presented for working-age men and women, first when the long-term unemployed are classified with the never worked in NS-SEC Class 8 (Table 10.3), and, second, when the long-term unemployed are classified by their last main job (Table 10.4). All logistic models control for age in five-year age groups. Intermediate occupations (NS-SEC Class 3) were selected as the reference category for these analyses because this class was both large enough to provide reliable estimates of odds ratios for men and women of working age and is near the middle of the class distribution. To reiterate, these class analyses for women are based on their own occupation.

Table 10.3 presents the odds ratios of self-assessed health and LLI for men and women when the long-term unemployed were combined with the never worked into a separate NS-SEC class. The results show a consistent class gradient in self-assessed health and LLI for men, with those in higher managerial and professional occupations (Classes 1.1 and 1.2) having significantly better health than the reference category of intermediate occupations (Class 3). Self-employed men in Class 4 (small employers and own account workers) or Class 5 (lower supervisory and technical occupations) did not have significantly higher odds of poor health than the reference category. The poorest health was found for men classified in routine occupations (Class 7), particularly using the health measure of LLI.

Table 10.3 *Logistic regression odds ratios of NS-SEC inequalities in health for men and women aged 18–59: separating the long-term unemployed and never worked*

	General health 'less than good'		Limiting longstanding illness (LLI)	
NS-SEC	Men	Women	Men	Women
1 Higher managerial and professional occupations				
1.1 Large employers and higher managerial occupations	0.53***	0.62**	0.55***	0.45**
1.2 Higher professional occupations	0.57***	0.66*	0.56***	0.94
2 Lower managerial/professional occupations	0.72***	0.83	0.72**	0.98
3 Intermediate occupations	1.00	1.00	1.00	1.00
4 Small employers and own account workers	0.95	0.96	0.94	0.95
5 Lower supervisory and technical occupations	1.16	1.59***	1.24	1.69***
6 Semi-routine occupations	1.39***	1.30**	1.26	1.22***
7 Routine occupations	1.66***	1.68***	1.72***	1.59***
8 Never worked and long-term unemployed	2.09***	2.51***	2.94***	3.12***
8.1 Long-term unemployed	2.07***	2.33***	2.43***	2.44***
8.2 Never worked	2.32***	2.71***	11.92***	3.79***
$N =$	10,481	12,025	11,892	12,555

Reference category: intermediate occupations.
* $p < 0.05$. ** $p < 0.01$. *** $p < 0.001$.

Unlike for men, the odds of reported morbidity for women in lower managerial or professional occupations (Class 2) and intermediate occupations (Class 3) were not significantly different on either health measure, and the odds ratio of reported LLI was only significantly lower for women in Class 1.1 compared with Class 3. The odds ratio of morbidity for women in lower supervisory and technical occupations (Class 5) was notably higher than for men, particularly for self-assessed health. Whilst these differences meant that class inequalities in reported morbidity were slightly weaker and less consistent for women than for men, for both sexes the odds ratios of morbidity were greatest for the long-term unemployed and never worked in Class 8. The odds ratio was increased at least twofold for self-assessed health and the odds of LLI were approximately three times higher than the reference category for women and men.

To highlight differences in the health of men and women who were long-term unemployed or never employed, the odds ratios of reported morbidity are also shown separately for these groups in Table 10.3. On both health measures, the odds were significantly increased for never employed men and women (Class 8.1) relative to the reference category of intermediate employees, reaching nearly twelve times higher for LLI reported by men. The odds ratios of morbidity were more than two times higher for men and women who were long-term unemployed (Class 8.2), supporting the assertion made earlier that the long-term unemployed have high reported morbidity. For both sexes, the odds ratios showed higher morbidity among the never worked than for the long-term unemployed, although it must be remembered that the definition of 'never worked' used here will include some adults who are unavailable for work. Both of these groups in Class 8 had poorer health than adults in routine occupations (Class 7).

Table 10.4 examines class inequalities in reported health when the long-term unemployed are classified by their last main job. This has been the practice in the past when analysing class inequalities in health using SC. For both sexes, the odds ratios of poor self-assessed health are broadly comparable with Table 10.3. Including the long-term unemployed in the NS-SEC therefore made little difference to the class patterning of health, although the odds ratios were slightly higher for men and women in occupational groups below the reference category of intermediate occupations (Class 3), indicating slightly stronger class inequalities in health.

An exception is found with using a measure of LLI where the results suggest a slight weakening of class differences in health for men, but not for women, when the long-term unemployed are classified by their last main job. The odds ratios of LLI in Table 10.4 for working-age men classified in semi-routine and routine occupations are lower than for these classes in Table 10.3. However, including long-term unemployed men in the classes slightly lowers the odds

Table 10.4   *Logistic regression odds ratios of NS-SEC inequalities in health for men and women aged 18–59: classifying the long-term unemployed by last main occupation*

	Self-assessed health 'less than good'		Limiting longstanding illness (LLI)	
NS-SEC	Men	Women	Men	Women
1 Higher managerial and professional occupations				
1.1 Large employers and higher managerial occupations	0.55***	0.63**	0.53***	0.44**
1.2 Higher professional occupations	0.58***	0.69*	0.53***	0.98
2 Lower managerial/professional occupations	0.74**	0.86*	0.67**	0.99
3 Intermediate occupations	1.00	1.00	1.00	1.00
4 Small employers and own account workers	1.06	1.04	0.90	0.97
5 Lower supervisory and technical occupations	1.20	1.67***	1.18	1.71***
6 Semi-routine occupations	1.43***	1.36***	1.16	1.25**
7 Routine occupations	1.69***	1.75***	1.60***	1.62***
8 Never worked	2.36***	2.77***	10.85***	3.76***
N =	10,481	12,025	11,892	12,555

Reference category: intermediate occupations.
* $p < 0.05$. ** $p < 0.01$. *** $p < 0.001$.

ratios of reported LLI for men in higher professional or managerial occupations (Classes 1.1 and 1.2). Thus, including the long-term unemployed accentuates the health 'advantage' of men in higher class positions but does little to alter the morbidity reported by lower occupational classes. This is a surprising finding given the percentage distribution of long-term unemployed men within the classes (see Figure 10.1) and may reflect poor health among long-term unemployed men in the reference category of intermediate occupations. The overall pattern of class differences in LLI changes little for working-age women irrespective of the method used to classify the long-term unemployed, with only a slight increase in the odds ratios among lower occupational groups when the long-term unemployed are included in each socio-economic class.

To summarise, the nine-class version of the NS-SEC used here generally shows somewhat weaker class gradients in health for working-age men and women than when the long-term unemployed are classified by their last main job.

A COMPARISON OF THE NS-SEC WITH OTHER SOCIO-ECONOMIC MEASURES FOR WORKING-AGE ADULTS

In this section, we examine how class differences in self-reported health using the NS-SEC differ from those found using established measures of SEG and SC in the GHS among working-age men and women. Differences between these three socio-economic measures are to be expected because the NS-SEC differs in its conceptual basis and operational categories from SEG and SC which utilise information about job skill and social status rather than employment relations. As such, each class measure is likely to be suggestive of different causal mechanisms linking occupation to self-reported health. It is further argued that changes in the nature and structure of British industry mean that distinctions between non-manual and manual occupations made using SEG and SC, for example, are increasingly outmoded and misleading (ONS, 2001).

The purpose of comparing these socio-economic measures is therefore to assess the extent to which the concept of employment relations underlying the derivation of the NS-SEC is associated with a different pattern of class inequality in health than that exhibited by SEG or SC. The analysis reported here focuses on adults of working age and is then repeated in the next section for older men and women (age 60+). For clarity, only the results for self-assessed health are reported. In Figures 10.2 and 10.3, a collapsed version of SEG is used alongside NS-SEC for working-age men and women respectively. (The occupational groups included in this eight-category collapsed SEG are given in the Appendix of this chapter.) To facilitate comparison, the long-term unemployed are classified by their last main job in all three class measures.

It must be stressed that SEG and SC are *not* directly comparable with the NS-SEC. In the NS-SEC, intermediate occupations (Class 3) refer to those jobs which do not involve any general planning or supervision (e.g. in sales, service, clerical or engineering occupations) and are 'mixed' in terms of employment regulation. There is no direct match between intermediate occupations in NS-SEC and the 'intermediate and junior non-manual' class of SEG which is based

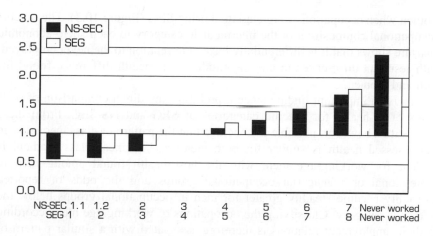

Figure 10.2 *Odds ratios of 'less than good' health for working-age men: comparing NS-SEC and SEG*

primarily on levels of job skill. The intermediate class in SEG includes some occupations that are 'redefined' in NS-SEC as professional or semi-routine according to the criteria of employment relations.

The differing composition of the reference category (intermediate occupations) in NS-SEC and SEG is highlighted in Figures 10.2 and 10.3 by the odds ratios of poor self-assessed health for the never employed (Class 8) using these two class measures. Whilst the composition of Class 8 remains constant in SEG and NS-SEC, the apparent health disadvantage of never employed men and women differs in magnitude according to whether NS-SEC or SEG is used. For men, the odds ratios of poor health were greatest for the never employed when NS-SEC was used (Figure 10.2), but morbidity was highest for never employed

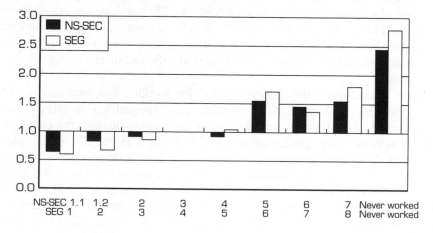

Figure 10.3 *Odds ratios of 'less than good' health for working-age women: comparing NS-SEC and SEG*

women when occupations were classified using SEG (Figure 10.3). The diverse occupational composition of the intermediate category in each socio-economic measure shows that it is differentially located in relation to the never employed, with resultant differences in the magnitude of the health difference found for men and women.

This is an important finding since it prohibits any direct comparison of odds ratios of ill-health for specific categories of SEG and NS-SEC. From these figures it is, however, possible to conclude that the pattern of class inequality in self-assessed health is similar for both measures. A linear class gradient is evident for working-age men, with the best health found among men in professional or managerial occupational groups and the odds of reported morbidity become steadily greater for men in occupational groups below the reference category. Classifying the occupations of working-age men according to their employment relations is therefore associated with a similar pattern of health inequality to SEG based primarily on levels of job skill. However, we should recall from Chapter 1 that SEG was much closer than SC to a truly sociological measure of class.

Figure 10.3 presents the same analysis for working-age women. On both socio-economic measures, class differences in self-assessed health were not as linear as for men owing to the high morbidity of women who were classified as skilled manual or as lower supervisory and technical occupations in NS-SEC (Class 5). Despite the differing composition of this occupational group and the reference category for NS-SEC and SEG, the results therefore show a similar pattern of class inequality in women's health.

These findings for working-age men and women typically show a linear relationship between class and health despite using very different classifications based on job skill or employment relations. The lack of continuity between NS-SEC and SEG in this analysis means that it is potentially misleading to make direct health comparisons.

For this reason, the change in log-likelihood ratio (LLR) is used for the purpose of comparing the efficacy of NS-SEC, SEG and SC for self-assessed health and LLI. Unaffected by the differential composition of the occupational categories in these classifications, this statistic reflects the variance in reported health accounted for by NS-SEC, SEG and SC after adjusting for age in five-year groups.

Table 10.5a shows the change in LLR for working-age men and women using NS-SEC, SEG and SC to examine class inequalities in self-assessed health and LLI. After adjusting for age in the logistic models, the change in LLR was consistently greater using NS-SEC than for either of the other class measures. This finding applied to both sexes and health measures and the efficacy of NS-SEC was particularly evident for women's self-assessed health and LLI reported by men. This finding suggests that the new NS-SEC classes are the most sensitive overall discriminator of health in this age group and that it performs well for both sexes. For men, SEG could account for more of the variance in self-assessed health and LLI than SC, but using SEG had little or no 'advantage' over SC for women's LLI and general health.

Table 10.5 *Comparison of change in log-likelihood ratios of ill-health, with addition of three different socio-economic measures* *

Socio-economic measures (change in df)	Self-assessed health 'less than good'		Limiting longstanding illness (LLI)	
	Men	Women	Men	Women
(a) Working-age adults (18–59)				
NS-SEC – classifying long-term unemployed by last main job, plus never worked (8)	**271.1**	**248.6**	**280.5**	**166.8**
SEG, plus never worked (8)	248.2	207.6	241.1	138.0
SC, plus never worked (6)	237.5	213.9	227.4	137.8
(b) Older adults (60+)				
NS-SEC – classifying the long-term unemployed by last main job, plus never worked (8)	**130.3**	99.3	**67.1**	**45.5**
SEG, plus never worked (8)	117.2	**129.6**	62.1	44.6
SC, plus never worked (8)	103.7	89.0	65.6	39.2

* All logistic models adjusted for age in five-year groups.

A COMPARISON OF THE NS-SEC WITH OTHER SOCIO-ECONOMIC MEASURES FOR OLDER ADULTS

Adults over the age of retirement are often omitted from studies of class inequalities in health. However, greater longevity means that a growing proportion of the UK population are in older age groups and, coupled with early retirement, more time than ever before is spent outside the labour market. It is important that class inequality in health is not neglected at this stage of the lifecourse and that these analyses take into account the different employment histories of older men and women. Studies focused on the older population show clearly that occupational position during working life continues to structure the chances of good health in old age, but in ways that may differ for men and women (Arber and Cooper, 1999).

Table 10.1 showed that the vast majority of older adults aged 60+, particularly women, are no longer in paid employment. Occupational class for these adults is therefore based on their last main occupation which, in some instances, may have been many years earlier. Changes over time in the structure of the labour market and working conditions mean that the experience of paid employment for the current generation of older adults was likely to differ greatly from that of working-age groups, particularly for women whose employment patterns have undergone substantial change over recent decades.

This section examines the extent of health inequality among men and women aged 60+ according to the occupational classification used. Of particular concern is to assess the extent to which the NS-SEC, which was designed primarily to reflect the occupational structure of the current labour market, can capture class inequality in older people's health. Odds ratios of reported health for the new occupational classification are presented alongside those for SEG.

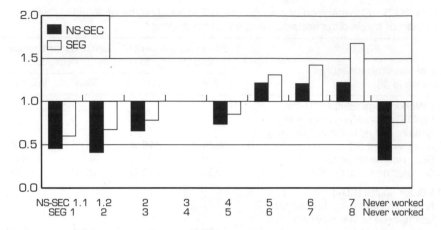

Figure 10.4 *Odds ratios of 'less than good' health for older men: comparing NS-SEC and SEG*

The ability of both socio-economic measures to discriminate older people's health is likely to depend on their capacity to represent labour market conditions and occupation-based influences on health that may extend from many years earlier. For clarity, the results shown here are based on self-assessed general health only.

The odds ratios of self-assessed health are shown in Figure 10.4 and Figure 10.5 using NS-SEC and SEG for older men and women respectively. A gradient in self-reported health was found using both measures of social class to represent older men, with the best health associated with more 'advantaged' occupational groups in the NS-SEC and SEG. However, in contrast to men of

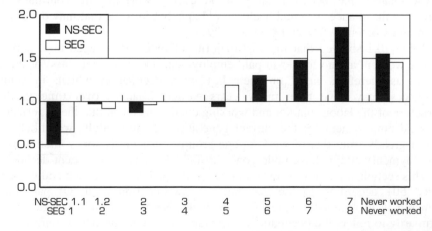

Figure 10.5 *Odds ratios of 'less than good' health for older women: comparing NS-SEC and SEG*

working age, Figure 10.4 shows better health among older men classified in self-employed occupational groups on SEG and NS-SEC (Class 4).

As discussed earlier for working-age adults, the odds ratio of morbidity for the never employed can reveal important compositional differences between NS-SEC and SEG. For the small proportion of never employed men aged 60+, the odds of poor self-assessed health are lower than for the reference category. However, this difference was of much greater magnitude using the NS-SEC (OR 0.3) than for SEG (OR 0.7) and this must arise from the different occupations included in the 'intermediate' reference category. By comparison, the poor reported health of never employed older women varies less according to the socio-economic classification used; the odds ratio is only slightly higher using the NS-SEC (Figure 10.5). In interpreting the gender difference in the reported health of never employed older men and women, it is important to consider gendered reasons for never employment, the relative proportion of men and women in this category, and to acknowledge the possibility of reverse causation.

Figure 10.5 presents the same results for older women. Despite difficulties associated with measuring class for older women, class variation in their self-assessed health is clearly evident from this figure. Older women who were currently or previously employed in unskilled manual occupations (SEG 8) or routine occupations (NS-SEC Class 7) had odds of poor health substantially higher than the reference category, whilst the best reported health was for those in professional or managerial occupations. However, the overall relationship between class and health for older women was less consistent than for older men and, in contrast to working-age women, there was no evidence that older women in the skilled manual occupations (SEG 6) or the lower supervisory/technical occupations (NS-SEC Class 5) had high reported morbidity comparable with women in unskilled manual occupations (SEG 8) or routine occupations (NS-SEC Class 7).

A difference between the two class measures is suggested for older self-employed women. When 'own account' workers were classified according to employment relations using the NS-SEC, their health was broadly comparable with the reference category of intermediate employees. However, when determined by job skill using SEG, the odds ratio of poor health was notably higher for self-employed older women relative to the reference category.

Table 10.5b shows the change in LLR for older men and women using NS-SEC, SEG and SC to examine class inequalities in self-assessed health and LLI. After adjusting for age, the change in LLR for older men's health was greater using NS-SEC than for either SEG or SC. However, the difference between these three class measures was greatest using a measure of self-assessed health and only marginal for LLI reported by older men. According to the change in LLR, NS-SEC had less explanatory power than SEG for older women's self-assessed health, although it could account for more of the variance in health than SC. There was little difference in the efficacy of NS-SEC, SEG and SC for LLI among older women.

In contrast to working-age adults where the NS-SEC clearly emerged as the best predictor of health for men and women, these results show that, for older people, the NS-SEC has a consistent advantage over other socio-economic measures for older men but not for older women. That the NS-SEC appears to be less relevant to understanding class inequality in the health of older people – especially older women – is not surprising because the concept of employment relations and working conditions underlying the NS-SEC is based on current labour market structure. The NS-SEC is therefore likely to be less applicable to the employment experienced by older people many years earlier, which instead may be particularly well suited to a concept of class based on skill (SEG). Of course, these results might be different were we to use a household measure of class.

DISCUSSION

The analysis presented in this chapter used GHS data to examine the relationship between occupational social class and reported health using the NS-SEC. Rather than base our results on the general adult population, we advocated a lifecourse approach which distinguishes between adults of working age (18–59 years) and older age (60 years and over). From this perspective, it was argued that generational and cohort differences in labour market structure, employment participation and non-employment between these two age groups have important implications for the relationships found between occupational position (based on current or last main job) and health.

Analysis of the GHS clearly showed that age-related differences in employment and occupational position could not be divorced from gender. At both lifecourse stages, men were more likely than women to be in paid employment and to work full-time hours, whilst at working age, a greater proportion of women were looking after home or family. Men and women were differentially distributed within the classes of the NS-SEC, particularly at older ages, highlighting occupational gender segregation and likely differences between the sexes in current employment relations and working conditions underlying this socio-economic classification.

A key issue concerns the classification of non-employed groups currently outside the paid labour market who are excluded from current employment relations. The analysis focused on two such groups: the long-term unemployed of twelve months or more, and the never employed, who were defined in this analysis as all adults who reported never having had a paid job (excluding full-time students). The likelihood of being long-term unemployed or never having had a paid job was associated with age and gender; long-term unemployment was concentrated among working-age adults, notably men, whilst never employment was greatest for older adults and women in particular.

One aim of the analysis was to examine how the method used to classify long-term unemployed adults of working age influenced the magnitude of social class inequality in reported health. The option recommended to users of the NS-SEC is to classify the long-term unemployed in a separate class with the never employed, but our findings showed clear gender differences in the composition of this class: men were most likely to be long-term unemployed and women dominated in the never worked group. Morbidity reported by adults in Class 8 will therefore primarily reflect the health of long-term unemployed men and never employed women. Added to this is the difficulty of interpreting a causal relationship between health, long-term unemployment and 'never employed', given both the high morbidity found among these non-employed groups and the links between long-term unemployment and class of previous occupation. As discussed earlier, our operational definition of 'never employed' will increase the likelihood of including adults who are 'unavailable for work', perhaps through ill-health or disability.

The pattern of odds ratios in reported health provided some evidence to suggest that class differences among lower occupational groups were slightly *weaker* when the long-term unemployed were combined with the never worked than when last main job was used to classify these adults. This suggests that the class-based distribution of long-term unemployed adults in the NS-SEC may serve to accentuate the health disadvantage of lower occupational groups when classified by their last main job. However, this finding depended to some extent on the health measure used, and was not evident for reported LLI among working-age men.

A key finding is that the NS-SEC 'outperformed' established measures of SEG and particularly SC according to the change in LLRs for two measures of reported health found in logistic models for working-age men and women. This result, in which the long-term unemployed were classified by their last main job, applied to both measures of reported health used in this analysis and strongly support the NS-SEC and the concept of employment relations as a sensitive discriminator of morbidity for men and women at this stage of the lifecourse. Unlike a recent study of mortality (Sacker et al., 2000), there was no evidence to suggest that the NS-SEC was a weak correlate of reported health for women. Class differences in reported health were clearly evident for women based on their own occupation. As we noted earlier, further analyses could compare the efficacy of using the NS-SEC for women's health based on the occupation of their husbands or the head of household.

As expected, because of its focus on current employment relations and working conditions, the 'advantage' of the NS-SEC over the skill-based measures of SEG and SC was less marked for older adults (age 60 and above) than for working-age adults. Nevertheless, the NS-SEC had greater explanatory power than SEG and a clear advantage over SC for older men's self-assessed health. These three class measures were found to be broadly comparable for LLI reported by men in this age group. For older women's health, there was little difference in the efficacy of NS-SEC, SEG and SC, with NS-SEC at least as good as SEG in distinguishing their health. This is despite the longer period of time older women are likely to have spent outside the labour market and changes in the nature of women's employment over the last few decades. Together, these results for working-age and older men and women show clear social class differences in reported health using the NS-SEC and find no evidence that this new socio-economic classification lacks discriminatory power in relation to other established measures of occupational class.

APPENDIX

Table 10.A1   *Collapsed SEG categories used in this analysis*

Collapsed SEG categories	Original SEG codes
1 Higher professional, employers and managers in large establishments	1, 3, 4
2 Lower professionals	5.1
3 Managers and employers in small establishments	2, 13
4 Intermediate and junior non-manual	5.2, 6
5 Non-professional, own account	12, 14
6 Skilled manual	8, 9
7 Semi-skilled and personal service occupations	7, 10, 15
8 Unskilled manual	11

NOTES

The GHS data used in this analysis were made available from the UK Data Archive on-line at MIMAS.

1 In the GHS, employment status refers to reported employment in the week before interview. Adults who were looking for work (including if temporarily sick) and those waiting to take up a job were classified as unemployed.

REFERENCES

Annandale, E. and Hunt, K. (2000) 'Gender inequalities in health: research at the crossroads', in E. Annandale and K. Hunt (eds) *Gender Inequalities in Health*. Buckingham: Open University Press. pp. 1–35.

Arber, S. (1996) 'Integrating non-employment into research on health inequalities', *Health and Social Policy*, 26: 445–81.

Arber, S. (1997) 'Insights about the non-employed and health: evidence from the General Household Survey', in D. Rose and K. O'Reilly (eds) *Constructing Classes: Towards a New Government Social Classification for the UK*. Swindon/London: ESRC/ONS. pp. 78–92.

Arber, S. and Cooper, H. (1999) 'Gender differences in health in later life: the new paradox?', *Social Science and Medicine*, 48: 63–78.

Arber, S. and Cooper, H. (2000) 'Gender and inequalities in health across the lifecourse', in E. Annandale and K. Hunt (eds) *Gender Inequalities in Health*. Buckingham: Open University Press. pp. 123–49.

Bennett, N., Jarvis, L., Rowlands, O., Singleton, N. and Haselden, L. (eds) (1996) *Living in Britain: Results of the 1994 General Household Survey*. London: The Stationery Office.

Dex, S. (1984) *Women's Work Histories: an Analysis of the Women and Employment Survey*, Department of Employment Research Paper, No. 46. London: DoE.

Drever, F. and Whitehead, M. (eds) (1997) *Health Inequalities: Decennial Supplement*. London: The Stationery Office.

Equal Opportunities Commission (2001) *Facts about Women and Men in Great Britain 2001*. London: EOC.

Ginn, J. and Arber, S. (1999) 'Changing patterns of pension inequality: the shift from state to private pension provisions', *Ageing and Society*, 19: 319–42.

Goldthorpe, J. (1997) 'The "Goldthorpe" class schema: some observations on conceptual and operational issues in relation to the ESRC Review of Government Social Classifications', in D. Rose and K. O'Reilly (eds) *Constructing Classes: Towards a New Government Social Classification for the UK*. Swindon/London: ESRC/ONS.

Idler, E.L. and Benyamini, Y. (1997) 'Self rated health and mortality: a review of twenty-seven community studies', *Journal of Health and Social Behavior*, 38: 21–37.

Macintyre, S. and Hunt, K. (1997) 'Socio-economic position, gender and health: how do they interact?', *Journal of Health Psychology*, 2: 315–34.

Mossey, J.M. and Shapiro, E. (1982) 'Self-rated health: a predictor of mortality among the elderly', *American Journal of Psychiatry*, 144: 1573–6.

Office for National Statistics (ONS) (1998) *Social Focus on Women and Men*. London: The Stationery Office.

Office for National Statistics (ONS) (1999) *Social Trends*, 29. London: The Stationery Office.

Office for National Statistics (ONS) (2001) *The National Statistics Socio-economic Classification: user manual*. http://www.statistics.gov.uk/methods_quality/ns_sec/

Rake, K. (ed.) (2000) *Women's Incomes over the Lifetime*, Cabinet Office, Women's Unit. London: The Stationery Office.

Rose, D. and O'Reilly, K. (eds) (1997) *Constructing Classes: Towards a New Government Social Classification for the UK*. Swindon/London: ESRC/ONS.

Rowlands, O., Singleton, N., Mager, J. and Higgins, V. (eds) (1997) *Living in Britain: Results of the 1995 General Household Survey*. London: The Stationery Office.

Sacker, A., Firth, D., Fitzpatrick, R., Lynch, K. and Bartley, M. (2000) 'Comparing health inequality in men and women: prospective study of mortality 1986–96', *British Medical Journal*, 320: 1303–7.

Stronks, K., Mheen, H. van de, Bos, J. van den and Mackenback, J.P. (1995) 'Smaller socio-economic inequalities in health among women: the role of employment status', *International Journal of Epidemiology*, 24: 559–68.

Wadsworth, M. (1991) *The Imprint of Time: Childhood, History and Adult Life*. Oxford: Clarendon Press.

11

Old and New Social Class Measures

A comparison

Anthony Heath, Jean Martin and Roeland Beerten

INTRODUCTION

In devising the National Statistics Socio-economic Classification (NS-SEC) a great deal of attention was given to the need to preserve continuity with earlier classifications such as Social Class based on Occupation (SC) and Socio-economic Groups (SEG), on which many scholars have in the past relied. As we saw in Chapter 1, the new classification therefore has a number of 'short' versions designed for analytic purposes and a 'long' operational version with a very much larger number of categories. The categories in the operational version can be combined so as to preserve the main distinctions made in SC and SEG. Thus by combining specific categories of the operational version of NS-SEC it is possible to reach what is hoped to be a reasonable approximation to the old SC and thus provide continuity over time.

However, the final version of NS-SEC is based on a new classification of occupations (SOC2000) whereas the SC and SEG schemes which it replaces were based on an earlier classification of occupations (SOC90). Changes between the two versions of SOC are substantial and have introduced discontinuities which mean that approximations to SC derived from SOC2000 will be less accurate than would have been the case had there been no change to the underlying occupational classification. Our aim in this chapter is twofold: to explore whether a collapsed version of NS-SEC designed to approximate SC will meet the needs of those who need continuity with SC; and also to examine how the eight-class analytic version of NS-SEC compares with SC in the analyses described below. Thus the first part of the chapter compares SC with the approximation derived from NS-SEC while the second part compares SC with the eight-class analytic version of NS-SEC.

CONGRUENCE BETWEEN SC AND SCapprox

We begin in the first section of this chapter by exploring the extent of congruence between SC and its approximation – SCapprox – which was created by cross-tabulating SC by the operational version of NS-SEC and assigning each category or sub-category of the operational version to the SC class where the highest proportion of its cases lay. Thus if a particular NS-SEC operational category or sub-category was split over several SC classes, all the cases in that category were assigned to the same class in SCapprox. The main reason for this splitting over the SC classes is that the SC takes no account of employment status whereas NS-SEC has separate categories for employers and the self-employed (except in the case of professional occupations). In particular self-employed workers are spread over a number of the SC classes (depending on their occupational skill level) whereas they are brought together in the new classification. However, even the operational version of NS-SEC does not separate them out in sufficient detail to allow us to recreate SC with complete accuracy.

SC originally distinguished five classes, which are usually known by the Roman numerals I, II, III, IV and V. Subsequently Class III was split into non-manual and manual categories. For ease of exposition we continue to use Roman numerals when referring to the SC, and arabic numerals for the SCapprox. We thus have the following classifications:

	SC	SCapprox
Professional	I	1
Managerial and technical	II	2
Skilled non-manual	IIInm	3
Skilled manual	IIIm	4
Semi-skilled	IV	5
Unskilled	V	6

For our analyses we use the first wave of the British Household Panel Survey (BHPS). This first wave, conducted in 1991, constituted a representative probability sample of British households and contains indicators of the three chosen outcome variables (as well as the information required to construct both the old SC and NS-SEC). Since all members of responding households were interviewed, this also provides a representative sample of individuals in Great Britain. For our analysis we excluded respondents who were aged under 18 years, those who were in the armed forces, and those who had never had a job (or for whom there was inadequate information on their occupations). Note that, where respondents were not currently in employment, we have used information on their last main job to assign them to a social class. After exclusions, we have a total of 8,778 respondents for our analysis.

In Table 11.1 we cross-tabulate the original SC by the SCapprox. Comparing the marginal distributions we can see that both classifications produce broadly the same class profiles, with small top and bottom classes and three large classes of more or less equal size representing the managerial and technical, skilled non-manual and skilled manual classes. The main difference in the two profiles is that the SCapprox Class 4 at 24.3 per cent is rather larger than the equivalent SC Class IIIm (21.9 per cent). This increase in size is partly a result of some occupations from SC Class IV being 'promoted' to Class 4 of SCapprox but also from other occupations moving 'down' from Classes II and

Table 11.1   *Comparison of SC and SCapprox*

SC	SCapprox						All	Row %
	1	2	3	4	5	6		
I	**339**	37					376	4.3
II	21	**1,945**	47	148	31		2,192	25.0
IIInm		44	**2,027**	162	18		2,251	25.6
IIIm		48	43	**1,619**	201	8	1,919	21.9
IV		44	54	157	**1,086**	122	1,463	16.7
V		4		44	73	**456**	577	6.6
All	360	2,122	2,171	2,130	1,409	586	8,778	100
Col.%	4.1	24.2	24.7	24.3	16.1	6.7	100	

IIInm. The operational version of the NS-SEC from which our approximation to SC is derived does not allow these to be separately identified and placed in the correct SC class.

Looking at the cross-tabulation in more detail we can see that a total of 7,472 respondents, 85.1 per cent of the total, lie on the main diagonal. These respondents are the ones who are classified in exactly the same way in the two classifications. With this relatively high degree of congruence we would expect to find in the later sections of this chapter that the associations with the outcome variables we examine will also be rather similar.

However, we should note that the off-diagonal cases are not distributed symmetrically about the diagonal. Of the 14.9 per cent off-diagonal cases, 6.1 per cent are in the lower left quadrant while 8.8 per cent are in the upper right. This indicates that when respondents are not allocated to the correct class in SCapprox compared with SC they are somewhat more likely to be allocated to a lower than to a higher class.

Table 11.2 shows, for each class of SC, the proportion of respondents allocated to the correct class in SCapprox and the proportions allocated to a higher or lower class. This shows that the degree of congruence is relatively high for the professional class and the two other non-manual classes (around 90 per cent). However, as would be expected from our examination of the marginal distributions, the three manual classes are more problematic. Thus we find that only 74 per cent of respondents classified as Class IV (the semi-skilled

Table 11.2   *Equivalence of SC and SCapprox*

SC		Percentage of SC allocated to:		
		correct class	higher class	lower class
I	Professional	90.2	–	9.8
II	Managerial/technical	88.7	1.0	10.3
IIInm	Skilled non-manual	90.0	2.0	8.0
IIIm	Skilled manual	84.4	4.7	10.9
IV	Semi-skilled	74.2	17.4	8.4
V	Unskilled	79.0	21.0	–

class) in the SC get allocated to the equivalent class (Class 5) in the SCapprox, while 79 per cent of Class V and 84 per cent of Class IIIm are correctly allocated to Class 6 and Class 4 respectively. Clearly in the case of the two extreme classes, respondents can only be misallocated in one direction. They are also the smallest classes and so will have less influence on the overall results. But Table 11.2 reveals the asymmetry of the misallocations: respondents in Classes IV and V are particularly likely to have been misallocated to a higher rather than to a lower class. We therefore need to check carefully what effect these misallocations have had on the pattern of associations.

ASSOCIATIONS WITH OUTCOME MEASURES

To assess whether SCapprox will be adequate for users of the previous SC, we consider the associations with three variables, namely political party support, smoking and housing tenure, using the BHPS data described above. We have chosen these three as they provide a variety of outcomes that are indicative of the broad spectrum of outcomes with which social class is associated.

We first make a global comparison of the associations between SC and SCapprox and these three outcomes; then in the next section we conduct a more detailed investigation of those groups which are treated differently in the two versions of SC.

In the BHPS party support is derived from a series of questions: respondents were asked whether they generally thought of themselves as a supporter of any one political party or, failing that, as a little closer to one political party than to the others. They were then asked for the name of the party. (A small residual group who answered no to the first two questions were asked 'If there were to be a general election tomorrow, which political party do you think you would be most likely to support?' Their responses are also included.)

For ease of analysis we have collapsed the responses into a binary variable distinguishing Conservatives (coded 1) from all others (coded 0). Respondents who answered 'don't know', 'none' or gave other answers are also included in the category 0 along with Labour, Liberal Democrat, Scottish Nationalist, Plaid Cymru, Green and other Parties. (Our measure is derived from variable AVOTE in the BHPS.)

Our measure of smoking is more straightforward and is derived from a question which simply asked 'are you a smoker?' This gives us a binary variable, distinguishing those who smoked (coded 1) from those who reported that they were non-smokers (coded 0). (Variable ASMOKER in the BHPS.)

In the case of housing tenure we distinguish owners (coded 1) from those who rented (coded 0). The category of owner includes both those who reported that they owned their property outright and those who owned with a mortgage. In the category 0 we include those who rented from a local authority, from a housing association, from an employer, rented privately either furnished or unfurnished, together with other rented. (This measure is derived from variable ATENURE in the BHPS.)

While collapsing the responses to binary variables means that we lose some information, it does mean that we can use the same, relatively simple, technique of logistic regression to assess the associations with all three outcome variables. Thus, we regress our three outcomes separately on SC and on SCapprox. We can then compare the goodness of fit and the parameter estimates based on the SC with those based on the SCapprox. What we are hoping for, first, is that the fit when an outcome is regressed on SCapprox will be at least as good as the fit obtained when the same outcome is modelled on SC. Second, we are hoping that the parameter estimates, which can be interpreted as log odds ratios, will be reasonably similar whether SC or SCapprox is used. If the parameter estimates are similar, then one will be more optimistic that a transfer to the approximate version will not disrupt continuity over time.

Note that the goodness of fit can vary independently of the parameter estimates, so in principle it is possible that we may achieve one objective but not the other. However, in practice if the parameter estimates were to change substantially, it is likely that the goodness of fit would also change.

Table 11.3 compares the results when we model support for the Conservative Party. As we can see, the fit (strictly speaking the improvement in fit over that of the no association model) is lower when SCapprox is used (305.7) than it is with SC (325.2), but the difference is relatively small. Moreover, most of the parameter estimates are very similar. These parameter estimates contrast the log odds of Conservative support in each of the upper five classes with the odds in the reference category of the unskilled class (Class V in the SC and Class 6 in the SCapprox). The biggest discrepancy concerns the skilled manual class (0.54 in the SC and 0.64 in the SCapprox). As we saw earlier, this is the class which displayed the largest overall change in size between the two classifications. Even here, however, the difference is less than the standard error.

Table 11.4 gives the results for smoking and shows a very similar picture. Again the fit is not as good when SCapprox is used (down from 166.2 to 148.5) but most of the parameter estimates are very close to each other. Here the exception is the semi-skilled manual Class IV/5 (a parameter estimate of 0.00 in SC but –0.11 in SCapprox). Once again, however, the differences are relatively small compared with the standard errors. Thus, whether we use SC or SCapprox, we are unable to reject the null hypothesis that the odds of smoking are the same in all three of the lowest classes.

Table 11.3   *Logistic regression of support for the Conservative Party*

SC	Log odds	SE	SCapprox	Log odds	SE
I	1.11	0.15	1	1.18	0.15
II	1.21	0.11	2	1.24	0.11
IIInm	1.15	0.11	3	1.18	0.11
IIIm	0.54	0.12	4	0.64	0.11
IV	0.30	0.12	5	0.35	0.12
V*	0.00		6*	0.00	
Improvement	325.2 (5 df)		Improvement	305.7 (5 df)	

* Reference category.

Table 11.4   *Logistic regression of smoking*

SC	Log odds	SE	SCapprox	Log odds	SE
I	-1.22	0.17	1	-1.18	0.17
II	-0.62	0.10	2	-0.64	0.10
IIInm	-0.50	0.10	3	-0.54	0.10
IIIm	-0.07	0.10	4	-0.10	0.10
IV	-0.00	0.10	5	-0.11	0.10
V*	0.00		6*	0.00	
Improvement	166.2 (5 df)		Improvement	148.5 (5 df)	

* Reference category.

Table 11.5 shows greater differences for housing tenure. The fit is down from 605.8 to 569.8 and the parameter estimates for SCapprox are in all cases rather lower than their equivalents for SC, the decline ranging between 0.13 and 0.19. However, these parameter estimates simply compare the five higher classes with the lowest class (the reference category). It is therefore useful to examine the nature of the differences in more detail by comparing the differences between the parameter estimates for adjacent classes, rather than just in relation to the reference category (Tables 11.6 to 11.8).

The estimates reported in Tables 11.6 to 11.8 for the differences between adjacent classes have been derived from the results reported in the previous three tables. Thus in the case of party support, Table 11.3 showed that the estimate for SC Class I was 1.11 while that for Class II was 1.21. Subtracting the second figure from the first we obtain a difference of –0.10. This represents the difference between these two classes as shown in Table 11.6, and it can be

Table 11.5   *Logistic regression of housing tenure*

SC	Log odds	SE	SCapprox	Log odds	SE
I	2.12	0.17	1	1.93	0.17
II	1.81	0.10	2	1.68	0.10
IIInm	1.58	0.10	3	1.45	0.10
IIIm	1.08	0.10	4	0.93	0.10
IV	0.52	0.10	5	0.35	0.10
V*	0.00		6*	0.00	
Improvement	605.8 (5 df)		Improvement	569.8 (5 df)	

* Reference category.

Table 11.6   *Differences between estimates for adjacent classes: support for Conservative Party*

SC		SCapprox		Difference
I/II	-0.10	1/2	-0.06	-0.04
II/IIInm	0.06	2/3	0.06	0.00
IIInm/IIIm	0.61	3/4	0.54	-0.07
IIIm/IV	0.24	4/5	0.29	0.05
IV/V	0.30	5/6	0.35	0.05

Table 11.7   *Differences between estimates for adjacent classes: smoking*

SC		SCapprox		Difference
I/II	–0.60	1/2	–0.54	–0.06
II/IIInm	–0.12	2/3	–0.11	–0.01
IIInm/IIIm	–0.43	3/4	–0.44	0.01
IIIm/IV	–0.07	4/5	–0.01	–0.06
IV/V	–0.00	5/6	–0.11	0.11

interpreted as the log odds ratio comparing party support in the top two classes. Comparing these top two classes, we can see that the log odds ratios based on SC and SCapprox are very similar for all three outcomes. Thus the differences are –0.04 in the case of party support and –0.06 and –0.06 for smoking and tenure. (We use a negative sign to indicate that the SCapprox exhibits a smaller log odds ratio between adjacent classes than does the SC; in other words, that it exhibits less discriminatory power.)

The log odds ratios contrasting the managerial/technical and skilled non-manual classes show that for these classes the SC and SCapprox are also very similar: there is no difference in the case of partisanship and tenure, and a difference of only –0.01 for smoking. Moving on down and contrasting the skilled non-manual and skilled manual classes, we find that the differences are again small for smoking and tenure (0.01 and 0.02 respectively), while for partisanship the difference is –0.07. In other words, it appears that in SCapprox the estimated relationships between these top four classes and our three outcomes are very close to those obtained when SC is used. This conclusion is in line with the high degree of congruence between SC and SCapprox that Table 11.2 showed in the allocation of respondents to these four classes.

The log odds ratios between the next two classes, that is between the skilled and semi-skilled manual classes, show small discrepancies. Thus the difference is 0.05 in the case of partisanship, –0.06 in the case of smoking, and 0.02 in the case of tenure. We had anticipated, from the relatively large misallocations involved, that there might be relatively large discrepancies between these two classes, but in the event there do not seem to be major consequential problems.

Looking at the two bottom classes, however, we find larger differences between SC and SCapprox. Although in the case of party support the estimates only differ by 0.05, in the case of smoking they differ by 0.11 and in the case

Table 11.8   *Differences between estimates for adjacent classes: housing tenure*

SC		SCapprox		Difference
I/II	0.31	1/2	0.25	–0.06
II/IIInm	0.23	2/3	0.23	0.00
IIInm/IIIm	0.50	3/4	0.52	0.02
IIIm/IV	0.56	4/5	0.58	0.02
IV/V	0.52	5/6	0.35	–0.17

of tenure by –0.17. It is this large difference of –0.17 that accounts for the decline in the parameter estimates found in Table 11.5. However, these differences do not show a consistent pattern in their direction and it is not clear how to interpret the findings. In practice, given the small size of Class V, researchers often combine it with Class IV in order to give sufficiently large numbers for analysis. Given the present ambiguous findings, this might be a wise strategy to follow with SCapprox.

The above regressions do not allow for the impact of any other variables on our three outcome measures. One might, for example, wish to use a social class measure in a multivariate analysis, and it is important to know whether SCapprox will give acceptable continuity with SC for these purposes too. A problem here is likely to arise only if the reallocations of respondents between SC and SCapprox were patterned with respect to other variables of interest. Gender and educational level are prime suspects, since both are closely linked with social class position. Thus if our reallocations disproportionately involved, say, men, this could lead to problems of continuity in analyses which controlled for gender.

We therefore repeated the analyses with gender as a control variable. Little difference in the results was found. We also repeated the analyses controlling for highest educational qualification (classified as: degree, A-level or equivalent, GCSE grades A–C or equivalent, lower qualifications, no qualifications). Here we also found that the patterns were very similar for SC and SCapprox.

COMPARISON OF SC AND THE EIGHT-CLASS VERSION OF THE NS-SEC

The first part of this chapter presented results that reassure users of SC that a reasonably good approximation of that classification can be derived from the NS-SEC: the SC approximation produces broadly similar patterns of relationships, although the overall fit tends to be somewhat lower than that obtained by the SC. In the second part we explore the differences between the SC and the eight-class version of the NS-SEC itself. Here we are primarily interested in the discriminatory power of the NS-SEC and whether it offers an improvement over SC. In particular, does the new classification identify important differences between occupations within a given SC social class with respect to our three outcome measures? Putting the same question rather differently, does the SC classification group together occupations that are in fact relatively heterogeneous in their patterns of party support, smoking and housing tenure?

First we examine the extent of congruence between the two classifications. Table 11.9 presents a cross-tabulation of NS-SEC by SC, showing the extent to which the SC classes are split across the eight classes of the NS-SEC.

Comparison with Table 11.1 shows, as we would expect, a much less close correspondence between the NS-SEC and SC than between the latter and its approximation. However, the two classifications were not designed to be equivalent at this level of aggregation and, given that they have different numbers of classes, we cannot measure the degree of correspondence in quite the same way as we did earlier. In particular, we cannot straightforwardly

Table 11.9 Comparison of eight-class version of the NS-SEC and SC

NS-SEC	SC						All	Row %
	I	II	IIInm	IIIm	IV	V		
1.1 Large employers & higher managerial occupations	2	**215**	1	1			219	2.5
1.2 Higher professional occupations	**347**	104					451	5.1
2 Lower managerial & professional occupations	27	**1,435**	321	20			1,803	20.5
3 Intermediate occupations		100	**1,214**	63	17		1,394	15.9
4 Small employers & own account workers		257	84	**272**	123	47	783	8.9
5 Lower supervisory & technical occupations		31	104	**801**	83	8	1,027	11.7
6 Semi-routine occupations		45	517	262	**645**	65	1,534	17.5
7 Routine occupations		5	7	501	595	**456**	1,564	17.8
All	376	2,192	2,248	1,919	1,463	577	8,775	100
Col. %	4.3	25.0	25.6	21.9	16.7	6.6	100	

identify a main diagonal in the way that we did in Table 11.1. If one were to attempt to derive SC from this eight-class version of the NS-SEC by assigning all of a given category to its modal SC class (shown in bold in Table 11.12), the proportion of correctly assigned cases would only be 57 per cent (rather than the 85 per cent congruence that we obtained with SCapprox using the operational version of the NS-SEC).

Given the larger number of classes in the NS-SEC, it is not surprising that there is considerable spread in the way members of the six SC classes are allocated to the new classification. Only in the case of Classes I and V do we find that most of their members are assigned to a single NS-SEC class. In all the other cases there is substantial diversity. For example, members of SC Class II are now spread across all eight classes of the NS-SEC, some going to Class 1.1 (large employers and higher managerial occupations), others to Class 1.2 (higher professional occupations), to Class 2 (lower managerial and professional occupations), to Class 3 (intermediate occupations), to Class 4 (small employers and own account workers) and a few to Classes 5, 6 and 7.

Looking at the detail of each of the NS-SEC classes we can see that Class 4, small employers and own account workers, is drawn from a very wide spread of SC classes; this is, of course, because Class 4 is based on employment status rather than purely on occupation, as in the case of the SC. Classes 6 and 7 (semi-routine and routine occupations) are also notable with their members drawn from several different SC classes. In particular, a number of occupations that the SC treats as non-manual (and places in IIInm) have been 'demoted' on the grounds of their relatively disadvantaged terms and conditions of employment. It is naturally of considerable interest to know whether these allocations have led to more coherent categories with reduced within-category diversity in terms of our three outcomes.

ASSOCIATION WITH OUTCOME MEASURES

If the allocations have produced more coherent categories, then we would expect to find that the discriminatory power or fit of the new eight-category NS-SEC classification would be superior to that of the SC. We therefore carry out similar regression analyses to those in the first part of the chapter, regressing our binary measures of party support, smoking and tenure on the SC and NS-SEC respectively.

The fit of the models is shown in Table 11.10. We do not present the parameter estimates for individual classes as no direct correspondence between classes in the two classifications is intended and the comparison of the

Table 11.10   Model improvement for SC and NS-SEC8

	SC (5df)	NS-SEC8 (7df)	Difference
Party	325.2	347.1	21.9
Smoking	166.5	164.9	−1.6
Tenure	605.8	641.1	35.3

Table 11.11   *Logistic regressions using the NS-SEC*

NS-SEC	Party	SE	Smoking	SE	Tenure	SE
1.1	1.32	0.12	−0.70	0.13	1.98	0.15
1.2	1.01	0.11	−1.02	0.14	1.72	0.15
2	0.91	0.08	−0.68	0.08	1.41	0.08
3	0.96	0.08	−0.60	0.08	1.44	0.09
4	1.21	0.10	−0.20	0.09	1.23	0.10
5	0.32	0.09	−0.14	0.09	0.73	0.08
6	0.29	0.08	0.09	0.08	0.38	0.07
7*	0.00		0.00		0.00	

* Reference category.

parameter estimates is not therefore meaningful. We must also be careful in comparing the fits of the two sets of models since they involve different numbers of degrees of freedom and are not nested. For the extra two degrees of freedom (corresponding to its extra two categories) the NS-SEC improves the fit (−2 log likelihood) by 21.9 in the case of party support and 35.3 in the case of tenure. However, in the case of smoking there is a slight deterioration in the fit, despite the extra two degrees of freedom, which is disappointing.

Table 11.11 shows the parameter estimates when our three outcome variables are regressed on the NS-SEC. For all three outcomes Classes 2 and 3 are very similar to one another but all the other classes are substantially distinct from each other on some or all of the outcomes. We can also see that there is in general a hierarchical relation between the categories and the outcomes, with support for the Conservatives and home-ownership tending to decline, and smoking to increase, as we move from Class 1 to Class 7, although there is at least one exception for each outcome. Thus Class 4 is distinctive with respect to partisanship, being much more likely to support the Conservatives than any other apart from Class 1.1, but is not 'out of order' with respect to the other two outcomes. This is consistent with other research on the partisanship of the self-employed and small employers. Class 1.2 (higher professional occupations) is distinctive with respect to smoking but is not 'out of order' with respect to the other two outcomes. Again, this is consistent with previous research. In general, then, the NS-SEC appears to provide good discriminatory power but one needs to bear in mind that the patterns of association may vary from one outcome to another.

EXPLORING SUBDIVISIONS OF SC CLASSES

Table 11.10 gives us a global assessment of the discriminatory power of the two classifications. We now turn to a more detailed examination, in particular looking at respondents from a given class of SC who have been reallocated to a variety of NS-SEC classes. We want to find out whether the estimates indicate greater homogeneity in NS-SEC classes than in SC classes. As we noted earlier, two classes of the NS-SEC categorisation are of particular interest: Class 4, which has brought together all the small employers and own account (non-professional) workers irrespective of their occupational positions; and Class 6, which has placed in a single semi-routine category respondents who were distributed across non-manual and manual classes in the SC scheme. Conversely, it is interesting to examine the heterogeneity of the SC classes, some of which, such as Class II, are spread across many different NS-SEC classes.

To explore these questions we first create a composite variable which has categories corresponding to each of the occupied cells in Table 11.9 (apart from the smallest cells, which we merge with their column neighbours). This gives us a composite variable with twenty-six categories. This composite variable thus contains virtually all the distinctions made by SC and NS-SEC. In this sense, the SC and NS-SEC are nested within the composite variable.

The parameter estimates obtained when the three outcomes are regressed on the composite measure are shown in Tables 11.12 to 11.14. (More detailed tables are given in the Appendix showing the standard error of each estimate and the *n* for the category. The two tables are laid out so as to facilitate comparisons down the columns, that is the heterogeneity within SC classes, and along the rows, that is the heterogeneity within NS-SEC classes.)

We begin by examining the SC classes and the extent of their internal heterogeneity. As we noted above, SC Class II is of especial interest since its occupations are spread across all eight of the NS-SEC classes. (For this analysis, however, as mentioned above, we have amalgamated the smallest cell with the adjacent one.) We can see from Tables 11.12 to 11.14 that some of these components of Class II differ in their patterns of party support, their housing tenure and, to a lesser extent, their smoking. We take as our reference

Table 11.12 *Comparison of NS-SEC and SC regression estimates for Conservative Party support*

NS-SEC	SC					
	I	II	IIInm	IIIm	IV	V
1.1 Large employers & higher managerial occupations		**0.00**				
1.2 Higher professional occupations	**-0.39**	0.02				
2 Lower managerial & professional occupations	-0.38	**-0.45**	-0.18			
3 Intermediate occupations		-0.47	**-0.30**	-1.05		
4 Small employers & own account workers		0.32	-0.06	**-0.22**	-0.33	-0.99
5 Lower supervisory & technical occupations		-0.30	-0.57	**-0.96**	-2.46	
6 Semi-routine occupations		-0.71	-0.58	-1.25	**-1.31**	-1.24
7 Routine occupations				-1.27	-1.17	**-1.60**

Table 11.13   *Comparison of NS-SEC and SC regression estimates for smoking*

NS-SEC		I	II	IIInm	IIIm	IV	V
					SC		
1.1	Large employers & higher managerial occupations		**0.00**				
1.2	Higher professional occupations	**–0.50**	0.17				
2	Lower managerial & professional occupations	–0.84	**0.03**	0.02			
3	Intermediate occupations		0.50	**0.05**	–0.09		
4	Small employers & own account workers		0.27	0.36	**0.63**	0.70	0.61
5	Lower supervisory & technical occupations		0.23	0.56	**0.57**	0.47	
6	Semi-routine occupations		–0.58	0.47	0.62	**0.76**	0.59
7	Routine occupations				0.78	0.62	**0.72**

category the II/1.1 cell. Compared with this reference category, the Class II respondents who have been allocated to NS-SEC Class 2 (lower professional and managerial occupations) show significant differences in patterns of party support (–0.45, SE 0.15) and housing tenure (–0.73, SE 0.24), as do those

Table 11.14   *Comparison of NS-SEC and SC regression estimates for housing tenure*

NS-SEC		I	II	IIInm	IIIm	IV	V
					SC		
1.1	Large employers & higher managerial occupations		**0.00**				
1.2	Higher professional occupations	**–0.42**	–0.36				
2	Lower managerial & professional occupations	0.30	**–0.73**	–0.71			
3	Intermediate occupations		–0.77	**–0.68**	–0.56		
4	Small employers & own account workers		–0.70	–0.85	**–0.47**	–1.60	–1.84
5	Lower supervisory & technical occupations		–1.33	–1.18	**–1.37**	–1.86	
6	Semi-routine occupations		–1.32	–1.39	–1.92	**–1.92**	–2.44
7	Routine occupations				–1.70	–2.13	**–2.58**

allocated to Class 3, where the differences are of similar magnitude and where there is in addition an almost significant difference with respect to smoking (0.50, SE 0.27). Those allocated to Classes 4, 5 and 6 are also notable showing much lower levels of home ownership (-0.70, SE 0.28, -1.33, SE 0.46, and -1.32, SE 0.40 respectively) than the reference category. The original SC Class II does therefore seem to have been rather heterogeneous, particularly with respect to housing tenure.

We turn next to SC Class IIInm (skilled non-manual workers). The members of this class too have been reallocated across a variety of NS-SEC classes, some being 'promoted' to the lower professional and managerial occupations (Class 2), others being 'demoted' to the semi-routine occupations (Class 6). Again, Tables 11.12 to 11.14 show some differences in their outcome patterns although in general there is not as much heterogeneity as with Class II. We can treat the cell IIInm/3 as the 'core' of SC Class IIInm and it is useful to compare the parameter estimates for the other categories with that for this core cell. What we find is that the groups who have been 'demoted' to Classes 5 and 6 are less likely than the core group to support the Conservatives or to own their homes, but are more likely to smoke. (To draw these inferences we need to subtract the parameter estimate for the cell in question from that of the core cell. Thus in the case of the respondents demoted to Class 6, the difference in parameter estimates for party support is $0.58-0.30 = 0.28$; for smoking is $0.47-0.05 = 0.42$; and in the case of tenure is $1.39-0.68 = 0.71$.)

The members of Class IIIm (skilled manual workers) are also spread over a range of NS-SEC classes. We can treat cell IIIm/5 as the 'core' cell and compare the other four cells with it. There are some differences in the expected direction between the estimate for the core cell and those for the respondents demoted to Classes 6 and 7 (although the differences are very modest in the case of smoking). There are also some larger differences in the case of the respondents 'promoted' to Classes 3 and 4. Most notably, the promoted groups are much more likely to be home-owners than the core group (with differences of 0.81 and 0.90 in the parameter estimates).

SC Class IV is also spread across a number of NS-SEC classes. This time several of the differences in parameter estimates are in unexpected directions and the pattern is harder to interpret. However, the divisions within SC Class V between the self-employed (moved to NS-SEC Class 4) and the remainder are all in the expected direction.

The patterns, therefore, are not always clear cut and vary according to the outcome. Nevertheless it is evident that SC Classes II and IIIm were particularly heterogeneous. In general, there are larger differences with respect to party support and housing tenure than there are with smoking, but even with respect to smoking there have been some important improvements obtained by the reallocation. Some of these involve substantial groups such as the 517 respondents demoted from Class IIInm to Class 6 and the 63 respondents promoted from Class IIIm to Class 3. So even in the case of smoking, where there was no overall improvement in fit, there are some groups whose behaviour was out of line with their place in the SC classification.

Another way to explore these parameter estimates is to consider the diversity within NS-SEC classes. We can again use Tables 11.12 to 11.14 for this purpose, but this time comparing parameter estimates within a given row rather than within a given column.

We pass over Class 1.1, since over 90 per cent are drawn from a single SC class, and begin with Class 1.2 (higher professional occupations) which brings together two groups that were divided between SC Classes I and II. As we can see, this reallocation makes excellent sense in the case of tenure, where the parameter estimates are very similar, but works less well for the other two outcomes.

Class 2 (lower managerial and professional occupations) is composed of two main groups drawn from SC Classes II and IIInm. These two groups are very similar to each other with respect to smoking and tenure, although they are less similar in party support.

We pass over Class 3, since well over 80 per cent are drawn from a single SC class, and move on to Class 4 (small employers and own account workers). Previous research has shown that these self-employed workers tend to be more inclined to support the Conservative Party than would be expected on the basis of their occupations alone. This tendency is also apparent in Table 11.12: within each SC class, the respondents assigned to NS-SEC Class 4 stand out as the most Conservative group in that class. Looking along the row we see that the parameter estimates for those members of Class 4 drawn from Classes IIInm, IIIm and IV are relatively similar (at –0.06, –0.22 and –0.33). However, the parameter estimate for those drawn from Class II is rather more distinct at +0.32, probably reflecting a larger proportion of employers in this group. Ideally one might distinguish small employers from own account workers (as is done in Goldthorpe's class schema) but the numbers are not sufficient to warrant this distinction in the eight-class version of the NS-SEC. It should also be noted that the estimate (–0.99) for the small number of respondents drawn from Class V is out of line with the rest of this category.

We pass over Class 5, where 80 per cent are drawn from a single SC class, and move on to Class 6. Class 6 groups together the semi-routine workers from three main SC classes (IIInm, IIIm and IV). The outcome on which its members stand out most clearly is their housing tenure. The three groups that have been demoted to Class 6 have parameter estimates that are in each case closer to that of the core 6/IV cell than to the core cells of the SC classes from which they originate. However, with respect to the other two outcomes the findings are less encouraging.

Finally, Class 7 (routine occupations) brings together three main groups of unskilled workers from SC Classes III, IV and V. This is perhaps the least successful reallocation, since the parameter estimates for the demoted groups tend in general to be closer to the estimates for the core cell of the SC class from which they originate than to the estimates for the 7/V cell, which can be thought of as the core of Class 7. However, it may be worth recalling the results of Table 11.11 which shows that, despite these reallocations, Class 7 in the NS-SEC remains fairly distinct from Class 6 with respect to both party support and housing tenure.

CONCLUSIONS

Continuity with the SC will not be exact but our analysis in this chapter suggests that the approximation derived from the operational version of the NS-SEC should not cause any major disruption to users of the SC. The main difference to which we drew attention in the first part of this chapter involved SC Class IIIm; the approximation allocates 24.3 per cent of respondents to this class, compared with 21.9 per cent in the SC itself. This expansion is caused both by movements up from Class IV and movements down from Classes II and IIInm. We also saw that, in the case of the top three classes, there was very considerable congruence between the two versions. There was least congruence in the case of Class IV.

We are encouraged by three findings in particular:

- 85 per cent of respondents in the BHPS are treated identically in the old SC and in the new approximation (SCapprox).
- The SC has been especially popular in the analysis of class differences in health, and our analysis of smoking indicated that the parameter estimates for SC and SCapprox were close and should raise little problem of continuity.
- On balance the misallocations – respondents who are not in the same class of the approximation as they were in the SC proper – have not produced major reductions in explanatory power and have not altered the relativities between the classes except perhaps in the relation between Classes IV and V.

However, while SCapprox permits a high degree of continuity, we feel that the new eight-class version of the NS-SEC represents an overall improvement over the SC, allowing greater discriminatory power with respect to two of our three outcome variables.

- For both party support and housing tenure the fit with the NS-SEC is substantially better than that achieved by the SC.
- With the exception of Classes 2 and 3, which are very similar to one another with respect to our three outcomes, all the other categories are substantially distinct from each other on some or all of the outcomes.
- A number of SC classes, most notably Classes II and IIIm, appear to be rather heterogeneous in their composition. This is particularly evident with respect to housing tenure.
- The classes of the NS-SEC display in general a fair degree of internal homogeneity. In particular, Class 4 brings together self-employed workers who are relatively homogeneous in their party support; Class 6, the semi-routine employees, also brings together several groups that were widely spaced out in the SC but are rather similar to each other with respect to housing tenure.

Nevertheless, the results vary according to the outcome selected. Our results are most encouraging in the case of housing tenure, perhaps reflecting the conceptual basis of the new classification. Users of both SC and the new classification need to bear in mind that patterns of association with social class may well vary from one outcome to another. This serves to illustrate the importance of the earlier discussion of analytic issues in Chapter 2.

APPENDIX

Table 11.A1　*Logistic regression using composite of SC and NS-SEC8 (SC order)*

	Party	SE	Smoking	SE	Tenure	SE	N
I/1.2	**−0.39**	**0.18**	**−0.50**	**0.22**	**−0.42**	**0.28**	**347**
I/2	−0.38	0.41	−0.84	0.63	0.30	0.77	27
II/1.1 (ref. cat.)	0	0	0	0	0	0	215
II/1.2	0.02	0.24	0.17	0.28	−0.36	0.37	104
II/2	**−0.45**	**0.15**	**0.03**	**0.18**	**−0.73**	**0.24**	**1,435**
II/3	−0.47	0.25	0.50	0.27	−0.77	0.34	100
II/4	0.32	0.19	0.27	0.22	−0.70	0.28	257
II/5	−0.30	0.40	0.23	0.44	−1.33	0.46	31
II/6	−0.71	0.35	−0.58	0.47	−1.32	0.40	45
IIIN/2	−0.18	0.18	0.02	0.21	−0.71	0.27	321
IIIN/3	**−0.30**	**0.15**	**0.05**	**0.18**	**−0.68**	**0.24**	**1,214**
IIIN/4	−0.06	0.26	0.36	0.29	−0.85	0.36	84
IIIN/5	−0.57	0.24	0.56	0.26	−1.18	0.32	104
IIIN/6	−0.58	0.17	0.47	0.19	−1.39	0.25	517
IIIM/3	−1.05	0.31	−0.09	0.35	−0.56	0.41	63
IIIM/4	**−0.22**	**0.19**	**0.63**	**0.21**	**−0.47**	**0.29**	**272**
IIIM/5	**−0.96**	**0.16**	**0.57**	**0.18**	**−1.37**	**0.24**	**801**
IIIM/6	−1.25	0.20	0.62	0.21	−1.92	0.26	262
IIIM/7	−1.27	0.17	0.78	0.19	−1.70	0.25	501
IV/4	−0.33	0.23	0.70	0.25	−1.60	0.30	123
IV/5	−2.46	0.42	0.47	0.29	−1.86	0.32	83
IV/6	**−1.31**	**0.17**	**0.76**	**0.18**	**−1.92**	**0.24**	**645**
IV/7	−1.17	0.17	0.62	0.19	−2.13	0.24	595
V/4	−0.99	0.35	0.61	0.35	−1.84	0.38	47
V/6	−1.24	0.32	0.59	0.31	−2.44	0.34	65
V/7	**−1.60**	**0.18**	**0.72**	**0.19**	**−2.58**	**0.25**	**456**

Entries in bold indicate the cells on the diagonal of the SC/NS-SEC8 cross-tabulation.

Table 11.A2   *Logistic regression using composite of SC and NS-SEC8 (NS-SEC order)*

	Party	SE	Smoking	SE	Tenure	SE
1.1/II (ref. cat.)	0	0	0	0	0	0
1.1/I	−0.39	0.18	−0.50	0.22	−0.42	0.28
1.2/II	0.02	0.24	0.17	0.28	0.36	0.37
2/I	−0.38	0.41	−0.84	0.63	0.30	0.77
2/II	−0.45	0.15	0.03	0.18	−0.73	0.24
2/IIInm	−0.18	0.18	0.02	0.21	−0.71	0.27
3/II	−0.47	0.25	0.50	0.27	−0.77	0.34
3/IIInm	−0.30	0.15	0.05	0.18	−0.68	0.24
3/IIIm	−1.05	0.31	−0.09	0.35	−0.56	0.41
4/II	0.32	0.19	0.27	0.22	−0.70	0.28
4/IIInm	−0.06	0.26	0.36	0.29	−0.85	0.36
4/IIIm	−0.22	0.19	0.63	0.21	−0.47	0.29
4/IV	−0.33	0.23	0.70	0.25	−1.60	0.30
4/V	−0.99	0.35	0.61	0.35	−1.84	0.38
5/II	−0.30	0.40	0.23	0.44	−1.33	0.46
5/IIInm	−0.57	0.24	0.56	0.26	−1.18	0.32
5/IIIm	−0.96	0.16	0.57	0.18	−1.37	0.24
5/IV	−2.46	0.42	0.47	0.29	−1.86	0.32
6/II	−0.71	0.35	−0.58	0.47	−1.32	0.40
6/IIInm	−0.58	0.17	0.47	0.19	−1.39	0.25
6/IIIm	−1.25	0.20	0.62	0.21	−1.92	0.26
6/IV	−1.31	0.17	0.76	0.18	−1.92	0.24
6/V	−1.24	0.32	0.59	0.31	−2.44	0.34
7/IIIm	−1.27	0.17	0.78	0.19	−1.70	0.25
7/IV	−1.17	0.17	0.62	0.19	−2.13	0.24
7/V	−1.60	0.18	0.72	0.19	−2.58	0.25

Part IV
Further reflections on the NS-SEC

In the two chapters in this final part of the book we reflect upon some of the key issues raised in previous chapters. In particular, in Chapter 12 we return to the issue of the unit of class composition, previously discussed in Chapter 1. Through an examination of lower sales, service and clerical occupations, we draw analysts' attention to circumstances where a household measure of class may be superior to an individual measure. In Chapter 13, we summarise other key points made in previous chapters.

Naturally, we acknowledge that, however rigorous the procedures used to create it may be, no socio-economic classification is ever perfect. For instance, we have seen in Chapter 4 that there are indications of employment relations differences between higher managerial and higher professional occupations that might lead some analysts to want to regard these, as SEG and SC did, as separate classes rather than as sub-divisions of the same class. However, the flexible structure of the NS-SEC allows for these alternatives and also, therefore, for further research on this issue. It may simply be that these two groups look different from one another when analysed using our crude and partial measures of employment relations. More problematic, perhaps, is that some occupations proved to be particularly difficult in terms of their precise class allocation.

This is illustrated by our discussion in Chapter 12 of lower sales, service and clerical occupations. We know from comparative analyses of social mobility that the class positions of these occupations are variable across societies. This is not surprising given that the relevant occupations generally have mixed forms of employment relations and are expanding rapidly. The extent to which the mix of employment relations tends towards the service relationship or the labour contract appears to be changing in the direction of the latter. This might indicate the emergence of a new, white-collar, post-industrial working class – and, moreover, one which is largely feminised. Some of the implications of all this for class analysis will be explored.

In Chapter 13 we draw together the main points raised in the studies presented in Parts II and III, provide some background for the key debates in these areas and identify issues that may benefit from more research.

12
The Problem of Lower Sales, Service and Clerical Occupations

David Rose and David J. Pevalin

INTRODUCTION

In allocating occupation by employment status units to NS-SEC classes, of especial concern to us, and Chapter 4 highlights this, was how best to allocate low-grade clerical, sales and service occupations. In Chapter 4, Mills and Evans suggested that occupations such as these appeared to be outliers of Class 3. Our own analysis of LFS data suggested that they did not belong with the intermediate occupations in Class 3. Superficially, in terms of raw SRS scores, they looked more similar to occupations in Class 5 but detailed analysis showed that the pattern of scores was in fact very different. Lower clerical, sales and service workers have SRS scores that are highly influenced by the fact that many of them are employed by large bureaucratic organisations. They tend, therefore, to be salaried and to have longer periods of notice. Occupations in Class 5 are more typified by high scores on autonomy and promotion prospects. As a further complicating factor, lower clerical, sales and service occupations also include many part-time employees, especially married women and students. In the end we placed most of these occupations in Class 6, but in their own operational sub-categories – L12.1, L12.2, L12.6 and L12.7. A few went to Class 7, L13.1. Hence, as with higher managerial and higher professional occupations, this means that they may be separately analysed and further investigated. Nevertheless, we always knew these occupations would cause some problems for classification because of past experience with them when using the Goldthorpe class schema. In this chapter, we are going to discuss lower clerical, sales and service work in more detail. We do this not just for its intrinsic interest, but also, and most especially, because of the issues raised in relation to the unit of class composition as discussed in Chapter 1.

In what follows, we begin with a general discussion of the class position of lower sales, service and clerical occupations. Since Goldthorpe's treatment of this issue was pertinent to our deliberations in the ESRC Review, we next discuss how his schema deals with the relevant occupations. Independent criterion validation studies of Goldthorpe's schema in relation to these occupations will also be considered. In the remainder of the chapter, we examine the characteristics of lower sales, service and clerical occupations in the context of the NS-SEC. Finally we discuss the implications of our empirical data on these occupations and their incumbents in relation to the unit of class composition.

LOWER CLERICAL, SALES AND SERVICE OCCUPATIONS IN THE CLASS STRUCTURE

When John Goldthorpe elaborated his original class schema by sub-dividing three of his original seven classes, thereby producing his 'eleven-class' model, *inter alia* he highlighted the issue of the class position of lower sales and service occupations. In the eleven-class version, Goldthorpe created a new class for this group of occupations through a sub-division of the intermediate Class III between IIIa and IIIb. It is the latter class that contains lower sales and service occupations.

The reasons these occupations have proved of continuing interest to class analysts are, first, because they highlight the problems of seeing the old 'manual/non-manual' divide as synonymous with middle and working class positions. More broadly, therefore, they pose questions about the nature of class structures in post-industrial societies. Second, they raise central issues concerning the unit of class composition, that is whether and under what circumstances we should assign individuals to class positions based on their own or their household's class situation. This in turn relates to the much-debated issue of class and gender as well as to the class position of part-time employees. It is with aspects of these latter two issues that we shall mainly be concerned here. Finally, lower sales and service workers constitute one of the most dynamic elements in the class structure. As Table 12.1 shows, the proportion of the workforce in Goldthorpe's Class IIIb has been growing significantly, as the economy has become increasingly post-industrial in character and thus service based. Moreover, given that Class IIIb provides only partial coverage of all lower sales and service jobs, as we shall demonstrate, Table 12.1 understates the true picture of growth. Something like 22 per cent of the economically active in 1997 were employed in the occupations delineated in Table 12.4.

It is thus vital that we understand where these occupations – such as shop assistants, call centre workers and the myriad of personal service occupations in the public and private sectors, as well as some lower-level clerical work – fit into the overall structure of class positions and why.

To put the matter baldly, do lower sales and service occupations constitute an element of the intermediate, 'lower middle' class of white-collar employees,

Table 12.1   *Growth of Goldthorpe's Class IIIb over time* *

	1984[1]	1991[2]	1997[3]
All	4.4	7.3	8.9
Males	0.3	1.9	2.6
Females	10.3	13.6	16.2
n	1,315	6,151	63,262

* As a percentage of those currently working.
[1] Social Class in Modern Britain.
[2] Wave 1 of the British Household Panel Survey.
[3] Winter quarter of the 1996/97 Labour Force Survey.

alongside most clerical and secretarial jobs? That is, do they belong in NS-SEC Class 3? Or are they in fact a new element of the working class with employment relations more similar to those of assembly line work, driving and other semi-routine and routine occupations in Classes 6 and 7? If they form part of the working class, still further considerations arise.

It has been argued that lower sales and service workers may constitute a new post-industrial, post-Fordist working class – a 'service proletariat' (see Esping-Andersen, 1993). In that sense, another question must be addressed: is the class position of lower sales and service workers similar to or different from the traditional industrial working class? That is, if lower sales and service work may be defined as essentially 'working class' in nature, how far are differences between these two elements of the working class a matter of mere 'situs'. In other words, are employees in both traditional manual and service work essentially in the same class? Or are they, in fact, two different classes, one a post-industrial and the other an industrial working class with different employment relations and little mobility between the two? The way we have constructed the NS-SEC, with an operational 'long' version that may be collapsed to analytic 'short' versions, will eventually allow us to shed some light on this matter. We can look inside the classes we have created by using the operational categories and sub-categories. In this chapter we are merely going to undertake a preliminary examination of the issues surrounding the allocation of lower sales and service occupations within the NS-SEC in order to illustrate the problems these occupations pose for analysts.

Goldthorpe's Class IIIb, 'lower grade routine non-manual employees', although apparently an intermediate class position, is in fact an element of the working class (see below). As we shall see, in the NS-SEC most of these Class IIIb occupations, along with other similar ones which were allocated by Goldthorpe to either his Class IIIa or Class VII, are allocated to the clerical, sales and services sub-divisions of category L12 of the operational version of the NS-SEC. Thus, they are predominantly in NS-SEC Class 6, semi-routine occupations in the working class, rather than operational category L7, the intermediate Class 3. However, as we have noted, the allocation of these occupations to Class 6 was perhaps the least satisfactory we made for any significant group of employee occupations. In fact, one might argue that, for the most part, lower sales and service occupations belong neither in Class 3 nor in Class 6 but rather form a separate and largely feminised element of the working class. This is precisely as Goldthorpe would have expected and predicted, as we shall soon explain. Whether this element may also then be characterised as a post-industrial service proletariat is beyond the scope of this chapter, but is a matter we hope to investigate in future research.

In order to develop our argument, first we need to identify the lower clerical, sales and service group more precisely in terms of the constituent occupations and their demographics. This will involve recounting the history of the group in relation to the development of the Goldthorpe class schema and its validation. Who are they? Why did Goldthorpe separate them into Class IIIb? What considerations make this group especially problematic in terms of its class allocation?

In the process we shall see that the overwhelming fact about this group of occupations is that it is mainly filled by married women, most of whom are working part time. Among men, students working part time are a significant element. These are therefore occupations that are typical both of the trend towards a post-industrial, 'flexible' labour market (Dex and McCulloch, 1997) and to the debates that surround the meaning and significance of work for married women (Hakim, 1995; cf. Ginn et al., 1996). Once we could define the majority of the working class as 'industrial', 'blue collar', full time, male, manual and muscular. Now large parts of that class are white collar, female, non-manual and working part time in sales and services.

LOWER SALES AND SERVICE OCCUPATIONS AND THE GOLDTHORPE CLASS SCHEMA

We begin by recounting the way in which Goldthorpe and his colleagues have dealt with the class position of lower sales and service occupations. Initially, some of these occupations were seen as part of an undivided Class III of 'routine non-manual employees' (Goldthorpe with Llewellyn and Payne, 1980). Other sales and service occupations were allocated to the semi- and unskilled working class, Class VII (see Table 12.4). At that time, the Goldthorpe classes were described as groupings of occupations that shared similar work and market situations (see Lockwood, 1958/1989). In these terms, Class III occupations had lower incomes than those in Classes I and II (the higher and lower 'service' classes) and even than some occupations in Class VI (skilled manual workers). However, they had greater security than Class VI and were regarded by management as 'staff' rather than 'workers'. They formed a 'white-collar labour force' that was functionally associated with, but marginal to, Classes I and II. Along with lower grade technicians and the supervisors of manual workers in Class V, Goldthorpe thus saw Class III as an intermediate class between the service class and the working class.

We must recall, however, that this first version of the Goldthorpe schema was devised for a study of social mobility among men only. At the time of this study, in 1972, men in Class III constituted less than 10 per cent of the sample, the smallest of the employee classes. Had it existed, Class IIIb would then have constituted less than 1 per cent for men. However, we estimate that about 40 per cent of economically active and retired women would have fallen into Class III in 1972, of whom something like a quarter (10 per cent of the total) would have been in Class IIIb. Thus, when Goldthorpe confronted his feminist critics by addressing the class mobility of women (Goldthorpe with Llewellyn and Payne, 1987: Ch. 10), it became necessary for him to sub-divide Class III. He thus distinguished between Class IIIa (higher grade routine non-manual) and Class IIIb (lower grade routine non-manual) 'in order to make the schema more suited to the class allocation of women' (ibid.: 279). His aim was

to isolate in IIIb occupations which are very largely filled by women and which, moreover, *in terms of their characteristic employment relations and conditions, would seem to entail straightforward wage-labour rather than displaying any of the*

quasi-bureaucratic features associated with other positions covered by Class III.
(ibid.: 280, emphasis added)

Thus, from the outset Goldthorpe had no doubt that the lower sales and service
occupations that he allocated to Class IIIb (such as shop (sales and retail)
assistants, shop cashiers, checkout operators, lower level attendants and receptionists) should *not* be seen as part of an intermediate class. Rather, and
particularly for women, they were to be combined with Class VII as part of the
semi- and unskilled working class, a class that already included other sales and
service occupations such as care assistants, street traders, restaurant and bar
workers, cleaners and shelf fillers. The comparable SOC2000 occupational unit
groups allocated to Class IIIb are given in Table 12.2.

Almost simultaneously, the Essex class project, using national survey data
collected in 1984, had arrived at a similar conclusion to Goldthorpe about the
class character of these occupations. As the Essex team explained, work
situation data seemed to show that Class IIIb was more similar to Class
VII than to the rest of Class III (Marshall et al., 1988: Ch. 5). Subsequent
analyses showed similar findings for the market situation (Rose and Birkelund,
1991; cf. Birkelund and Rose, 1997). The Essex team concluded that creating
Class IIIb when classifying women by their own employment fulfilled
Goldthorpe's intended objective (Marshall et al., 1988: 309). They noted that:

> this largely female group is more or less indistinguishable from the working class as
> conventionally defined. They are . . . significantly less likely to be in positions of
> trust, positions which give individuals control over their labour . . . than are those
> involved in routine clerical tasks (in Class IIIa). These personal service workers
> would seem to have more in common . . . with members of the skilled and unskilled
> working class. For women in these positions Class III may be a proletarian – rather
> than an intermediate – class location. (ibid.: 121)

Table 12.2   *SOC2000 OUGs in Goldthorpe Class IIIb*

OUG code	Title of OUG
4141	Telephonists
4216	Receptionists
5496	Floral arrangers, florists
6111	Nursing auxiliaries and assistants
6113	Dental nurses
6121	Nursery nurses
6122	Childminders and related occupations
6123	Playgroup leaders/assistants
6124	Educational assistants
6213	Travel and tour guides
6214	Air travel assistants
6231	Housekeepers and related occupations
7111	Sales and retail assistants
7112	Retail cashiers and checkout operators
7113	Telephone salespersons
7125	Merchandisers and window dressers
9244	School midday assistants

Moreover, Marshall and his colleagues found evidence for asymmetry: that is, many aspects of beliefs and identity for women in Class IIIb were more conditioned by their husband's class position than by their own. This confirmed Goldthorpe's own findings using the 1983 British Election Study data (Goldthorpe with Llewellyn and Payne, 1987; Goldthorpe and Payne, 1986).

We have seen that Goldthorpe created Class IIIb in order to respond to his feminist critics. In a later comparative project (the Comparative Analysis of Social Mobility in Industrial Societies or CASMIN project) Erikson and Goldthorpe (1992) returned to this debate. Here Class IIIb is now described as 'routine non-manual employees, lower grade (sales and services)'. Class III as a whole is described as covering a range of non-manual positions existing at the fringes of bureaucracies. Along with Class V (lower technical and supervisory) it is again defined as an intermediate class, that is as a class with 'mixed' employment relations. Readers are reminded by Erikson and Goldthorpe of the distinction made between Classes IIIa and IIIb and of the fact that it is only implemented in analyses where women are involved. Thus, Class IIIb is combined with Class IIIa in most of the CASMIN analyses. The only exception is when Erikson and Goldthorpe examine the class mobility of women. For this purpose Class IIIb is collapsed with Class VII in order

> to isolate in Class IIIb a range of routine and very-low skill non-manual positions which are largely occupied by women and to which (especially *when* held by women) very little ambiguity in fact attaches. That is to say, these positions tend, in contrast to those retained in Class IIIa, to be more-or-less undifferentiated in their conditions of employment from those of non-skilled manual workers. Thus, in analyses in which the sub-division is applied, Class IIIb is usually collapsed with Class VIIa. (ibid.: 44, emphasis in the original)

Do criterion validation studies justify Goldthorpe's approach?

Criterion validation and Class IIIb

The Goldthorpe class schema has been subjected to a number of *ex-post* validation studies (see Chapter 2, the introduction to Part II and also Goldthorpe, 1997). These studies have been designed to assess the criterion validity of the schema – how well it measures or captures the underlying concept of employment relations. For our present purposes we need only refer to two such studies using national sample survey data for 1984 and 1996 respectively.

Evans, using techniques derived from psychological approaches to validation, has pioneered investigations of the validity of the Goldthorpe schema. In his first paper on this issue (Evans, 1992), he used employment relations and conditions data from the Essex class project (Marshall et al., 1988). With regard to Class IIIb, Evans noted that in some respects it was more similar to Class V than to Class IIIa in employment relations terms. Indeed, on some of the measures he analysed, Class IIIb was hardly better placed than Class VII. However, and reflecting occupational sex segregation, in the Essex data set only one male respondent was in Class IIIb and very few women were in Class

V. Once Evans controlled for sex, he found more similarity between women in Classes IIIb and IIIa than between women in Classes IIIb and VII. Thus, he concluded that it was preferable to collapse Class IIIb with Class IIIa and not with Class VII. Nevertheless, he noted both that the then government occupational classification (*Classification of Ocupations 1980*) appeared to make difficulties for an adequate operationalisation of IIIb and that his statistical models showed little difference in explained variance whichever choice was made.

Since 1984, as we have seen in Table 12.1, Class IIIb occupations have greatly expanded as a proportion of the workforce. While still dominated by women, there are also more men now in these occupations. Evans' most recent validation of the Goldthorpe schema used 1996 ONS Omnibus Survey data on employment relations, data collected as part of the ESRC Review process (see O'Reilly and Rose, 1997; 1998). In this study (Evans and Mills, 2000) on seven of the nine employment relations items, Class IIIb was shown to have values closer to Class VII than to Class IIIa. On this basis, Evans and Mills concluded that 'though IIIb occupations do not have the same employment relations (as Class VII), there does appear to be a substantial amount of overlap' (ibid.: 650). In other words, what seemed a marginal situation in 1984 in terms of how Class IIIb should be regarded – intermediate or working class – by 1996 was looking more clear cut. Goldthorpe appears to have been vindicated on this issue.

In summary, therefore, Goldthorpe is clear that Class IIIb is part of the working class for women and should always be treated as such where women are involved in analysis. Validation studies appear to support this view. The fact that Class IIIb otherwise collapses with Class IIIa in the CASMIN project would appear to be partly the result of cross-national variability of employment relations for lower level administrative, clerical and service jobs. Whatever the case, whether Class IIIb should only be operationalised as part of the working class for women and should otherwise be ignored is an empirical matter. What is certain is that we can separate the treatment of Class IIIb neither from the

Table 12.3   *Some characteristics of the Goldthorpe classes* *

Goldthorpe classes	% part time	% married women	% married women working p/t	% married men	% with quals above A-level
I	9	18	5	50	62
II	18	32	12	31	45
IIIa	33	46	23	10	14
IIIb	70	49	39	4	7
IVa	9	22	7	59	11
IVb	21	17	11	52	7
IVc	12	16	7	57	12
V	11	13	6	53	8
VI	10	8	5	48	4
VIIa	39	27	19	28	3
VIIb	21	15	9	40	5

* Data from the winter quarter of the 1996/97 Labour Force Survey.

problem of the unit of class composition, to which we now briefly turn, nor from the associated effects of part-time working (cf. Chapter 6 in this volume). The reasons for this are clear from Table 12.3. This shows that Class IIIb has by far the highest rate of part-time employment, the highest proportion of both married women and married women working part time and the lowest proportion of married men.

THE UNIT OF CLASS COMPOSITION

When Erikson and Goldthorpe turn to the issue of class mobility among women, they reaffirm their commitment to the use of the household as the unit of class composition (see also Erikson, 1984; Goldthorpe, 1983). We have already discussed the issues surrounding this debate in Chapter 1. Erikson and Goldthorpe observe that 'it is by reference to the *empirical consequences* of different conceptual choices, and of different ways of rendering these choices operational' that analysts should evaluate the individual versus the household as the appropriate unit of class composition (1992: 231, emphasis in the original; cf. Sørensen, 1994). Their reasons for this choice are fully explained (ibid.: 232–5). Moreover, they observe that, although the labour market participation rates of married women have increased, they remain less attached to the workforce than men, have less continuous work histories and make less of a contribution to family income. They are more likely to leave work for family reasons or for reasons associated with their husband's employment. Thus they have less steady career development and more downward mobility. And, of course, we can add that they are more likely to work part time. In sum, for many married women, work does not reduce their dependency. On all these issues we shall have more to say later when we examine the situation of lower sales and service workers in the NS-SEC in more detail.

In order to reinforce their point, Erikson and Goldthorpe (ibid.: 236–7) offer the examples of two female, part-time shop assistants, one married to a man in Class VII and the other married to a man in Class I. The individual approach would place each woman in the same class (Class IIIb for Goldthorpe, Class 6 in the NS-SEC). Yet their positions in class terms are not really the same because of the effects of their husbands' different class positions. Their partners' class relations will lead to very different life chances for the two women concerned. Erikson and Goldthorpe repeat the findings concerning asymmetry from the Essex class project and the British Election Study data mentioned earlier in order to support their case: both women's political partisanship and their class identification are more related to their husband's class position than to their own (and see Marshall, 1997: Ch. 5). Again, we shall return to a re-examination of these issues later, using LFS and BHPS data.

This is the background against which we had to work in the ESRC Review. We now turn to an examination of our own findings with regard to the relevant occupations. In the final section we shall return to the problem of the unit of class composition.

LOWER SALES, SERVICE AND CLERICAL OCCUPATIONS IN THE NS-SEC

As we have already noted, the full range of lower sales and service occupational groups in SOC2000 is far wider than those encompassed by Goldthorpe's Class IIIb. To these we must also add lower level clerical occupations that might be thought to be similar in their class character. The full list of relevant OUGs and their Goldthorpe and NS-SEC class allocations for employees are given in Table 12.4. Driving and transport occupations are excluded. In constructing the NS-SEC we had to consider all of these occupational groups, not just those identified in Goldthorpe's Class IIIb.

As Table 12.4 shows, the majority of lower clerical, sales and service occupations have been allocated, *faute de mieux*, to NS-SEC Class 6. These include most of the occupations that comprise Goldthorpe's Class IIIb. These are therefore consistent allocations between the two schemata. Since Goldthorpe's Class VII would encompass both NS-SEC Classes 6 and 7, then those occupations in both Goldthorpe VII and NS-SEC Classes 6 and 7 are also homologous. However, there are a few occupational groups that are not

Table 12.4   *Lower sales, service and clerical occupations in SOC2000*

OUG code	Title of OUGs	Goldthorpe class	NS-SEC
3443	Fitness instructors	II	6/12.2
3449	Sports and fitness occupations n.e.c.	V	3/7.2
4133	Stock control clerks	IIIa	6/12.6
4137	Market research interviewers	IIIa	6/12.6
4141	Telephonists	IIIb	6/12.6
4150	General office assistants/clerks	IIIa	3/7.2
4216	Receptionists	IIIb	6/12.6
5496	Floral arrangers/florists	IIIb	7/13.1
6111	Nursing auxiliaries and assistants	IIIb	3/7.3
6112	Ambulance staff (excluding paramedics)	VI	3/7.2
6113	Dental nurses	IIIb	6/12.2
6114	Houseparents and residential wardens	IIIa	6/12.7
6115	Care assistants and home carers	VII	6/12.2
6121	Nursery nurses	IIIb	3/7.2
6122	Childminders and related occupations	IIIb	7/13.1
6123	Playgroup leaders/assistants	IIIb	6/12.7
6124	Educational assistants	IIIb	6/12.7
6131	Veterinary nurses and assistants	V	6/12.2
6211	Sports and leisure assistants	VII	6/12.2
6212	Travel agents	IIIa	3/7.2
6213	Travel and tour guides	IIIb	7/13.1
6214	Air travel assistants	IIIb	3/7.2
6215	Rail travel assistants	V/VII	3/7.2
6219	Leisure and travel service occupations n.e.c.	IIIb/VII	7/13.3
6221	Hairdressers, barbers	V	7/13.1
6222	Beauticians and related occupations	V	6/12.2
6231	Housekeepers and related occupations	IIIb	6/12.2

Table 12.4 *continued*

OUG code	Title of OUGs	Goldthorpe class	NS-SEC
6232	Caretakers	VII	6/12.2
6291	Undertakers and mortuary assistants	VII	6/12.2
6292	Pest control officers	VII	6/12.2
7111	Sales and retail assistants	IIIb	6/12.1
7112	Retail cashiers and checkout operators	IIIb	6/12.1
7113	Telephone salespersons	IIIb	6/12.1
7121	Collector salespersons and credit agents	IIIa	6/12.1
7122	Debt, rent and other cash collectors	IIIa	3/7.2
7123	Roundsmen/women and van salespersons	VII	7/13.3
7124	Market and street traders and assistants	VII	7/13.1
7125	Merchandisers and window dressers	IIIb	3/7.2
7129	Sales-related occupations n.e.c.	II/IIIa	3/7.2
7211	Call centre agents/operators	IIIa	3/7.2
7212	Customer care occupations	IIIa	3/7.2
9211	Postal workers etc.	VII	6/12.2
9219	Elementary office occupations n.e.c.	IIIa	6/12.6
9221	Hospital porters	VII	6/12.2
9222	Hotel porters	VII	7/13.1
9223	Kitchen and catering assistants	VII	6/12.2
9224	Waiters and waitresses	VII	7/13.1
9225	Bar staff	VII	7/13.1
9226	Leisure/theme park attendants	VII	7/13.1
9229	Elementary personal services n.e.c.	VII	7/13.1
9231	Window cleaners	VII	7/13.2
9232	Road sweepers	VII	7/13.4
9233	Cleaners/domestics	VII	7/13.4
9234	Launderers/dry cleaners/pressers	VII	7/13.2
9235	Refuse/salvage occupations	VII	7/13.4
9239	Elementary cleaning n.e.c.	VII	7/13.4
9241	Security guards	V	6/12.2
9242	Traffic wardens	V	6/12.2
9243	School crossing patrol attendants	V	7/13.1
9244	School midday assistants	IIIb	7/13.1
9245	Car park attendants	VII	7/13.4
9249	Elementary security n.e.c.	VII	6/12.2
9251	Shelf fillers	VII	6/12.1
9259	Elementary sales n.e.c.	VII	6/12.1

similarly treated, such as those in Goldthorpe Class IIIa but NS-SEC Class 6 or in Goldthorpe Class VII but NS-SEC Class 3.

Table 12.5 summarises the relationship of employees in Goldthorpe's Class IIIb in terms of their allocations within the NS-SEC. We can see that 61 per cent of those in Class IIIb go to NS-SEC Class 6 and a further 23 per cent to NS-SEC Class 7, so that in total 84 per cent go to positions consistent with Goldthorpe's original treatment of Class IIIb as an element of the working class. Only 16 per cent have been allocated to an intermediate position in the NS-SEC (Class 3) covering the occupational groups of nursing assistants, nursery nurses, air travel assistants and merchandisers and window dressers.

Since the majority of lower sales, service and clerical occupations are found in NS-SEC Class 6, we shall confine our subsequent analyses and discussion to the relevant components of this class (i.e. to operational sub-categories L12.1, L12.2, L12.6 and L12.7). We shall also make some comparisons with the rest of Class 6 (sub-categories L12.3, L12. 4 and L12.5). For convenience we shall refer to the former as Class 6A and the latter as Class 6B, a distinction we originally proposed to the Review team as being one worth incorporating into the NS-SEC.

Table 12.5   *Where do sales and service employees (S&S) go in the NS-SEC?* *

NS-SEC class	% of S&S	NS-SEC sub-category	% of S&S	S&S as % of NS-SEC sub-category
3	16	7.1	–	–
		7.2	13	74
		7.3	3	52
		7.4	–	–
6	61	12.1	27	99
		12.2	23	92
		12.3	–	–
		12.4	–	–
		12.5	–	–
		12.6	7	100
		12.7	4	100
7	23	13.1	11	100
		13.2	1	8
		13.3	†	2
		13.4	11	55
		13.5	–	–

* Data from the winter quarter of the 1996/97 Labour Force Survey.
† Less than 1%.

The characteristics of lower sales, service and clerical employees

Table 12.6 presents a summary of certain demographic and other characteristics of employees in Class 6A. We can see that 72 per cent of the class are women. While overall 62 per cent work part time, this is true for 71 per cent of women. Equally, 71 per cent of women in Class 6A said they did not want full-time work and 58 per cent of women in the class are married. Among men, only 38 per cent work part time and (we may assume) two-thirds of them do so because they are students. Only 38 per cent of the men are married. Not surprisingly, given all this, the mean age of part-time male employees in the class is only 26, compared with nearly 38 for women and 37 for full-time male employees.

In other words, the vast majority of women and a substantial minority of men in Class 6A have chosen to be part-time employees either (we may infer) for family- or education-related reasons. As Table 12.7 shows, other characteristics

Table 12.6 *Demographic characteristics of Class 6A [%]**

	All of 6A	Males in 6A	Females in 6A
Sex			
Male	28	–	–
Female	72	–	–
Work hours			
Full time	38	62	29
Part time	62	38	71
Why part time?[†]			
Student	24	64	16
Ill/disabled	1	2	1
Could not find f/t	13	21	12
Did not want f/t	61	13	71
Mean age [years]			
Full time	36.6	37.2	36.1
Part time	35.6	26.2	37.6
Industry			
Wholesale, retail	41	38	42
Education	7	3	8
Health, social	20	7	25
Others	32	52	24
Marital status			
Single	37	56	30
Married	53	38	58
Separated	3	2	3
Divorced	6	3	7
Widow	2	1	2
Education			
Degree	3	3	3
HE below degree	4	3	4
A-level	22	29	19
O-level	49	45	51
None	21	18	22

* Data from the winter quarter of the 1996/97 Labour Force Survey.
[†] % of part time workers in 6A.

of women in Class 6A are somewhat different from those found in Classes 5, 6B and 7. For example, 15 per cent had service class fathers, 32 per cent are married to service class men, 76 per cent earn less than half of their partner's income and only 15 per cent have a joint or dominant work position in Erikson's (1984) terms (see Chapter 1). While the proportion who regard themselves as working class is similar to Classes 5 and 7, at 51 per cent it is much lower than for the rest of Class 6. Similarly, identification with the Conservative Party is rather higher than for Classes 5, 6B and 7. Moreover, as Table 12.8 shows, married women in Class 6A are far more likely to identify with the working class when living with a man in Classes 6 or 7 and are equally less likely to feel closest to the Conservative Party. Even the proportion that smoke or who say they have excellent health varies between Class 6A women according to their partner's class.

Table 12.7   *Some characteristics of females in the NS-SEC classes (%)*

NS-SEC	Father in Goldthorpe Classes 1/2[†]	Partner in NS-SEC 1/2	Female pay < 50% of male pay	Joint or dominant work position	Self-identify as 'working class'	'Closest to' Conservative Party
1	45	71	26	85	29	31
2	36	53	32	61	34	33
3	23	39	49	37	43	42
4	22	21	55	62	29	59
5	16	25	50	46	51	25
6A	15	32	76	15	51	34
6B	8	13	41	53	69	19
7	11	26	75	15	50	23

* Data from Wave 1 of the British Household Panel Survey: households where both spouses working.
[†] All females.

Table 12.8   *Characteristics of married/cohabiting females in Class 6A by spouse's NS-SEC (%)*

Spouse's NS-SEC	Smoker	Self-rated health as excellent	Subjective 'working class'	'Closest to' Conservatives
1/2	25	35	32	44
6/7	31	23	54[†]	21[†]
Overall	28	29	43	34

* Data from Wave 1 of the British Household Panel Survey: households where both spouses working.
[†] Sig. at 5%.

CONCLUSIONS: THE IMPLICATIONS FOR THE UNIT OF CLASS COMPOSITION

All these findings of asymmetry are reminiscent of those we discussed earlier in relation to previous research by Goldthorpe and by the Essex class project team. Therefore, they raise the same questions when it comes to the appropriate unit of class composition. When dealing with a class such as 6A, it seems to us essential that a measure of household class is used. Indeed, we would generally regard a household measure as preferable to an individual one. As Cooper and Arber conceded in Chapter 10, using household class measures might significantly affect the results of analyses such as theirs, where gender is a significant factor. And as Goldthorpe has noted in correspondence with health researchers at University College London, and as we observed in Chapter 2, while it may be true that NS-SEC class is determined by an individual's employment relations, this does not imply that the NS-SEC is inherently an individual measure. Employment contracts have implications not only for individuals but for members of their immediate families, too. This is why we should not treat, say, a person in Class 6A married to a higher manager in the same way as a person in Class 6A married to a van driver. Similar considerations apply to full-time students who have paid work. In our view it makes much more sense to classify them to the class of their family household than to that of their part-time job. Alternatively, they should be classified as students (i.e. to L15) and then be ignored when using one of the NS-SEC analytic variables.

Of course, circumstances may alter cases. For example, if an analyst were interested in the effects of autonomy at work on health, then an individual measure would be more appropriate, although it would still be informative to examine the issues using a household measure, too. In studies which focus on students, it would be vital to collect information on their class of origin.

Naturally, we do not claim that our superficial analyses in this chapter absolutely prove our point. More work needs to be done. Rather, we are using our prima facie findings to indicate both why those occupations in Class 6A are difficult to classify and why they need to be treated with caution in analyses. In the latter case, we seek to amplify issues discussed in Chapter 2 concerning conceptual and analytic matters.

REFERENCES

Birkelund, G.E. and Rose, D. (1997) 'Women and social class: toward a more complete picture', *Sosiologisk Tidsskrift*, 5: 145–65.

Dex, S. and McCulloch, A. (1997) *Flexible employment: the future of Britain's jobs*. Basingstoke: Macmillan.

Erikson, R. (1984) 'Social class of men, women and families', *Sociology*, 18: 500–14.

Erikson, R. and Goldthorpe, J.H. (1992) *The Constant Flux*. Oxford: Clarendon Press.

Esping-Andersen, G. (ed.) (1993) *Changing Classes: Stratification and Mobility in Post-Industrial Societies*. London: Sage.

Evans, G. (1992) 'Testing the validity of the Goldthorpe class schema', *European Sociological Review*, 8: 211–32.

Evans, G. and Mills, C. (2000) 'In search of the wage-labour/service contract: new evidence on the validity of the Goldthorpe class schema', *British Journal of Sociology*, 51: 641–61.

Ginn, J., Arber, S., Brannen, J., Dale, A., Dex, S., Elias, P., Moss, P., Pahl, J., Roberts, C. and Rubery, J. (1996) 'Feminist fallacies: a reply to Hakim on women's employment', *British Journal of Sociology*, 47: 167–73.

Goldthorpe, J.H. (1983) 'Women and class analysis: in defence of the conventional view', *Sociology*, 17: 465–88.

Goldthorpe, J.H. (1997) 'The "Goldthorpe" class schema: some observations on conceptual and operational issues in relation to the ESRC Review of Government Social Classifications', in D. Rose and K. O'Reilly (eds) *Constructing Classes: Towards a New Social Classification for the UK*. Swindon/London: ESRC/ONS. pp. 40–8.

Goldthorpe, J.H. (with Llewellyn, C. and Payne, C.) (1980) *Social Mobility and Class Structure in Modern Britain*. Oxford: Clarendon Press.

Goldthorpe, J.H. (with Llewellyn, C. and Payne, C.) (1987) *Social Mobility and Class Structure in Modern Britain*, 2nd edition. Oxford: Clarendon Press.

Goldthorpe, J.H. and Payne, C. (1986) 'On the class mobility of women: results from different approaches to the analysis of recent British data', *Sociology*, 20: 531–55.

Hakim, C. (1995) 'Five feminist myths about women's employment', *British Journal of Sociology*, 46: 429–55.

Lockwood, D. (1958/1989) *The Blackcoated Worker*. London: Allen and Unwin/ Oxford: Clarendon Press.

Marshall, G. (1997) *Repositioning Class: Social Inequality in Industrial Societies*. London: Sage.

Marshall, G., Rose, D., Newby, H. and Vogler, C. (1988) *Social Class in Modern Britain*. London: Hutchinson.

O'Reilly, K. and Rose, D. (1997) 'Criterion validation of the interim revised social classification', in D. Rose and K. O'Reilly (eds) *Constructing Classes: Towards a New Social Classification for the UK*. Swindon/London: ESRC/ONS.

O'Reilly, K. and Rose, D. (1998) 'Changing employment relations? Plus ça change, plus c'est la même chose? Reflections arising from the ESRC Review of Government Social Classifications', *Work, Employment and Society*, 12: 713–33.

Rose, D. and Birkelund, G.E. (1991) 'Social class, gender and occupational segregation', Occasional Paper 1, ESRC Research Centre on Micro-Social Change, University of Essex, Colchester.

Sørensen, A. (1994) 'Women, family and class', *Annual Review of Sociology*, 20: 27–47.

13
The NS-SEC
Overview and conclusions

David Rose and David J. Pevalin

We designed this book to be an introduction to the NS-SEC complete with chapters illustrating both its adequacy as a measure of employment relations and conditions and its usefulness as a research tool. Not surprisingly, along the way the studies reported here have raised a number of issues. In this final chapter of the book we aim both to identify and draw together the pertinent points for future use of the classification and to indicate where further work may prove to be useful.

In Part I, we laid out a description and explanation of the NS-SEC. A fuller description of and technical information on the NS-SEC is provided in Rose and Pevalin with O'Reilly (2003) which complements the work presented in this volume. Rose and O'Reilly (1997; 1998) and O'Reilly and Rose (1998) provide the key summaries of the earlier stages of the Review. In the explanation of the conceptual basis of the NS-SEC given in Chapter 2, we briefly mentioned the other approaches to measuring socio-economic position, not only previous government classifications but other sociological approaches. We have previously described how these stand in relation to the NS-SEC (Rose and Pevalin, 2001) but perhaps it is worth reiterating the main points in order for new users to be aware of the larger debates in the area and to point them in the direction of the key texts (also see Mills and Evans in Chapter 4).

Apart from Goldthorpe's class schema, a number of occupational scales have also been derived by British academics for use in studies of social inequality. These are the Hall–Jones Scale, the Hope–Goldthorpe Scale and the Cambridge Scale. Very briefly, the Hall–Jones Scale (Hall and Jones, 1950) graded occupations according to their prestige and was used by Glass (1954) in his pioneering study of social mobility. While this scale was used in some important studies (e.g. Goldthorpe et al., 1969; Townsend, 1979), there were no clear guidelines published to show how occupations were coded to the scale by Glass, and the degree to which different uses of the scale were truly comparable is uncertain. The Hope–Goldthorpe Scale (Goldthorpe and Hope, 1974) was consciously produced to remedy the problems of the Hall–Jones Scale and was the first step in the Oxford mobility project before Goldthorpe abandoned the scale in favour of his class schema (see Marshall et al., 1988: 305–10). The Hope–Goldthorpe Scale was derived from a survey of the social standing of occupations so that jobs are ranked in terms of their social desirability. In that sense, it is not a prestige scale but a cognitive judgement about the desirability of different occupations.

The Cambridge Scale (CS) is based on the scaling of survey respondents' occupational friendship and marriage scores (Prandy, 1990; Stewart et al., 1980). Its originators regard the CS as a broad measure of social stratification and social inequality. Ultimately the scale measures the market outcomes of different jobs and the lifestyle associated with them. It is not an attempt to measure the social structure and the way this creates different market capacities in different sections of the population. Indeed, the theoretical position of the authors of the CS is one that rejects class analysis on the grounds that it is a static approach to what are fundamentally problems relating to social dynamics. Nor is CS a status scale. It is a measure of lifestyle determined by social experience and, ultimately therefore, significant social processes. It is designed to unite key features of both the social and the economic, and it raises questions about any attempt to analyse social inequality in terms of categorical measures.

In a series of articles over the last decade the authors of the CS have argued against the theoretical basis and empirical usefulness of the various Goldthorpe-based schemas (Blackburn and Prandy, 1997; Prandy, 1990; 1998a; 1999; Prandy and Blackburn, 1997). The programme of validating the Goldthorpe schema undertaken by Evans and Mills (Evans, 1992; 1996; Evans and Mills, 1998; 2000) has attracted particular critical attention (cf. Prandy and Blackburn, 1997). In response, this invoked a detailed critique of the CS from Evans (1998). Neither has the NS-SEC escaped attention with pointed critiques to be found in Blackburn (1998) and Prandy (1998b) followed by a response from Rose (1998).

There have been many other conceptual and methodological disputes between sociologists in the UK surrounding the issues discussed in Part I. In particular the continuing relevance of class analysis has been challenged. These are not exclusively British debates, but for British perspectives readers are referred to the work of Pahl (1989; 1993), Goldthorpe and Marshall (1992), Savage et al. (1992), Butler and Savage (1995), Lee and Turner (1996), Saunders (1996), Scott (1996), Marshall (1997: Ch. 1), Halpin (1999), Prandy (1998b), Blackburn (1998), Crompton (1998), Rose (1998) and Crompton et al. (2000).

The chapters in Part II have demonstrated the adequacy of the NS-SEC as a measure of employment relations. On the whole, the chapters show that the NS-SEC classes adequately group together occupational unit groups by employment status combinations that share similar employment relations and conditions. The authors of the four chapters in Part II have used a variety of techniques either to discriminate between classes or to assess the clustering of OUGs by employment status combinations in relation to their class allocation. All these analyses were conducted on the 'second tier' of the employment relations approach used in the conceptual derivation of the NS-SEC. That is, they were only concerned with the classification of employees through variation in employment relations and conditions, rather than with the 'first tier' of classification of employers, the self-employed, employees and the excluded.

It is worth reiterating at this point that the main methodological problem for all the chapters in Part II is that, for the most part, they use measures of employment relations and conditions that were specially collected for use in the construction of the NS-SEC and its *ex ante* validation. As Mills and Evans, Coxon and Fisher, and we have previously noted, it is then somewhat tautological to talk about these chapters as true criterion validation studies. We await *ex post* validation studies using other suitable measures of employment relations and conditions and other data. Nevertheless, the results of the analyses in these chapters have drawn attention to some problematic areas in the classification, such as distinctions between higher managerial and professional occupations and the proper classification of what Goldthorpe termed 'lower sales and service occupations'. We have left the former to further research but have attempted to detail the issues surrounding lower sales and service occupations in Chapter 12.

It would be easy to say that most researchers who may use the NS-SEC will be more interested in the results of the construct validation studies reported in the chapters in Part III. However, it is a concern for all who may use the NS-SEC to be assured that it is measuring what it purports to measure. Only then can plausible hypotheses be constructed to test the relationships and pathways between the NS-SEC and the outcome of interest to the researcher.

In Part III the construct validation studies aimed to illustrate the usefulness of the NS-SEC as a research tool. The authors of these chapters elaborated plausible social relationships between the classes of the NS-SEC and the outcomes studied. For example, Elias and McKnight in Chapter 7 hypothesised a direct link between the NS-SEC and risk of unemployment in that those in occupations with a 'labour contract' are more likely (and easily) to be made redundant and more likely to leave their current employer without first securing other employment. Using longitudinal data, they then demonstrated the prospective effect of class on experiences of unemployment in that those in NS-SEC Classes 6 and 7 are significantly more likely to experience unemployment than those in Classes 1 to 4.

Pevalin in Chapter 9 gives an example of hypothesising an indirect relationship from the NS-SEC to the outcome of his study – low-weight births. In this case what the NS-SEC directly measures, employment relations and conditions, has no direct bearing on his hypotheses. This is for two reasons. First, the father's NS-SEC class is used as a crude measure of household class. Second, the concept of employment relations is seen as central to defining socio-economic position and it is these positions, that exist independently of the individuals who happen to occupy them at any particular time, that determine material and symbolic advantages. It is from these advantages that processes, such as maternal nutrition and smoking, may link class with low-weight births.

The study of mortality by Fitzpatrick in Chapter 8 brings out a number of issues worth highlighting. The first one is the appropriate use of Census data to form the population denominators. Fitzpatrick details the differing distributions obtained by two methods of deriving the NS-SEC – one with full-employment status information and the other using the reduced method where size of establishment information is missing. From this Fitzpatrick advises that as the reduced method *has* to be used to derive the NS-SEC on the death registration data, the same derivation method should be used on the Census data. She also draws our attention to the potential differences between occupational information coded from relatively brief information, such as on the Census and death registers, and those coded using much more detailed information, such as the LFS.

A further point brought out in Fitzpatrick's chapter is the distinctive mortality patterns of the non-professional self-employed in NS-SEC Class 4 (cf. Pevalin in Chapter 9 in relation to low-weight births). Previously the people in this class would have been distributed across multiple SC classes, so that such differences could not be identified. While a distinctive pattern for the self-employed holds for adult and infant mortality and, to some extent, low-weight births, the reasons for this remain to be fully uncovered.

As we explained in Chapter 1, Class 8 – the never employed and the long-term unemployed – is an optional class as it cannot be operationalised on all government data. This class poses particular problems for health analyses and Cooper and Arber in Chapter 10 detail the operational and analytical issues. They expand on these initial problems to include a discussion of how gender and age are particularly relevant to the analysis of Class 8. Indeed, more generally, the changes to and the nature of female participation in the labour market over time and how these are adequately captured in occupational and socio-economic classifications remains an active debate (e.g. Crompton et al., 2000; Evans, 1996).

Finally, there remains the issue of continuity with the previous government classifications that we alluded to in Chapter 1. Heath, Martin and Beerten in Chapter 11 used the categories and sub-categories of the operational version of the NS-SEC to create an approximation to SC. They demonstrated that, with three common outcomes, this approximation had similar statistical associations to the normally derived measure of SC. For researchers interested in analysing longitudinal data or time series, this way of achieving a reasonable approximation to SC may prove useful. The Review has also provided a direct derivation of the NS-SEC from the previous occupational classification, SOC90, which can be used on data from 1991. In addition, as an academic, rather than official, exercise, we have produced derivation matrices for SC and SEG from the new occupational classification, SOC2000. *These matrices are not recognised as official by ONS.* However, they may be of use to researchers who prefer to continue their longitudinal or time series analyses using the previous government classifications. Needless to say, for all the conceptual reasons we outlined in Chapter 2, we recommend that the NS-SEC be applied retrospectively rather than taking SC and SEG forward.

CONCLUDING COMMENTS

We can note from both this chapter and the previous ones that the NS-SEC has the following features to commend it:

- It is conceptually clear and rigorous.
- It is simple to operationalise.
- Through both its nested properties and its various methods of derivation – full, reduced and simplified – it is very flexible in use.
- It also has both household- and individual-level versions.
- It offers a high degree of continuity and thus comparability with both SC and SEG.
- It provides an improved classification of women's employment positions.
- When fully operationalised, it enables comprehensive population coverage.
- It has clearer maintenance procedures than those that pertained to SC and SEG.
- It provides the possibility of a standardised tool for use in government, academia and the private sector.
- Above all, it provides both government and academic users with a tool which lends itself to the explanation of relationships, and thus to both more lucid policy recommendations and a better understanding of social processes.

We have no doubt that the NS-SEC will set new puzzles for analysts and will uncover fresh avenues of exploration. Some of these avenues have been explored in the chapters in Part III, but many more remain to be discovered.

REFERENCES

Blackburn, R.M. (1998) 'A new system of classes: but what are they and do we need them?', *Work, Employment and Society*, 12: 735–41.
Blackburn, R.M. and Prandy, K. (1997) 'The reproduction of social inequality', *Sociology*, 31: 491–509.
Butler, T. and Savage, M. (eds) (1995) *Social Change and the Middle Classes*. London: UCL Press.
Crompton, R. (1998) *Class and Stratification*. Cambridge: Polity Press.
Crompton, R., Devine, F., Savage, M. and Scott, J. (eds) (2000) *Renewing Class Analysis*. Oxford: Blackwell.
Evans, G. (1992) 'Testing the validity of the Goldthorpe class schema', *European Sociological Review*, 8: 211–32.
Evans, G. (1996) 'Putting men and women into classes: an assessment of the cross-sex validity of the Goldthorpe class schema', *Sociology*, 30: 209–34.
Evans, G. (1998) 'On tests of validity and social class: why Prandy and Blackburn are wrong', *Sociology*, 32: 189–202.
Evans, G. and Mills, C. (1998) 'Identifying class structure. A latent class analysis of the criterion-related and construct validity of the Goldthorpe class schema', *European Sociological Review*, 14: 87–106.
Evans, G. and Mills, C. (2000) 'In search of the wage-labour/service contract: new evidence on the validity of the Goldthorpe class schema', *British Journal of Sociology*, 51: 641–61.
Glass, D. (1954) *Social Mobility in Britain*. London: Routledge.

Goldthorpe, J.H. and Hope, K. (1974) *The Social Grading of Occupations*. Oxford: Clarendon Press.

Goldthorpe, J.H., Lockwood, D., Bechhofer, F. and Platt, J. (1969) *The Affluent Worker in the Class Structure*. Cambridge: Cambridge University Press.

Goldthorpe, J.H. and Marshall, G. (1992) 'The promising future of class analysis: a response to recent critiques', *Sociology*, 26: 381–400.

Hall, J. and Caradog Jones, D. (1950) 'Social grading of occupations', *British Journal of Sociology*, 1: 31–55.

Halpin, B. (1999) 'Is class changing? A work-life history perspective on the salariat', *Sociological Research Online*, 4, 3.

Lee, D. and Turner, B. (eds) (1996) *Conflicts about Class*. Harlow: Longman.

Marshall, G. (1997) *Repositioning Class: Social Inequality in Industrial Societies*. London: Sage.

Marshall, G., Newby, H., Rose, D. and Vogler, C. (1988) *Social Class in Modern Britain*. London: Hutchinson.

O'Reilly, K. and Rose, D. (1998) 'Changing employment relations? Plus ça change, plus c'est la même chose? Reflections arising from the ESRC Review of Government Social Classifications', *Work, Employment and Society*, 12: 713–33.

Pahl, R.E. (1989) 'Is the emperor naked?', *International Journal of Urban and Regional Research*, 13: 711–20.

Pahl, R.E. (1993) 'Does class analysis without class theory have a promising future? A reply to Goldthorpe and Marshall', *Sociology*, 27: 253–8.

Prandy, K. (1990) 'The revised Cambridge Scale of Occupations', *Sociology*, 24: 629–55.

Prandy, K. (1998a) 'Class and continuity in social reproduction: an empirical investigation', *Sociological Review*, 46: 340–64.

Prandy, K. (1998b) 'Deconstructing classes: critical comments on the revised social classification', *Work, Employment and Society*, 12: 743–53.

Prandy, K. (1999) 'Class, stratification and inequalities in health: a comparison of the Registrar-General's Social Class and the Cambridge Scale', *Sociology of Health and Illness*, 21: 466–84.

Prandy, K. and Blackburn, R.M. (1997) 'Putting men and women into classes: but is that where they belong? A comment on Evans', *Sociology*, 31: 143–52.

Rose, D. (1998) 'Once more unto the breach: in defence of class analysis yet again', *Work, Employment and Society*, 12: 755–67.

Rose, D. and O'Reilly, K. (eds) (1997) *Constructing Classes: Towards a New Social Classification for the UK*. Swindon/London: ESRC/ONS.

Rose, D. and O'Reilly, K. (1998) *The ESRC Review of Government Social Classifications*. London/Swindon: ONS/ESRC.

Rose, D. and Pevalin, D.J. (2001) 'The National Statistics Socio-economic Classification: unifying official and sociological approaches to the conceptualisation and measurement of social class', *Working Papers of the ESRC Research Centre on Micro-Social Change*, Paper 2001–4. Colchester: University of Essex.

Rose, D. and Pevalin, D.J. (with O'Reilly, K.) (2003) *The National Statistics Socio-economic Classification: Origins, Development and Use*. London: ONS.

Saunders, P. (1996) *Unequal but Fair? A Study of Class Barriers in Britain*. London: IEA.

Savage, M., Barlow, J., Dickens, P. and Fielding, A. (1992) *Property, Bureaucracy and Culture*. London: RKP.

Scott, J. (1996) *Stratification and Power*. Cambridge: Polity Press.

Stewart, A., Prandy, K. and Blackburn, R.M. (1980) *Social Stratification and Occupations*. London: Macmillan.

Townsend, P. (1979) *Poverty in the United Kingdom*. Harmondsworth: Allen Lane/ Pelican Books.

Index of Names

Index of Subjects